MEN'S OUTERWEAR DESIGN

MASAAKI KAWASHIMA

Fairchild Publications, New York

DEDICATION

To my colleagues and students in Japan and the United States, in appreciation.

Standard Book Number: 87005-196-2

Library of Congress Catalog Card Number: 77-79658

Printed in the United States of America

ACKNOWLEDGMENTS

No book issues from one hand or from one individual's experiences. Accordingly, I am indebted to the following colleagues and friends for their help, suggestions, inspiration and patience which they have offered me so generously during the preparation of this book: Itsuko Aoki, Ken and Miyako Aoki, Ed Gold and Olga Kontzias of Fairchild Publications, Shirley Goodman, Nancy Margolis, Pauline Newman, Edmund Roberts, Delmar Thompson, and Richard Weatherhead.

Jacket design by KENICHI AOKI

INTRODUCTION

This book presents to the classroom teacher and student, and also to those in the fashion industry and at home who may use it, a simplified method of pattern making for men's outerwear and a guide to the fundamentals of men's coats. The aim of the book is to provide further information in men's wear design and lead the person who works with it into more advanced study of men's fashion to the point where he or she may be able to create designs on paper and then translate these designs into men's outerwear. Because of the great variety in human shapes and proportions, the author has worked from "average" or "standard" or "normal" sizes. The author understands that these exist only in theory and hopes that the reader will adjust what is here presented to his or her own needs. The following paragraphs discuss the organization of the book and how the reader should use it.

The Organization and Use of the Book

For the convenience of the reader, the material presented is divided into six sections (as may be noted from a glance at the detailed Table of Contents). Each section concentrates upon the fundamentals of a basic step or element in the process of creating men's outerwear. Each element is described by means of a text, diagrams, and drawings. In most cases, the reader will note that the design drawing and text are on the left-hand page (the even-numbered pages), while the technical diagrams, with a step-by-step description, are on the right-hand page (on the odd-numbered pages). A brief description of each section follows.

Section I: Drafting Equipment and Body Measurements

Before learning the skills of a professional, one must have at hand the basic tools of the trade. This section lists the tools necessary for the beginner, shows how to use these tools to take accurate body measurements and draft them correctly on paper, and presents a size chart based on standards widely used in the fashion industry. The size chart may be used for the design of jackets, pants, shirts, sleeves, suits, and coats.

Section II: Pattern Fundamentals

Before the advanced student starts to make a basic pattern or "sloper," he or she should review the uses of the sixteen pattern fundamentals illustrated in this section.

Section III: Basic Coat Sloper

After the student has learned the basic fundamentals from which a design can be made, then he or she is ready for the next step. One begins with the basic coat sloper for the styling of multiple design variations.

Section IV: Fundamentals of Coat Design

Variations in design and styling details of robes, dress coats, raincoats, topcoats, and casual coats.

Section V: Fundamentals of Sleeve Design

The sleeve sloper is developed the same as in "Fundamentals of Men's Fashion Design: A Guide to Tailored Clothes." Here, nine basic sleeve slopers are dealt with: 1) the sleeve sloper, 2) the two-piece, 3) the three-piece, 4) the raglan, 5) the drop shoulder, 6) the squared armhole, 7) the diamond armhole, 8) the saddled sleeve, and 9) the yoke sleeve.

Section VI: Details of Outerwear

Before beginning the study of this section, the reader should be thoroughly acquainted with Section IV: Fundamentals of Coat Design. The collar and neckline design were purposely kept separate in order that the student could first master the skills of assembling a coat. Some basic collar designs and their variations are illustrated, along with their basic measurements. Notched collars, buttonholes, and cuff details are included.

TABLE OF CONTENTS

Page

SECTION I

DRAFTING EQUIPMENT

AND

BODY MEASUREMENTS

DRAFTING TOOLS

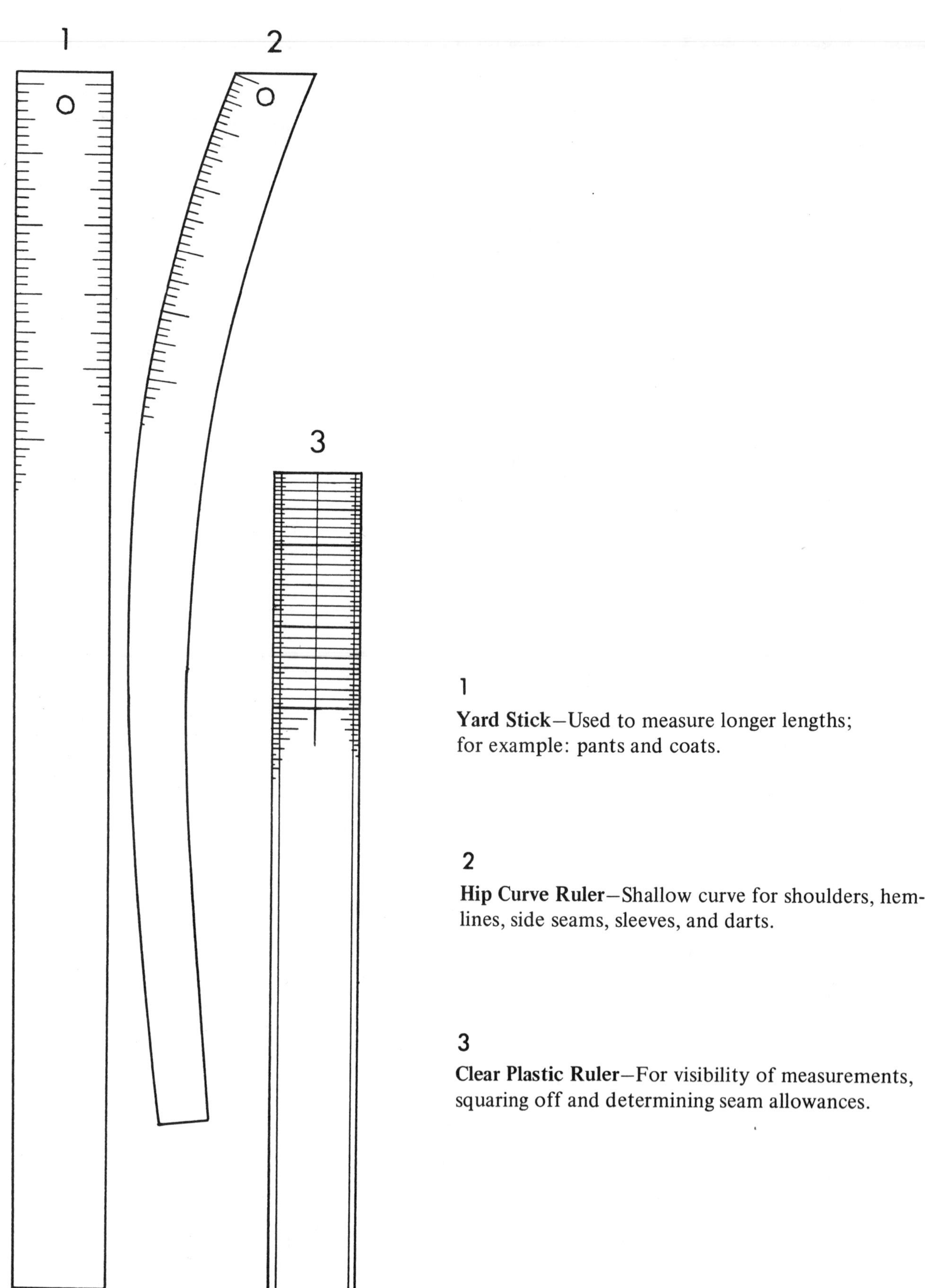

1

Yard Stick—Used to measure longer lengths; for example: pants and coats.

2

Hip Curve Ruler—Shallow curve for shoulders, hemlines, side seams, sleeves, and darts.

3

Clear Plastic Ruler—For visibility of measurements, squaring off and determining seam allowances.

DRAFTING TOOLS

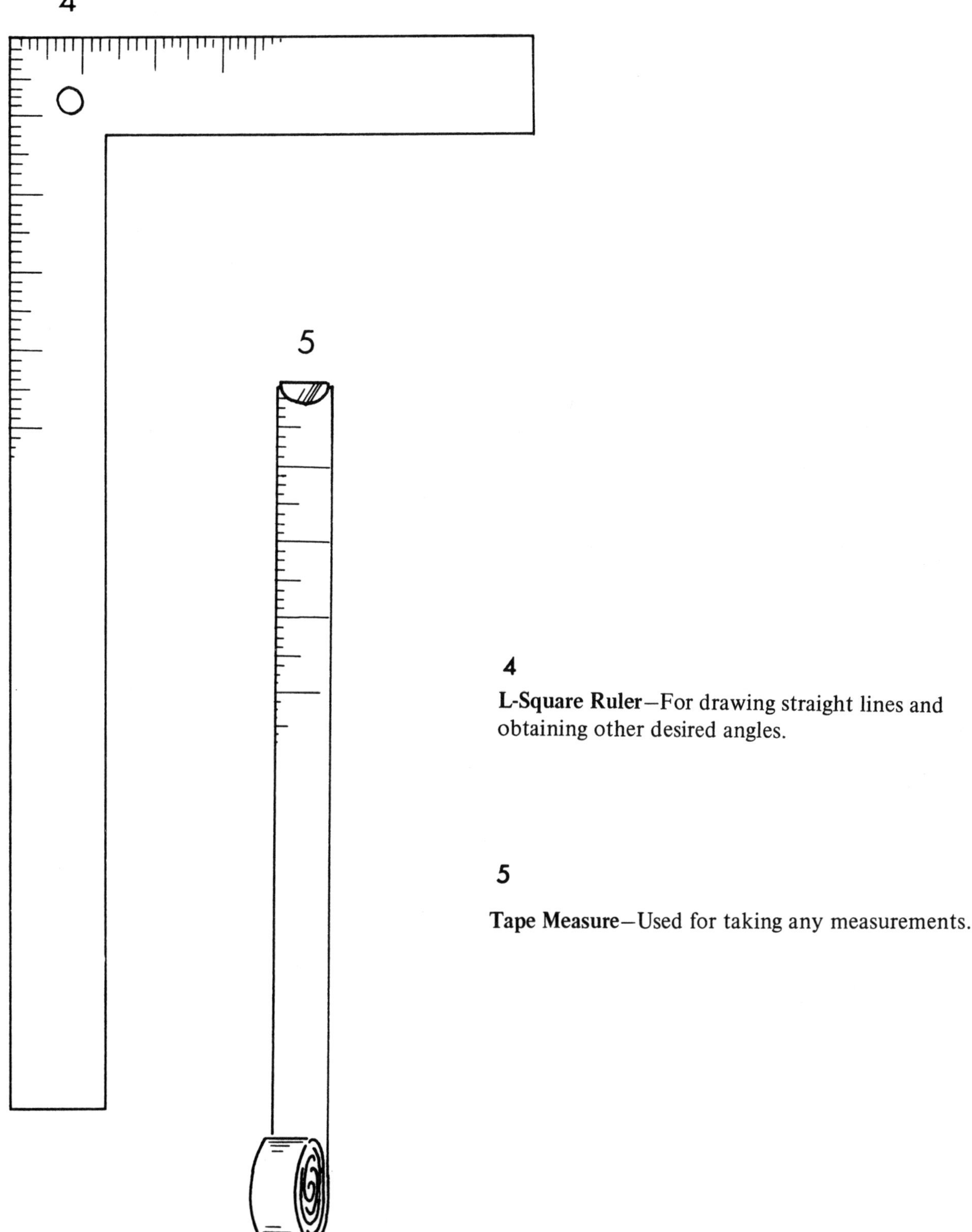

4

L-Square Ruler—For drawing straight lines and obtaining other desired angles.

5

Tape Measure—Used for taking any measurements.

DRAFTING TOOLS

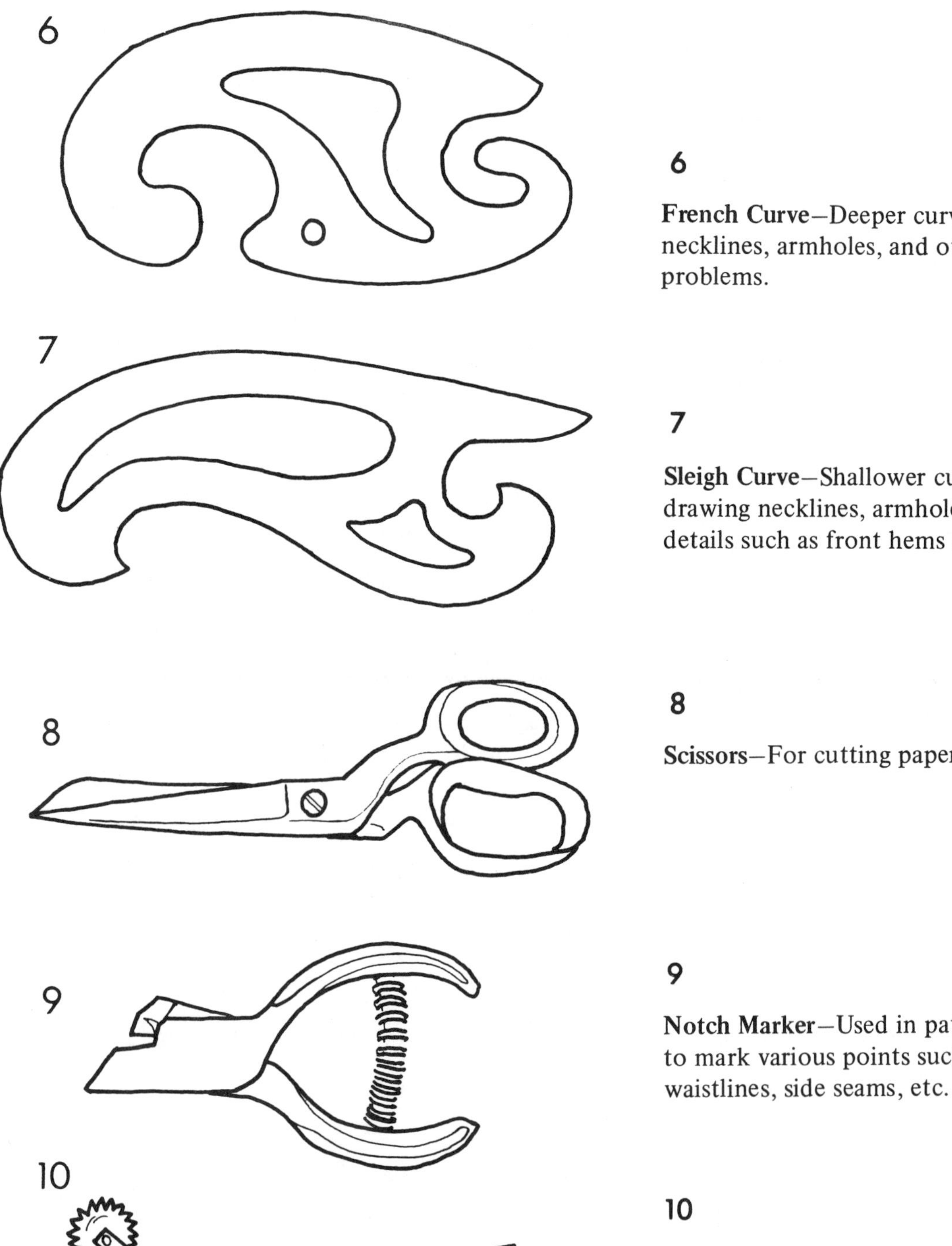

6

French Curve—Deeper curve used for necklines, armholes, and other design problems.

7

Sleigh Curve—Shallower curve used for drawing necklines, armholes, and other details such as front hems and pockets.

8

Scissors—For cutting paper and fabric.

9

Notch Marker—Used in pattern making to mark various points such as necklines, waistlines, side seams, etc.

10

Tracing Wheel—For carbon tracing on muslin and paper patterns.

NOTES

MEASUREMENTS

Jacket

A = Chest circumference

B = Waist circumference

C = Front chest measurement armhole to armhole

D = Sleeve length

E = Jacket length

F = Back waist length

G = Shoulder blade armhole to armhole

H = Shoulder length neck to armhole

Pants

I = Crotch depth. Take measurement by sitting person on solid-based flat chair surface. Measure from waist to chair surface.

J = Full pant length waist to hem

K = Hip measurement is usually 8" below waist

MEASUREMENTS

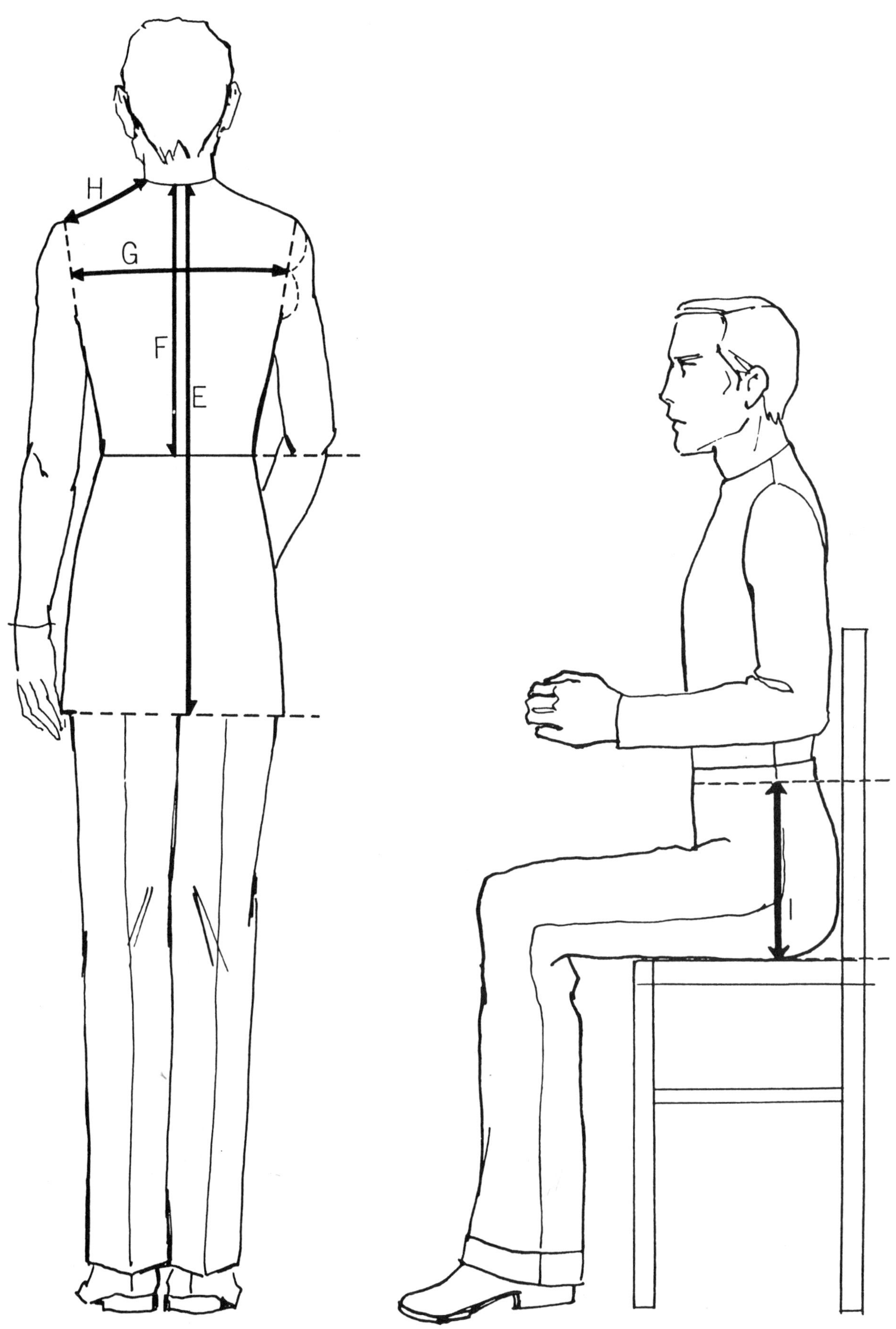

MEN'S SUIT AND COAT MEASUREMENTS

SHORT

SIZE	34	36	38	40	42	44
CHEST CIRCUMFERENCE	34	36	38	40	42	44
WAIST	28	30	32	34	36	38
HIP	34	36	38	40	42	44
FRONT CHEST	$14\frac{1}{2}$	15	$15\frac{1}{2}$	16	$16\frac{1}{2}$	17
BACK WAIST LENGTH	$16\frac{1}{2}$	$16\frac{3}{4}$	17	$17\frac{1}{4}$	$17\frac{1}{2}$	$17\frac{3}{4}$
SHOULDER BLADE	16	$16\frac{1}{2}$	17	$17\frac{1}{2}$	18	$18\frac{1}{2}$
SHOULDER LENGTH	$5\frac{7}{8}$	6	$6\frac{1}{8}$	$6\frac{1}{4}$	$6\frac{3}{8}$	$6\frac{1}{2}$
JACKET LENGTH	$28\frac{3}{4}$	29	$29\frac{1}{4}$	$29\frac{1}{2}$	$29\frac{3}{4}$	30
COAT LENGTH	ACCORDING TO DESIGN					
JACKET SLEEVE FULL LENGTH	$22\frac{3}{8}$	$22\frac{5}{8}$	$22\frac{7}{8}$	$23\frac{1}{8}$	$23\frac{3}{8}$	$23\frac{5}{8}$
COAT SLEEVE FULL LENGTH	JACKET SLEEVE LENGTH PLUS 3/8 INCH					
CROTCH DEPTH	$9\frac{1}{4}$	$9\frac{1}{2}$	$9\frac{3}{4}$	10	$10\frac{1}{4}$	$10\frac{1}{2}$
PANTS FULL LENGTH	41	$41\frac{1}{2}$	42	$42\frac{1}{2}$	43	$43\frac{1}{2}$

Note: For overcoat measurement, because of additional ease needed, use two sizes larger. For example, size 36 overcoat, use size 38 measurements.

MEN'S SUIT AND COAT MEASUREMENTS

SHORT

SIZE	35	37	39	41	43	45
CHEST CIRCUMFERENCE	35	37	39	41	43	45
WAIST	29	31	33	35	37	39
HIP	35	37	39	41	43	45
FRONT CHEST	$14\frac{3}{4}$	$15\frac{1}{4}$	$15\frac{3}{4}$	$16\frac{1}{4}$	$16\frac{3}{4}$	$17\frac{1}{4}$
BACK WAIST LENGTH	$16\frac{5}{8}$	$16\frac{7}{8}$	$17\frac{1}{8}$	$17\frac{3}{8}$	$17\frac{5}{8}$	$17\frac{7}{8}$
SHOULDER BLADE	$16\frac{1}{4}$	$16\frac{3}{4}$	$17\frac{1}{4}$	$17\frac{3}{4}$	$18\frac{1}{4}$	$18\frac{3}{4}$
SHOULDER LENGTH	$5\frac{15}{16}$	$6\frac{1}{16}$	$6\frac{3}{16}$	$6\frac{5}{16}$	$6\frac{7}{16}$	$6\frac{9}{16}$
JACKET LENGTH	$28\frac{7}{8}$	$29\frac{1}{8}$	$29\frac{3}{8}$	$29\frac{5}{8}$	$29\frac{7}{8}$	$30\frac{9}{8}$
COAT LENGTH	ACCORDING TO DESIGN					
JACKET SLEEVE FULL LENGTH	$22\frac{1}{2}$	$22\frac{3}{4}$	23	$23\frac{1}{4}$	$23\frac{1}{2}$	$23\frac{3}{4}$
COAT SLEEVE FULL LENGTH	JACKET SLEEVE LENGTH PLUS 3/8 INCH					
CROTCH DEPTH	$9\frac{3}{8}$	$9\frac{5}{8}$	$9\frac{7}{8}$	$10\frac{1}{8}$	$10\frac{3}{8}$	$10\frac{5}{8}$
PANTS FULL LENGTH	$41\frac{1}{4}$	$41\frac{3}{4}$	$42\frac{1}{4}$	$42\frac{3}{4}$	$43\frac{1}{4}$	$43\frac{3}{4}$

Note: For overcoat measurement, because of additional ease needed, use two sizes larger. For example, size 35 overcoat, use size 37 measurements.

MEN'S SUIT AND COAT MEASUREMENTS

REGULAR

SIZE	34	36	38	40	42	44
CHEST CIRCUMFERENCE	34	36	38	40	42	44
WAIST	28	30	32	34	36	38
HIP	34	36	38	40	42	44
FRONT CHEST	$14\frac{1}{2}$	15	$15\frac{1}{2}$	16	$16\frac{1}{2}$	17
BACK WAIST LENGTH	$17\frac{1}{2}$	$17\frac{3}{4}$	18	$18\frac{1}{4}$	$18\frac{1}{2}$	$18\frac{3}{4}$
SHOULDER BLADE	16	$16\frac{1}{2}$	17	$17\frac{1}{2}$	18	$18\frac{1}{2}$
SHOULDER LENGTH	$5\frac{7}{8}$	6	$6\frac{1}{8}$	$6\frac{1}{4}$	$6\frac{3}{8}$	$6\frac{1}{2}$
JACKET LENGTH	$29\frac{3}{4}$	30	$30\frac{1}{4}$	$30\frac{1}{2}$	$30\frac{3}{4}$	31
COAT LENGTH	ACCORDING TO DESIGN					
JACKET SLEEVE FULL LENGTH	$23\frac{3}{8}$	$23\frac{5}{8}$	$23\frac{7}{8}$	$24\frac{1}{8}$	$24\frac{3}{8}$	$24\frac{5}{8}$
COAT SLEEVE FULL LENGTH	JACKET SLEEVE LENGTH PLUS 3/8 INCH					
CROTCH DEPTH	$9\frac{3}{4}$	10	$10\frac{1}{4}$	$10\frac{1}{2}$	$10\frac{3}{4}$	11
PANTS FULL LENGTH	$41\frac{1}{2}$	42	$42\frac{1}{2}$	43	$43\frac{1}{2}$	44

Note: For overcoat measurement, because of additional ease needed, use two sizes larger. For example, size 36 overcoat, use size 38 measurements.

MEN'S SUIT AND COAT MEASUREMENTS

REGULAR

SIZE	35	37	39	41	43	45
CHEST CIRCUMFERENCE	35	37	39	41	43	45
WAIST	29	31	33	35	37	39
HIP	35	37	39	41	43	45
FRONT CHEST	$14\frac{3}{4}$	$15\frac{1}{4}$	$15\frac{3}{4}$	$16\frac{1}{4}$	$16\frac{3}{4}$	$17\frac{1}{4}$
BACK WAIST LENGTH	$17\frac{5}{8}$	$17\frac{7}{8}$	$18\frac{1}{8}$	$18\frac{3}{8}$	$18\frac{5}{8}$	$18\frac{7}{8}$
SHOULDER BLADE	$16\frac{1}{4}$	$16\frac{3}{4}$	$17\frac{1}{4}$	$17\frac{3}{4}$	$18\frac{1}{4}$	$18\frac{3}{4}$
SHOULDER LENGTH	$5\frac{15}{16}$	$6\frac{1}{16}$	$6\frac{3}{16}$	$6\frac{5}{16}$	$6\frac{7}{16}$	$6\frac{9}{16}$
JACKET LENGTH	$29\frac{7}{8}$	$30\frac{1}{8}$	$30\frac{3}{8}$	$30\frac{5}{8}$	$30\frac{7}{8}$	$31\frac{1}{8}$
COAT LENGTH	ACCORDING TO DESIGN					
JACKET SLEEVE FULL LENGTH	$23\frac{1}{2}$	$23\frac{3}{4}$	24	$24\frac{1}{4}$	$24\frac{1}{2}$	$24\frac{3}{4}$
COAT SLEEVE FULL LENGTH	JACKET SLEEVE LENGTH PLUS 3/8 INCH					
CROTCH DEPTH	$9\frac{7}{8}$	$10\frac{1}{8}$	$10\frac{3}{8}$	$10\frac{5}{8}$	$10\frac{7}{8}$	$11\frac{1}{8}$
PANTS FULL LENGTH	$41\frac{3}{4}$	$42\frac{1}{4}$	$42\frac{3}{4}$	$43\frac{1}{4}$	$43\frac{3}{4}$	$44\frac{1}{4}$

Note: For overcoat measurement, because of additional ease needed, use two sizes larger. For example, size 35 overcoat, use size 37 measurements.

MEN'S SUIT AND COAT MEASUREMENTS

LONG

SIZE	34	36	38	40	42	44
CHEST CIRCUMFERENCE	34	36	38	40	42	44
WAIST	28	30	32	34	36	38
HIP	34	36	38	40	42	44
FRONT CHEST	$14\frac{1}{2}$	15	$15\frac{1}{2}$	16	$16\frac{1}{2}$	17
BACK WAIST LENGTH	$18\frac{1}{2}$	$18\frac{3}{4}$	19	$19\frac{1}{4}$	$19\frac{1}{2}$	$19\frac{3}{4}$
SHOULDER BLADE	16	$16\frac{1}{2}$	17	$17\frac{1}{2}$	18	$18\frac{1}{2}$
SHOULDER LENGTH	$5\frac{7}{8}$	6	$6\frac{1}{8}$	$6\frac{1}{4}$	$6\frac{3}{8}$	$6\frac{1}{2}$
JACKET LENGTH	$30\frac{3}{4}$	31	$31\frac{1}{4}$	$31\frac{1}{2}$	$31\frac{3}{4}$	32
COAT LENGTH	ACCORDING TO DESIGN					
JACKET SLEEVE FULL LENGTH	$24\frac{3}{8}$	$24\frac{5}{8}$	$24\frac{7}{8}$	$25\frac{1}{8}$	$25\frac{3}{8}$	$25\frac{5}{8}$
COAT SLEEVE FULL LENGTH	JACKET SLEEVE LENGTH PLUS 3/8 INCH					
CROTCH DEPTH	$10\frac{1}{4}$	$10\frac{1}{2}$	$10\frac{3}{4}$	11	$11\frac{1}{4}$	$11\frac{1}{2}$
PANTS FULL LENGTH	42	$42\frac{1}{2}$	43	$43\frac{1}{2}$	44	$44\frac{1}{2}$

Note: For overcoat measurement, because of additional ease needed, use two sizes larger. For example, size 36 overcoat, use size 38 measurements.

MEN'S SUIT AND COAT MEASUREMENTS

LONG

SIZE	35	37	39	41	43	45
CHEST CIRCUMFERENCE	35	37	39	41	43	45
WAIST	29	31	33	35	37	39
HIP	35	37	39	41	43	45
FRONT CHEST	14 3/4	15 1/4	15 3/4	16 1/4	16 3/4	17 1/4
BACK WAIST LENGTH	18 5/8	18 7/8	19 1/8	19 3/8	19 5/8	19 7/8
SHOULDER BLADE	16	16 1/2	17	17 1/2	18	18 1/2
SHOULDER LENGTH	5 7/8	6	6 1/8	6 1/4	6 3/8	6 1/2
JACKET LENGTH	30 3/4	31	31 1/4	31 1/2	31 3/4	32
COAT LENGTH	ACCORDING TO DESIGN					
JACKET SLEEVE FULL LENGTH	24 3/8	24 5/8	24 7/8	25 1/8	25 3/8	25 5/8
COAT SLEEVE FULL LENGTH	JACKET SLEEVE LENGTH PLUS 3/8 INCH					
CROTCH DEPTH	10 1/4	10 1/2	10 3/4	11	11 1/4	11 1/2
PANTS FULL LENGTH	42	42 1/2	43	43 1/2	44	44 1/2

Note: For overcoat measurement, because of additional ease needed, use two sizes larger. For example, size 35 overcoat, use size 37 measurements.

SECTION II

PATTERN FUNDAMENTALS

COAT AND JACKET PARTS

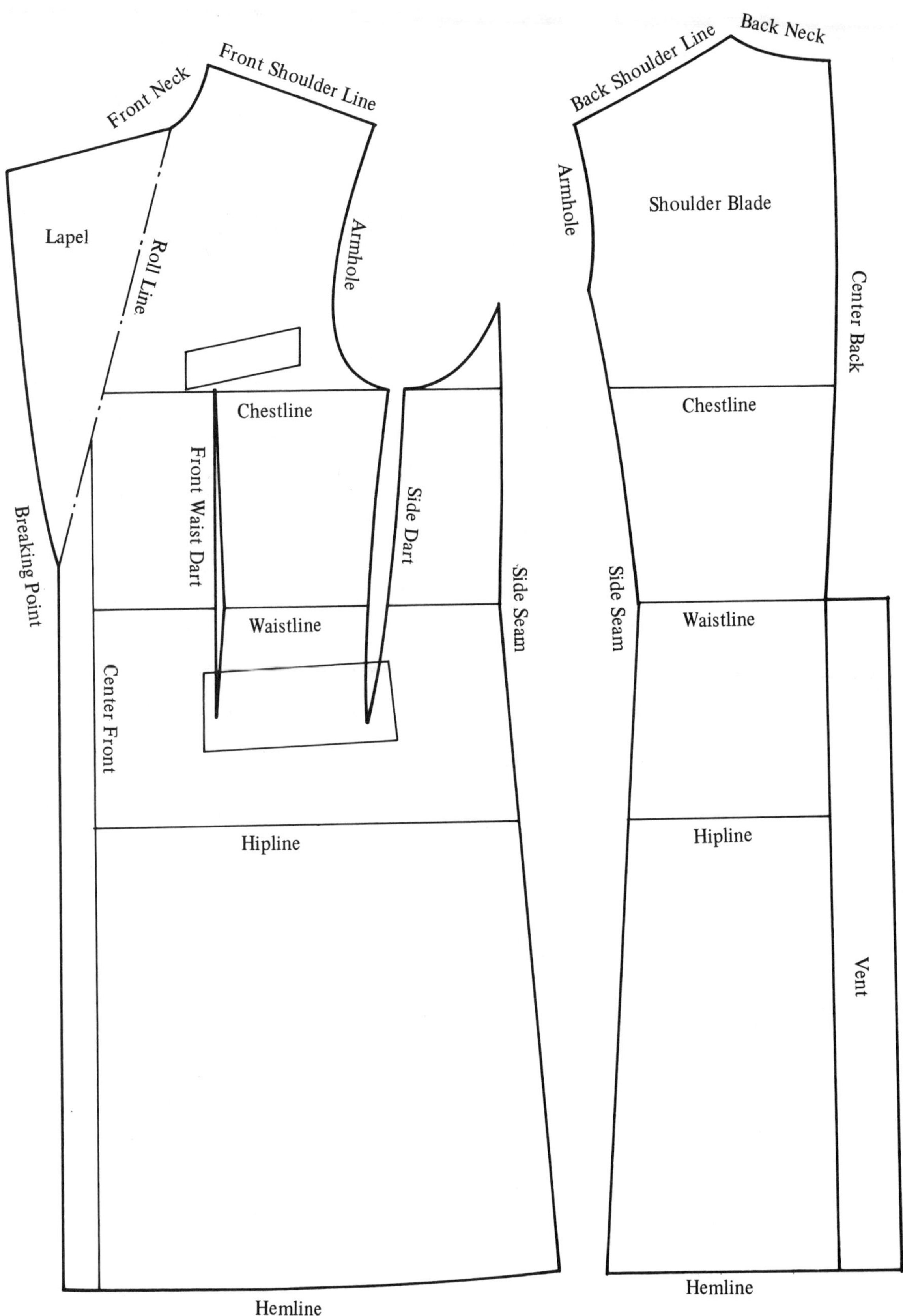

COLLAR AND SLEEVE PARTS

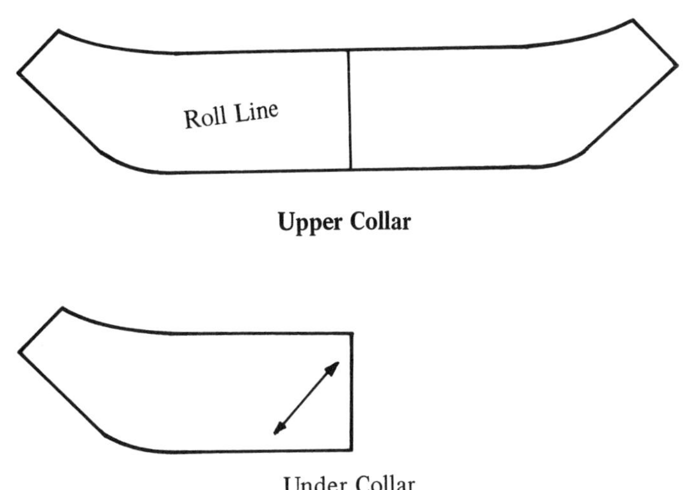

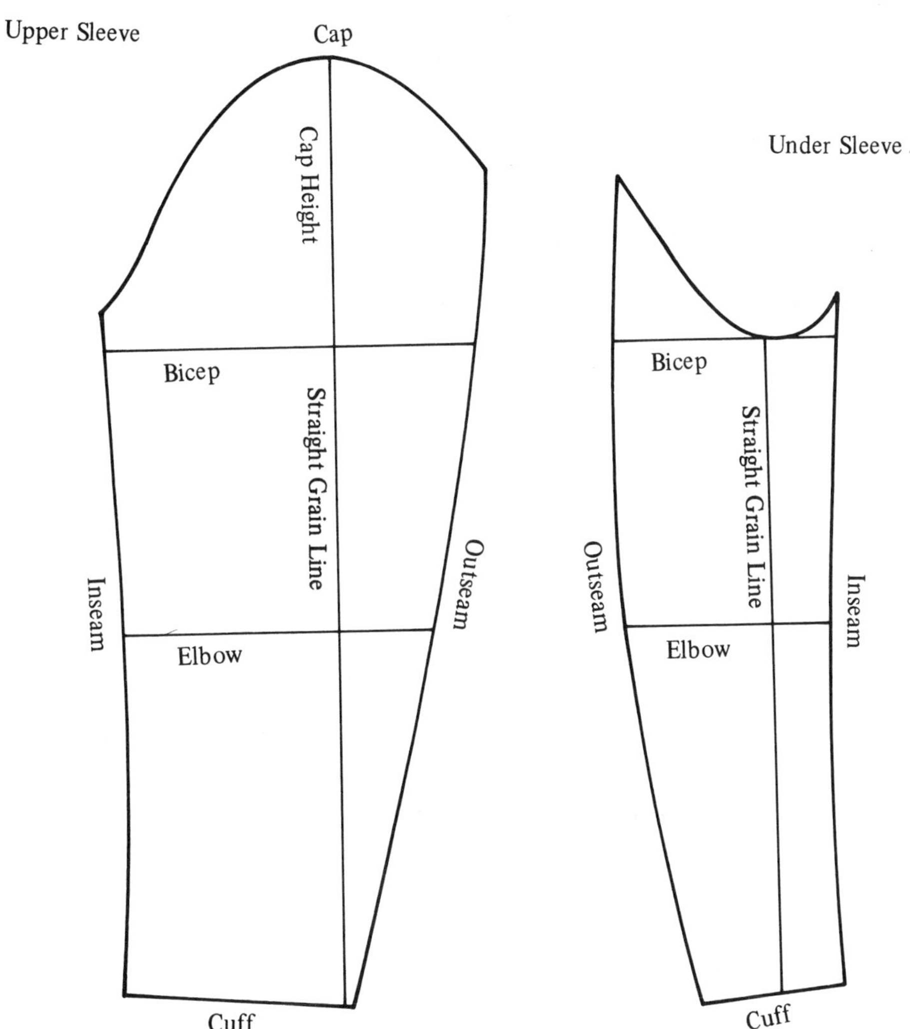

COAT AND JACKET GRAIN LINES

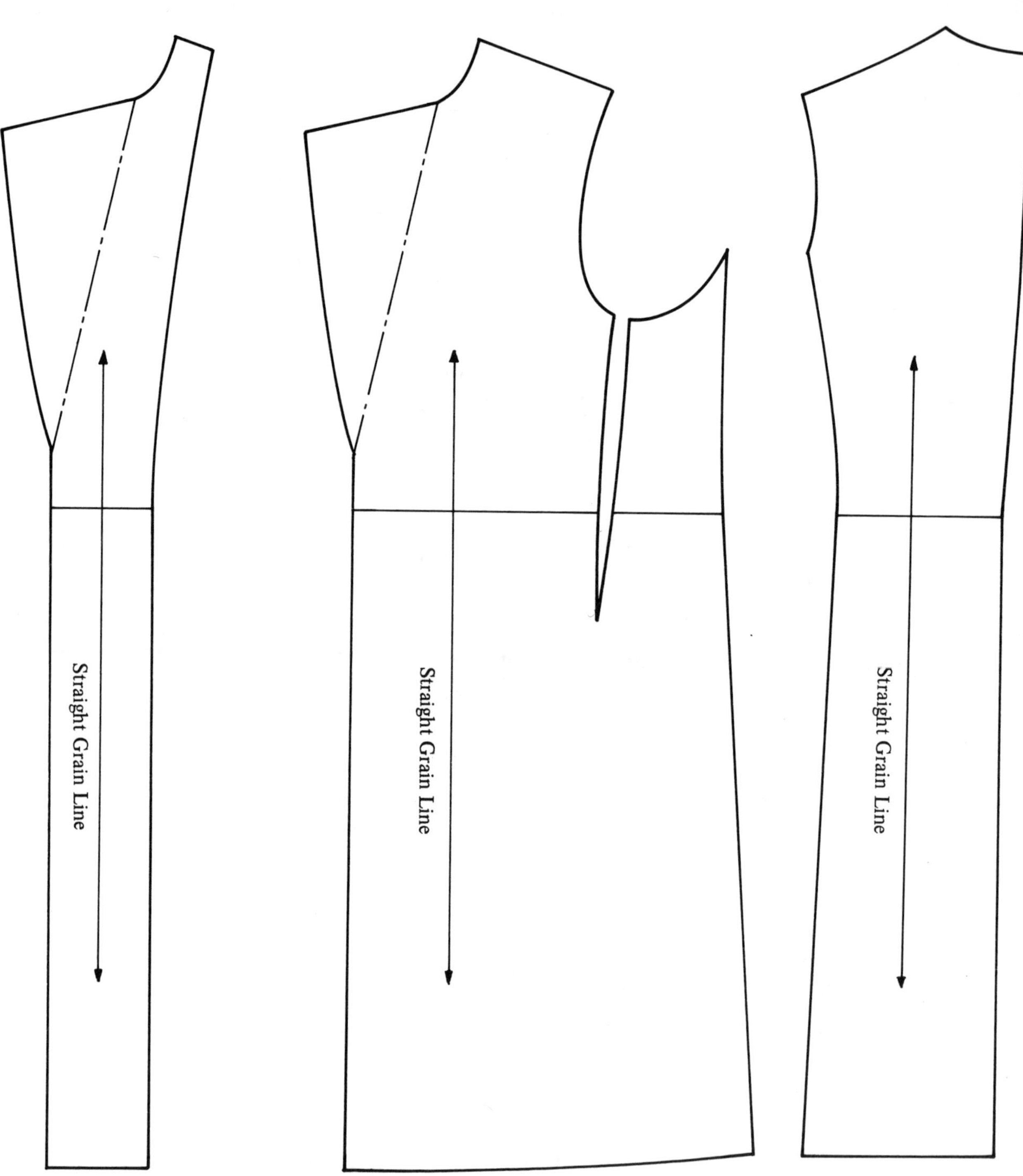

Front Coat Facing **Front Coat** **Back Coat**

COLLAR AND SLEEVE GRAIN LINES

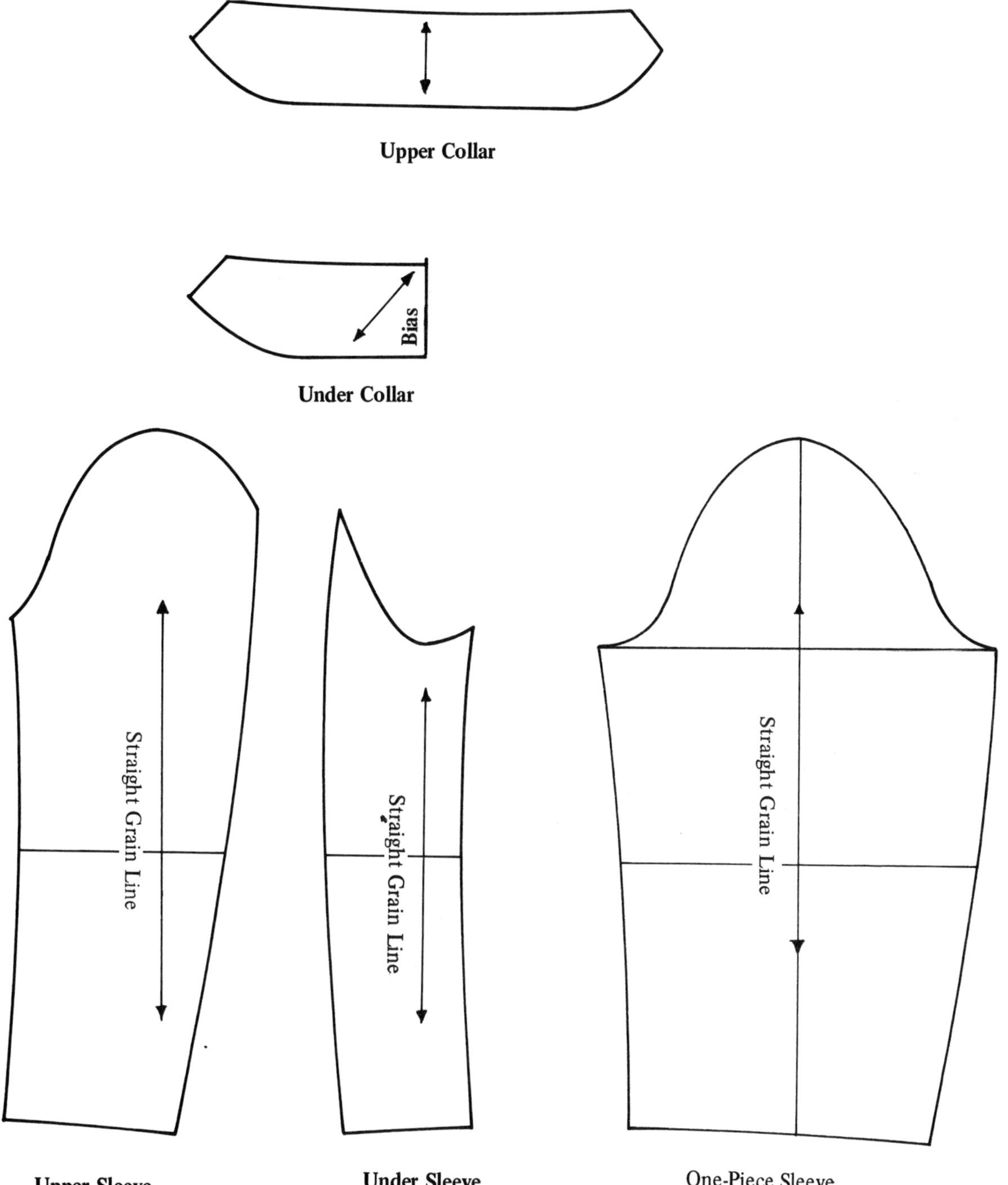

Upper Collar

Under Collar

Upper Sleeve

Under Sleeve

One-Piece Sleeve

COAT AND JACKET CROSSMARKS

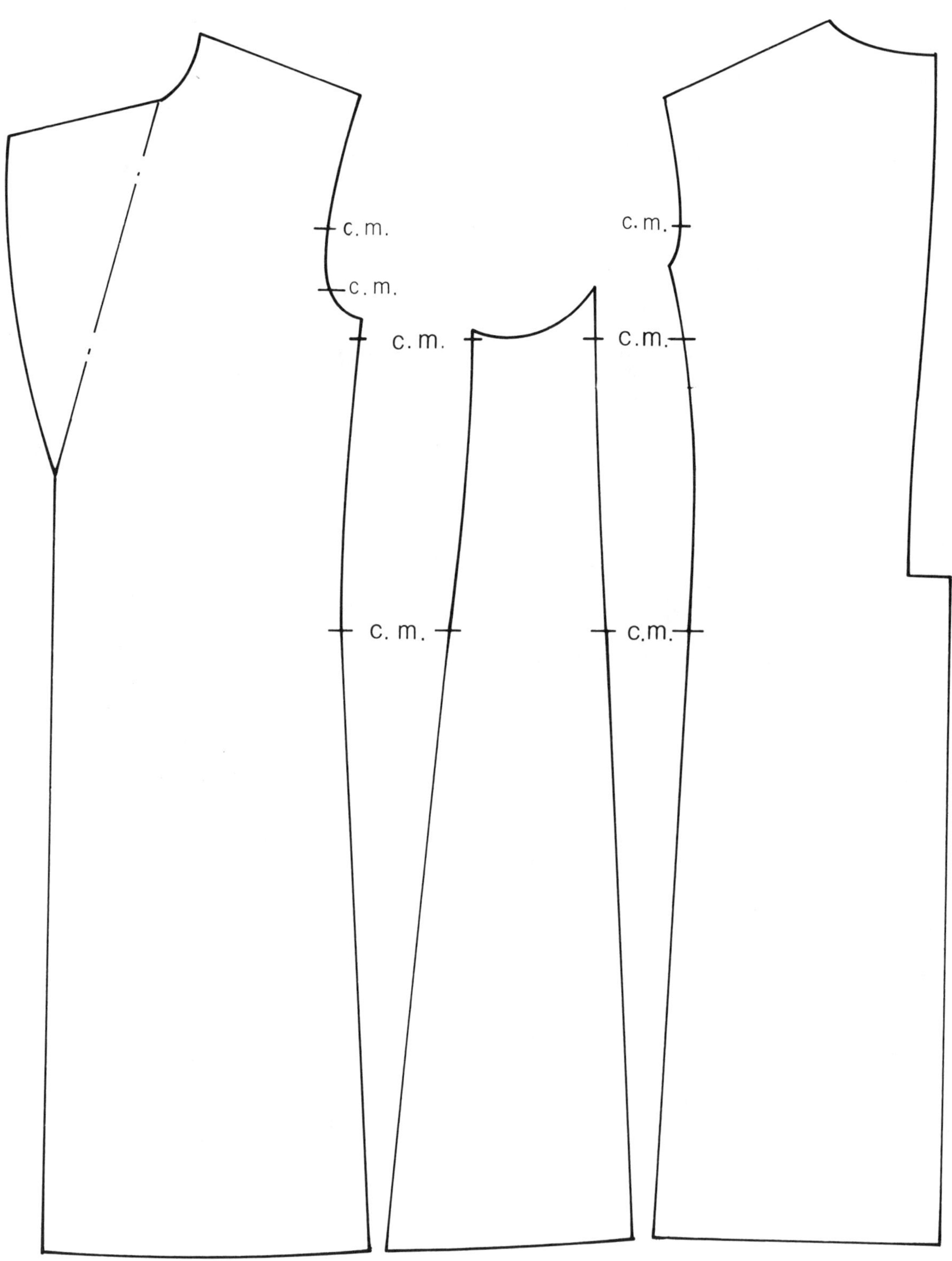

Front Coat Side Coat Back Coat

COLLAR AND SLEEVE CROSSMARKS

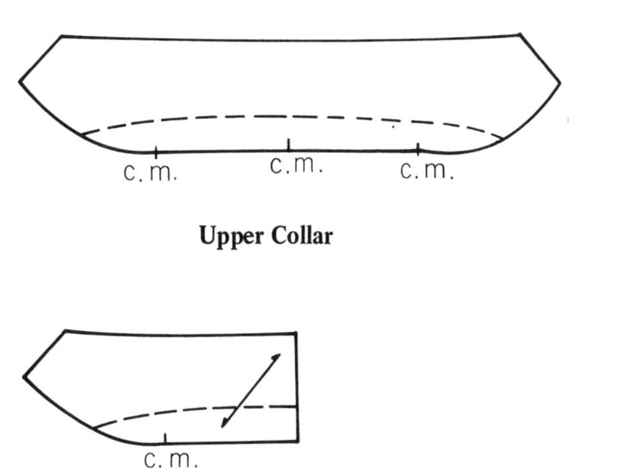

Upper Collar

Under Collar

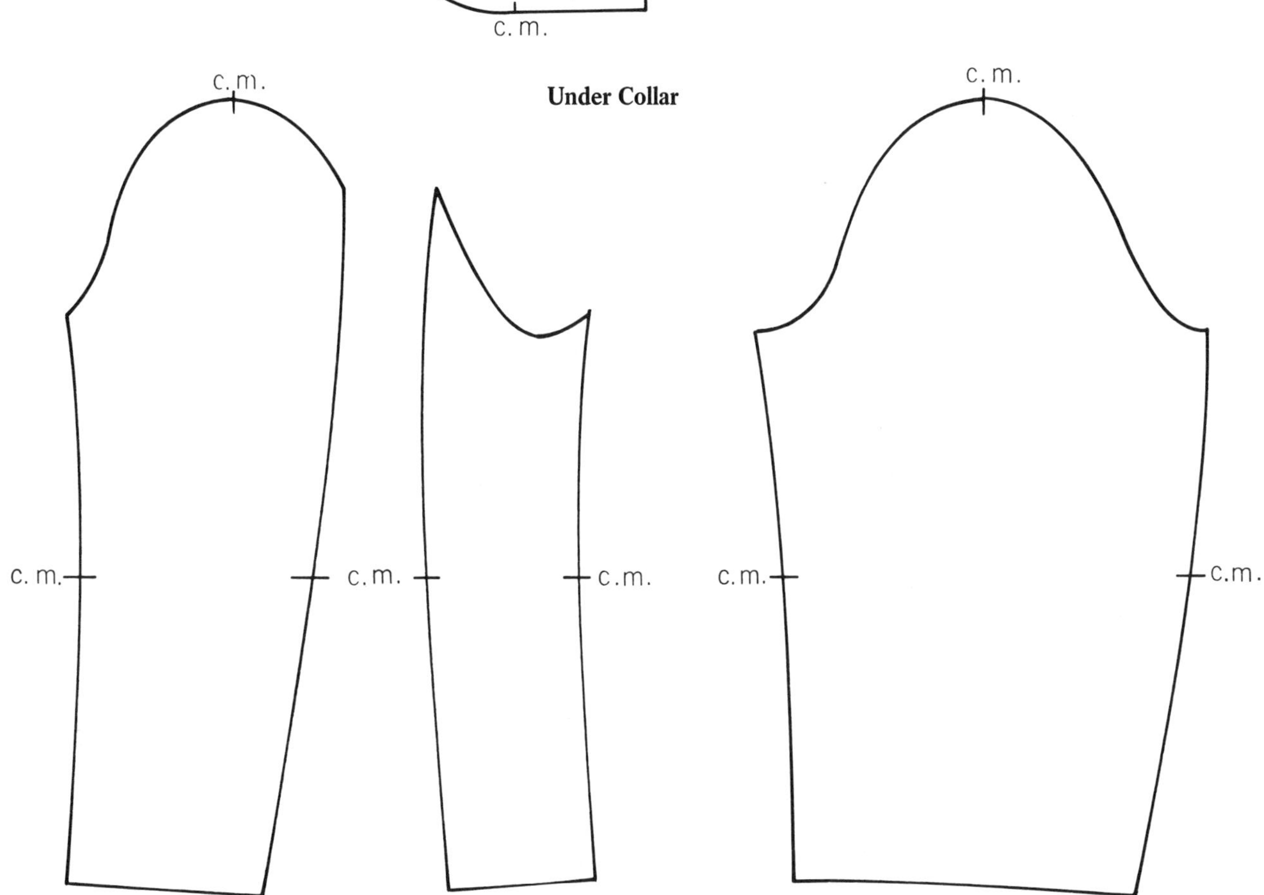

Upper Sleeve

Under Sleeve

One-Piece Sleeve

COAT AND JACKET SEAM ALLOWANCES

Note: These seam allowances are for finished garments. For first fitting add extra seam allowances.

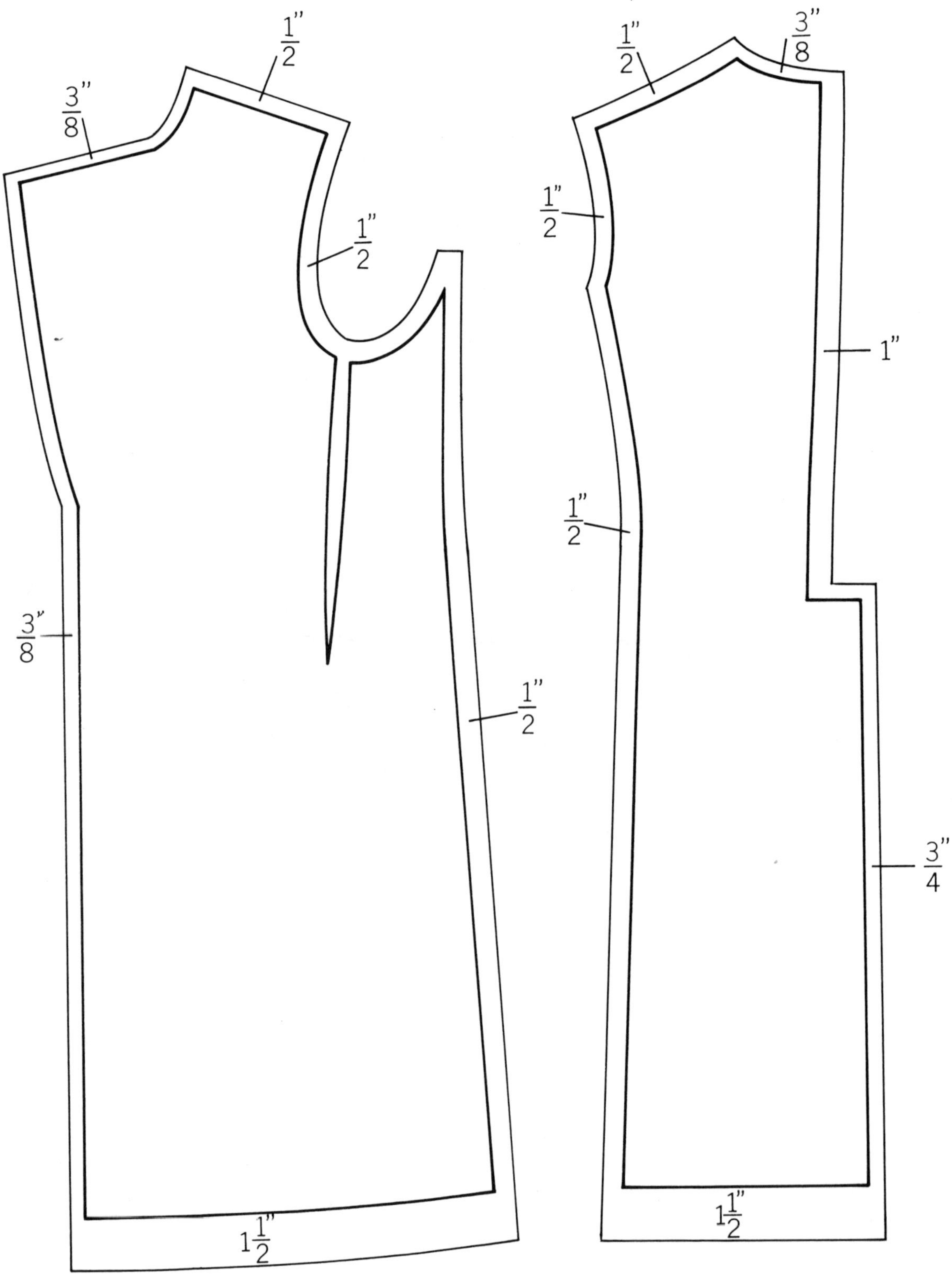

Front Coat **Back Coat**

COLLAR AND SLEEVE SEAM ALLOWANCES

Note: These seam allowances are for finished garments. For first fitting add extra seam allowances.

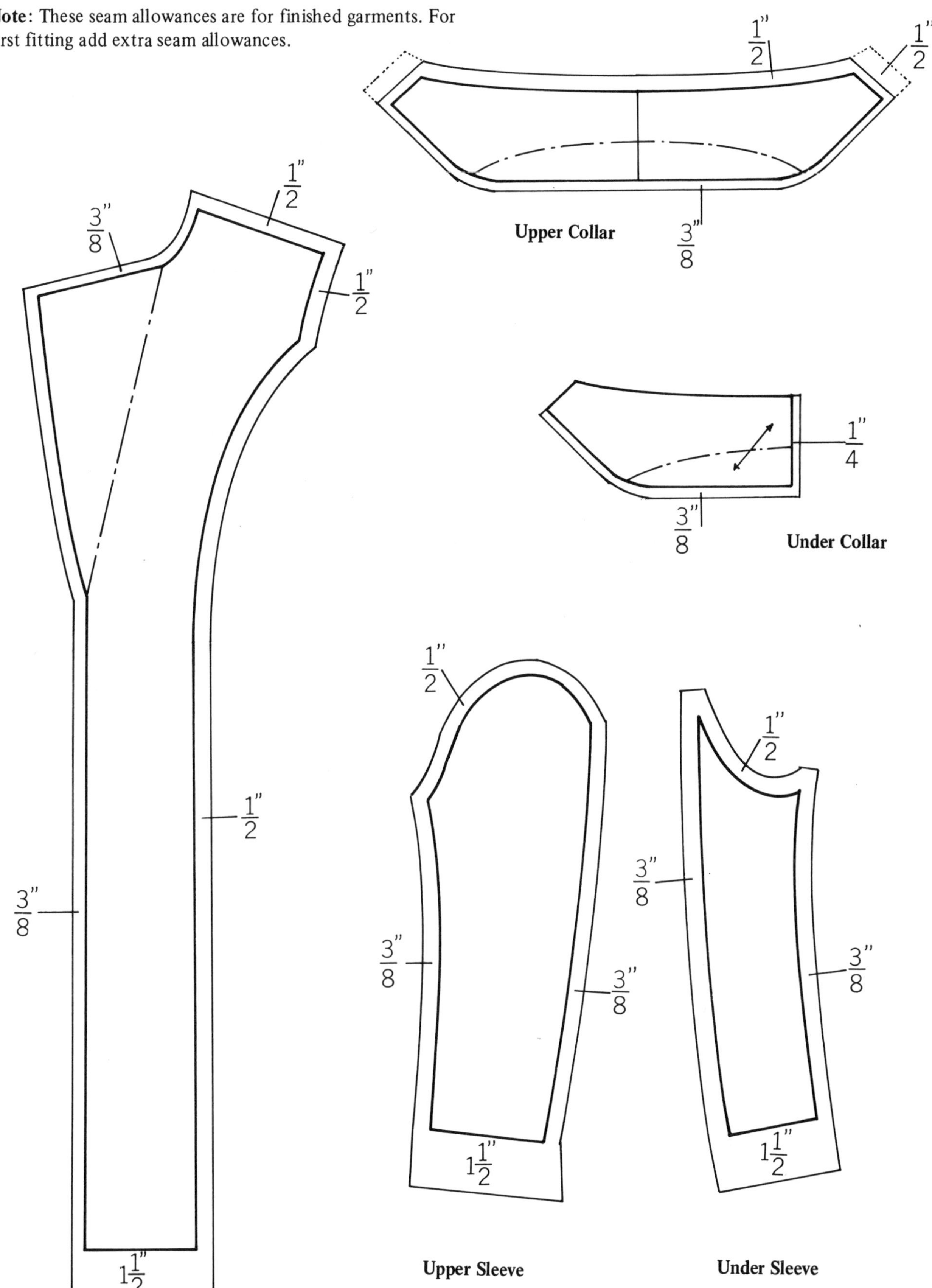

CASUAL COAT AND JACKET FACING

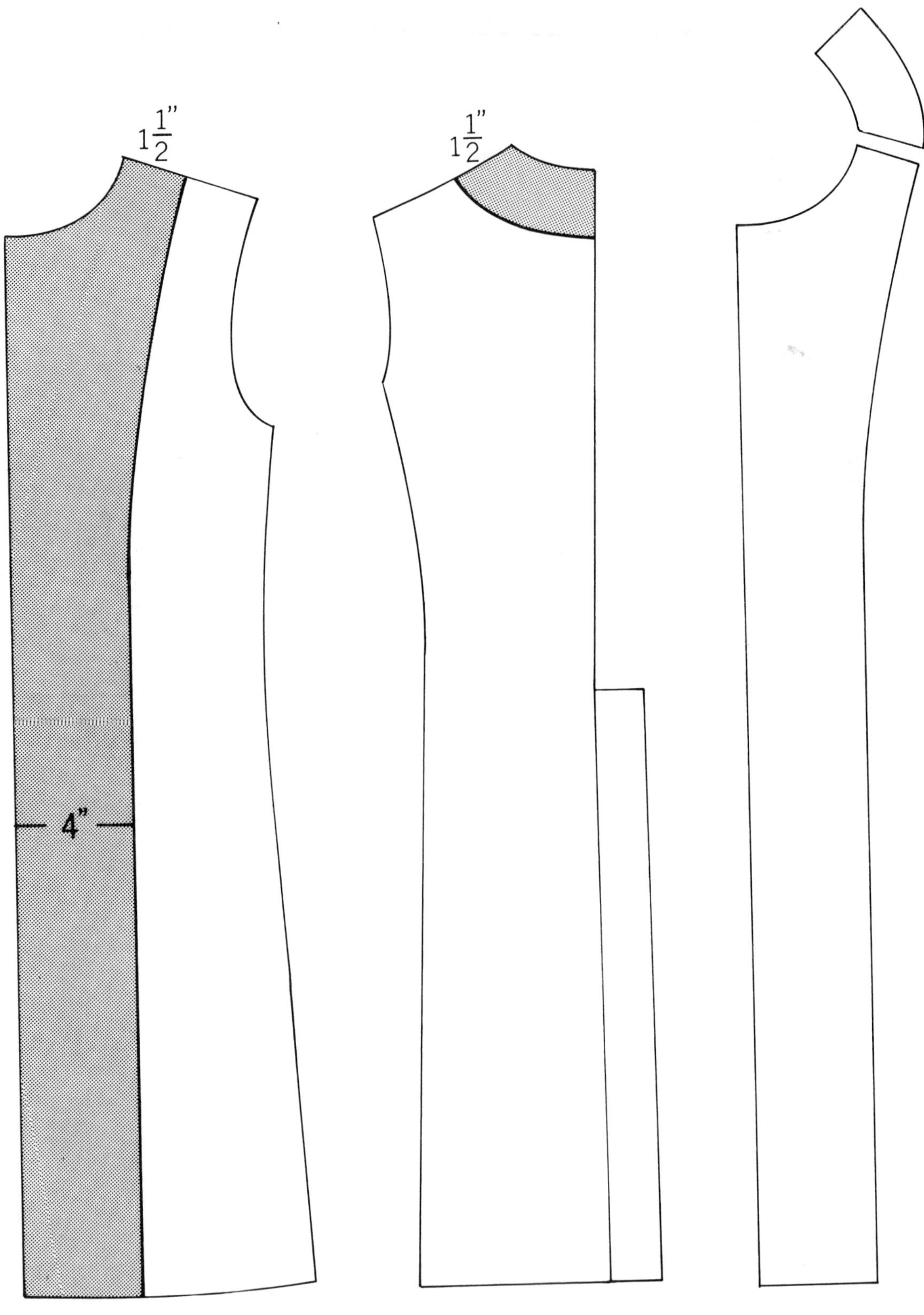

Front Coat

Back Coat

Front Coat Facing

TAILORED COAT AND JACKET FACING

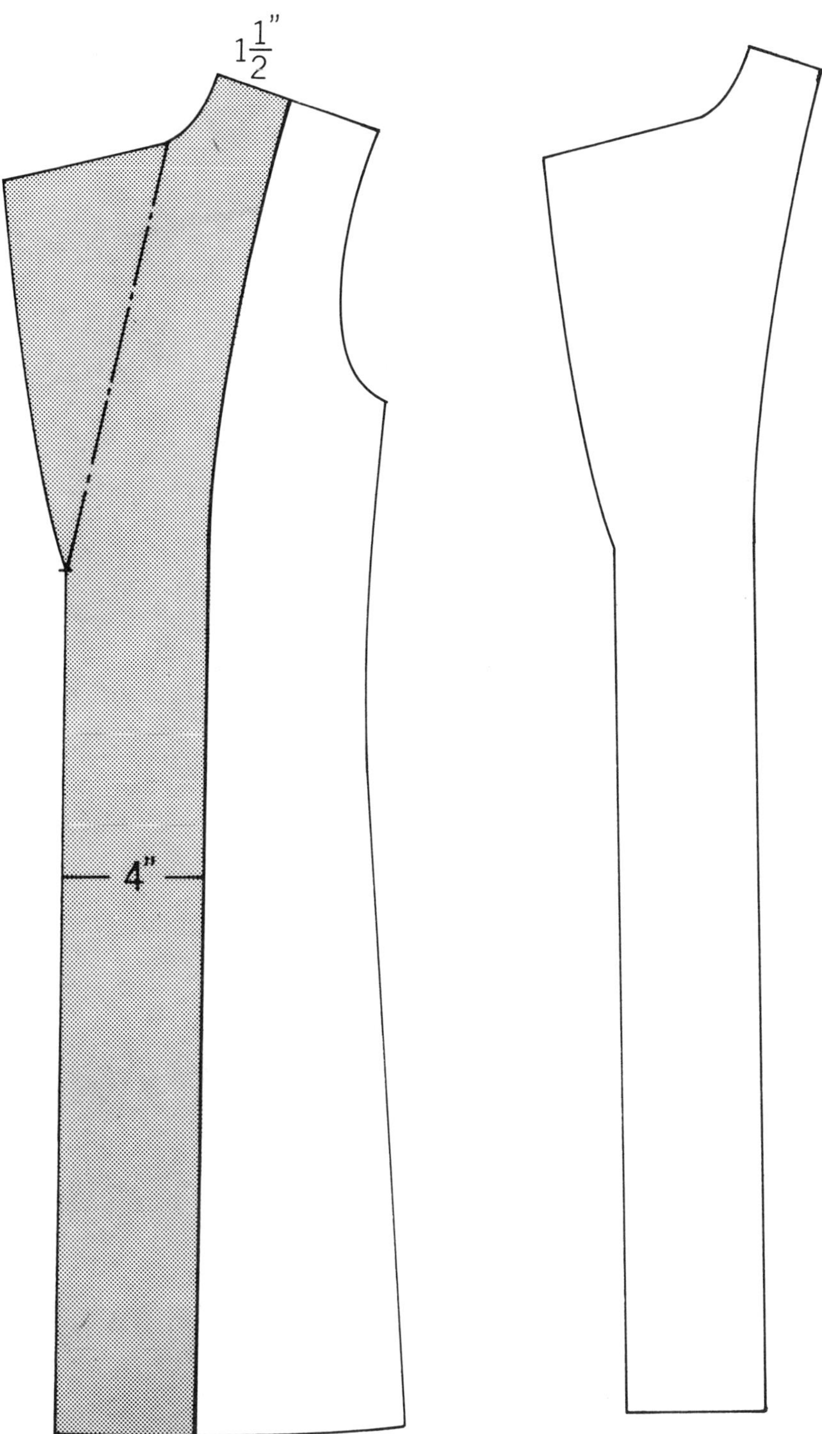

Front Coat

Front Coat Facing

BUTTON SIZE CHART

SIZE 14 – 1/3"

SIZE 16 – 3/8"

SIZE 18 – 7/16"

SIZE 20 – 1/2"

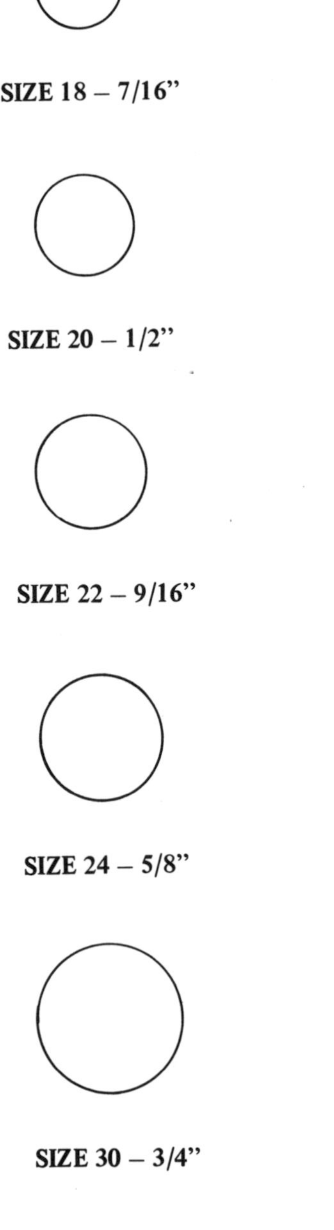

SIZE 22 – 9/16"

SIZE 24 – 5/8"

SIZE 30 – 3/4"

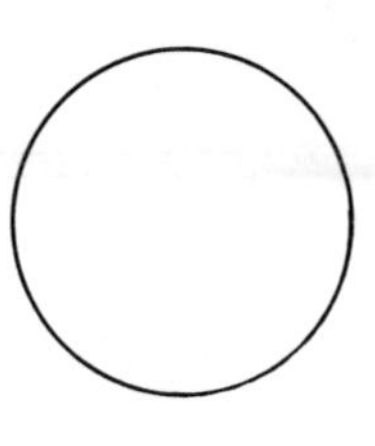

SIZE 36 – 7/8"

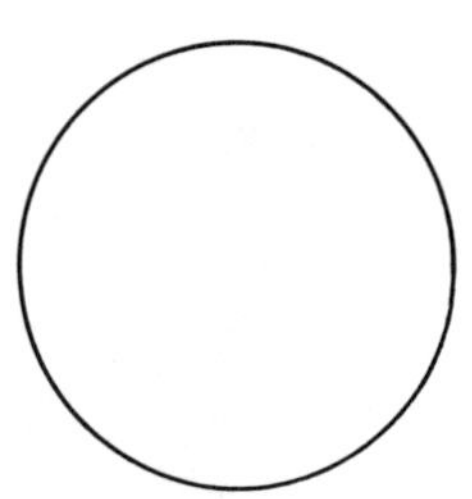

SIZE 45 – 1-1/8"

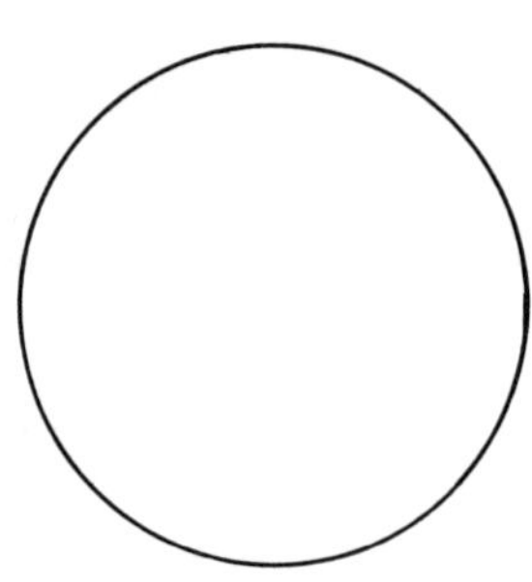

SIZE 55 – 1-3/8"

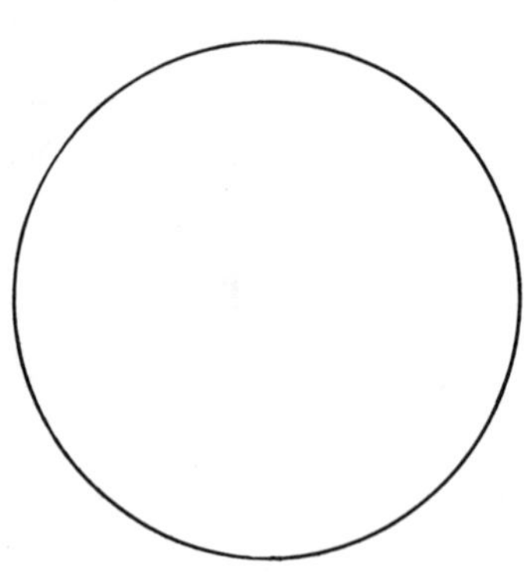

SIZE 70 – 1-3/4"

NOTES

BLENDING PROCEDURE

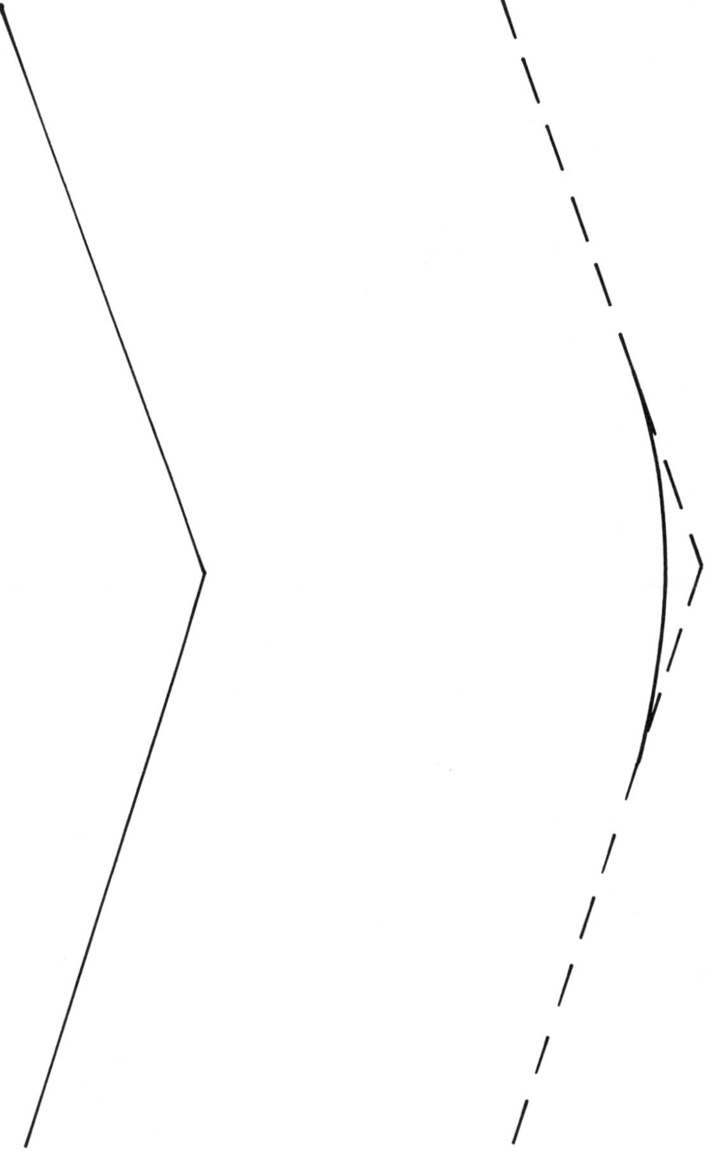

When lines intersect and create an angle, a smooth "blended" line is needed. See **Diagram A.** This line gives continuity to your patterns. See **Diagram B.**

All patterns in this book should blend connecting points with a curve to form smooth, clean lines.

SQUARING-OFF PROCEDURE

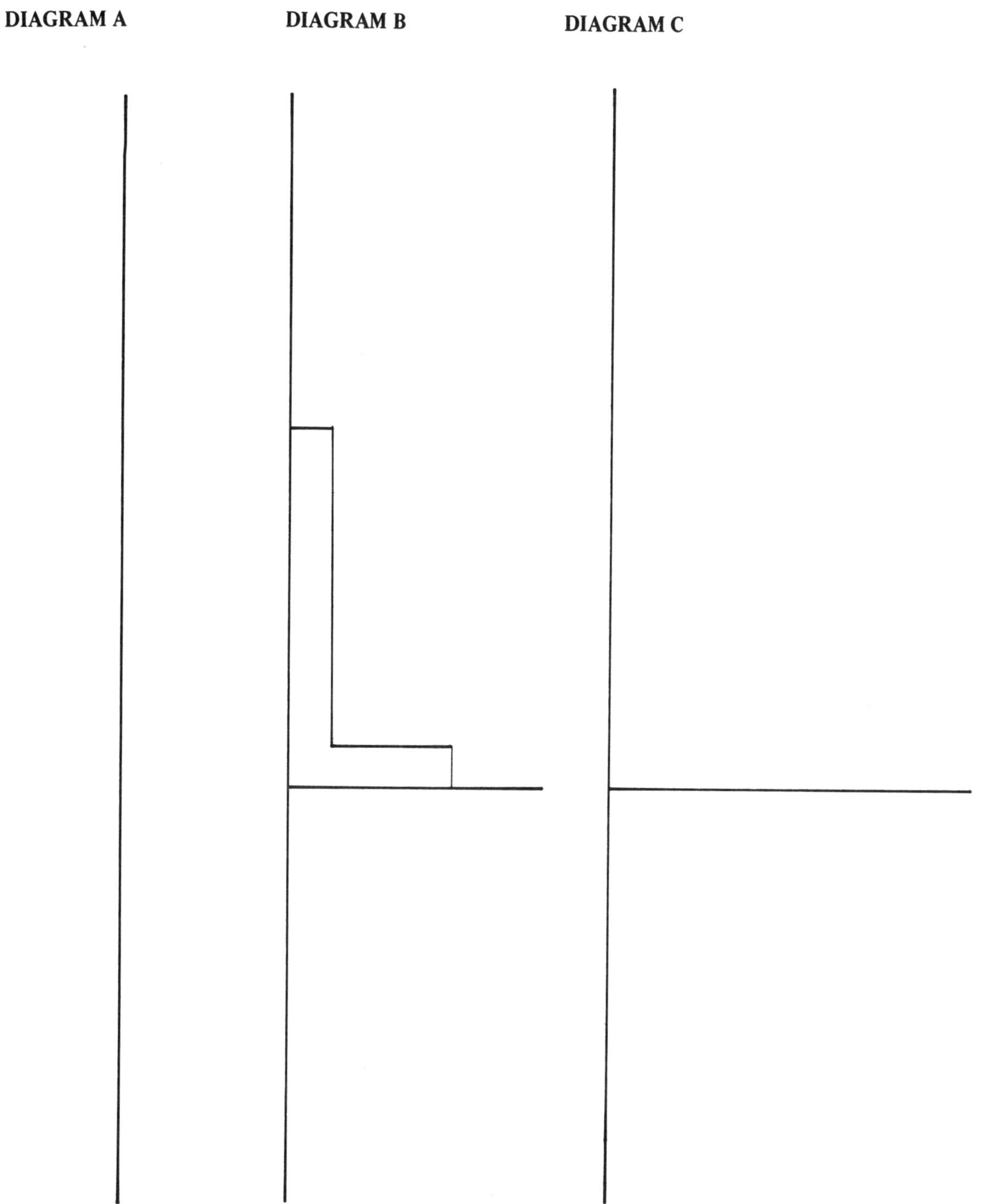

Place L-square.
Draw a line on right angle.

Remove L-square.

SECTION III

FUNDAMENTALS OF BASIC COAT SLOPER DESIGN

BASIC COAT SLOPER

DIAGRAM A

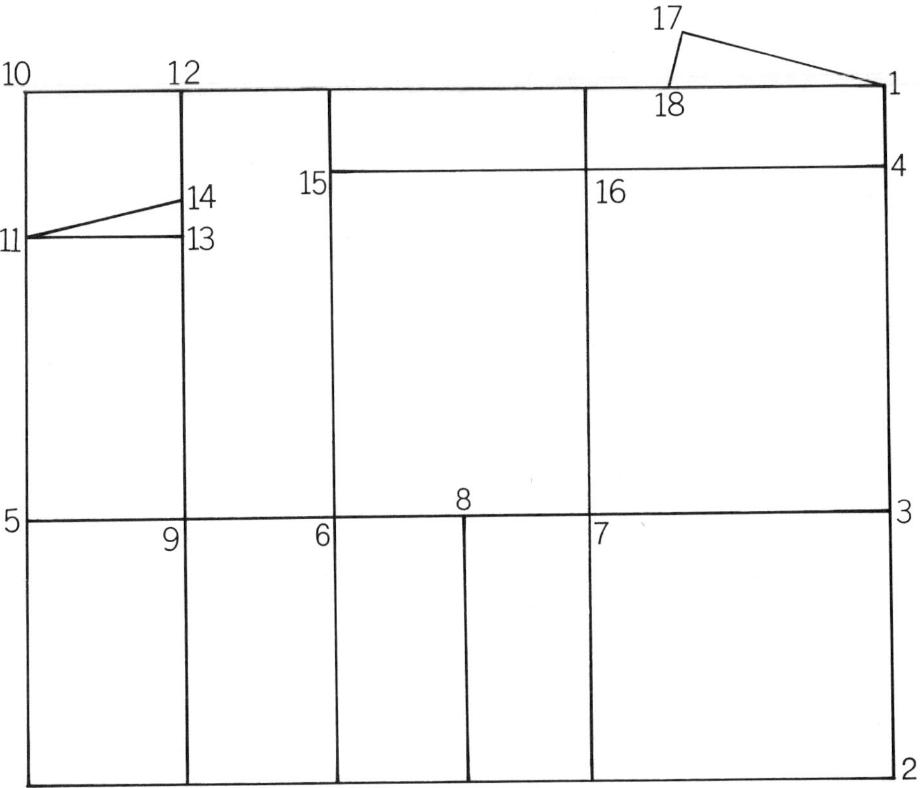

In order to draft the Basic Coat Sloper, the following measurements are needed. Note: For overcoat measurement, because of additional ease needed, use two sizes larger. For example for a size 36 overcoat, use size 38 jacket measurements.

1/2 chest circumference – scale + 3-1/2" for ease center front to center back.
1/2 chest front.
1/2 shoulder blade.
Back waist length (neck to waist).

Note: Scale = 1/2 Original Chest Measurement.

See **Size Chart**, pages 8–13.

1 = back neck point.
1 to 2 = back waist length (center back).
1 to 3 = 1/2 scale (1/4 chest measurement) + 1-1/2".
1 to 4 = 1/6 of 1 to 3.
Square off to the left from 1, 4, 3, and 2.
3 to 5 = scale (1/2 chest measurement) + 3-1/2".
5 to 6 = 1/2 front chest measurement.
3 to 7 = shoulder blade + 1/4".
8 = 1/2 7 to 6.
9 = 1/2 5 to 6.
Square up and down from 5, 9, 6, and 7.
Square down from 8 (See diagram).
10 = intersection of lines squared from 1 and 5.
10 to 11 = 10 to 12 - 1/2".
Square off 11 to 13.
13 to 14 = 3/4".
Connect 14 to 11.
1 to 17 = 5-1/2".
17 to 18 = 1-1/2".
17 is located on a squared line 1 to 18 (1-1/2") (see diagram).

BASIC COAT SLOPER

DIAGRAM B

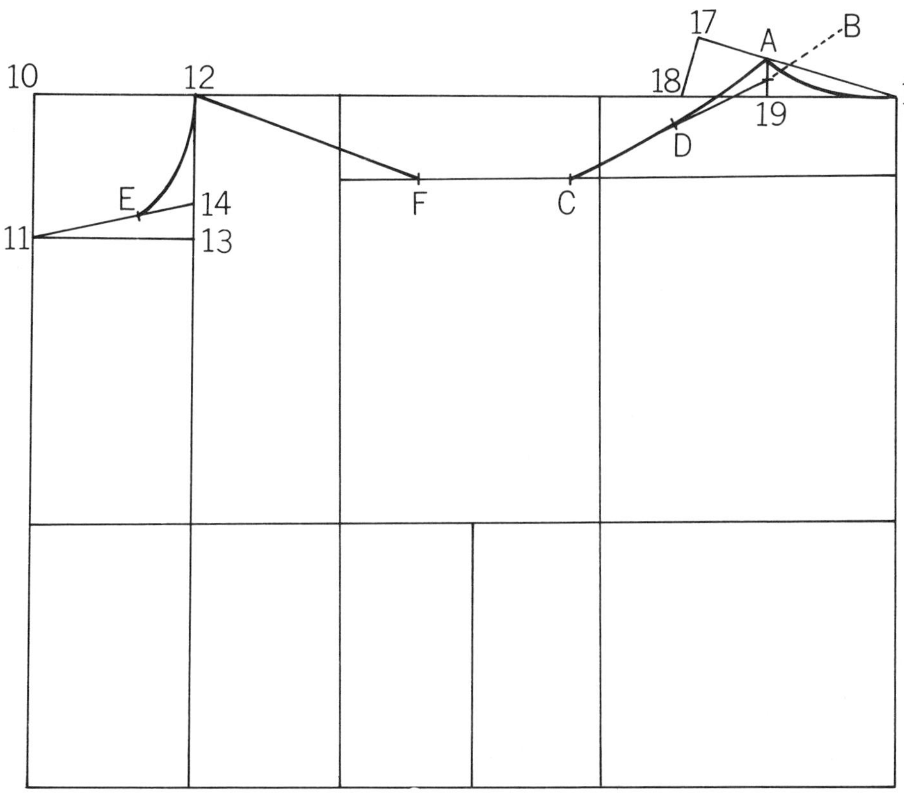

In order to draft neck and shoulder lines, the following measurements are needed:

Shoulder length.
1 to 19 = 10 to 12 - 3/4".
Square up 19 to A.
B = 1/2 of A to 19.
B to C = shoulder length + 1/8".
Connect B to C with straight line.
D = 1/2 of B to C.
Connect A to D with sleigh curve ruler.
Connect A to 1 with sleigh curve ruler to finish back neckline.
14 to E = 1/3 of 14 to 11.
Connect 12 to E with sleigh curve ruler to finish front neckline.
12 to F = A to C - 3/8".

BASIC COAT SLOPER

DIAGRAM C

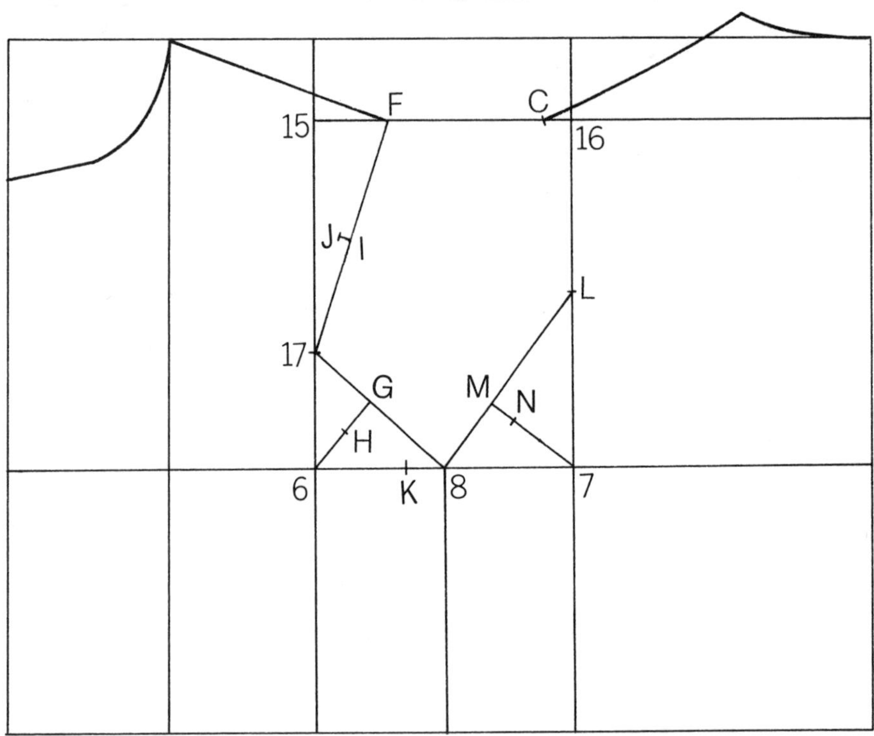

Front Armhole

Preparation:
6 to 17 = 1/3 of 6 to 15.
Connect 17 to F and 17 to 8 with a straight line.
To locate G, square off along the line between 17 and 8 into 6.
H = 1/2 of G to 6.
I = 1/2 of 17 to F.
I to J = 1/4".
K to 8 = 1/3 of 8 to 6.

Back Armhole

Preparation:
L = 1/2 of 7 to 16.
Connect L to 8 with straight line.
To locate M, square off along the line between L to 8 into 7.
M to N = 1/3 of M to 7.

BASIC COAT SLOPER

DIAGRAM D

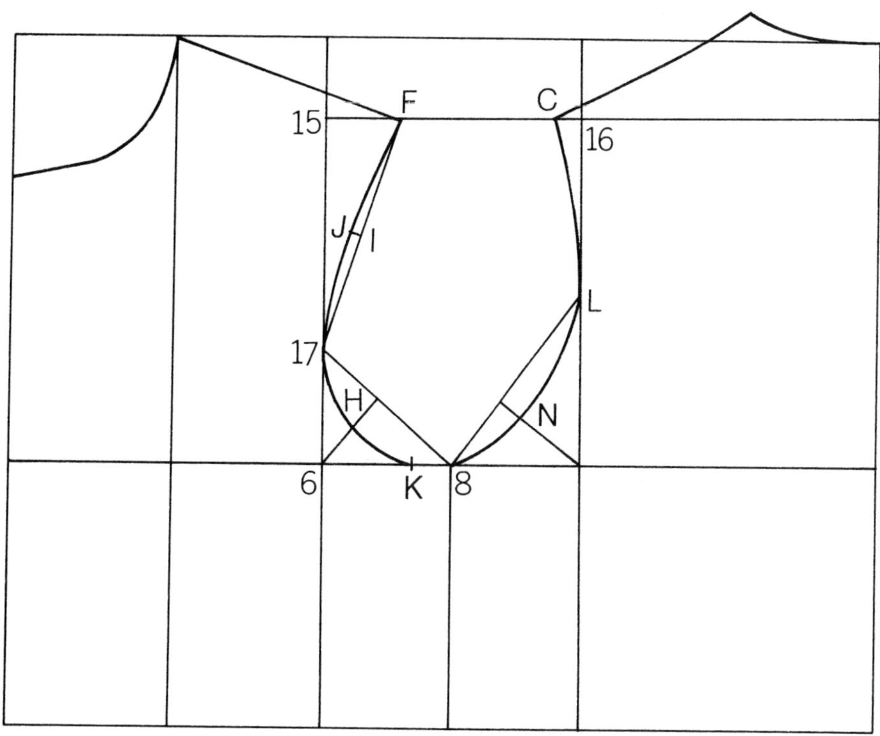

Completion of Armhole

Front
Connect F to J to 17 with sleigh curve ruler.
Connect 17 to H to K with sleigh curve ruler to finish front armhole.

Back
Connect L to N to 8 with sleigh curve ruler.
Connect L to C with sleigh curve ruler to finish back armhole.

CROSSMARK FOR COAT SLOPER ARMHOLE AND SLEEVE CAP

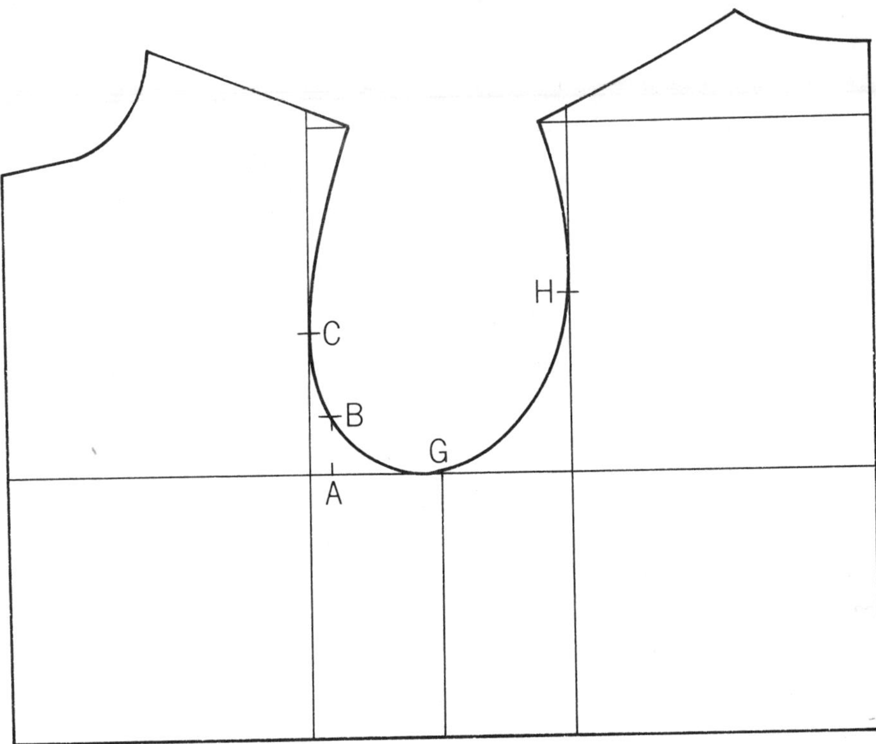

Coat Sloper

Square up A to B = 1-1/2".
B to C = 2 1/4".
Square up D to E = 1-1/2".
E to F = 2 1/2" = 1/4" ease.
G = intersection of armhole and sideseam.
G to H = I to J.
K = top of sleeve.
Keep same crossmark for two piece and other types of sleeve.

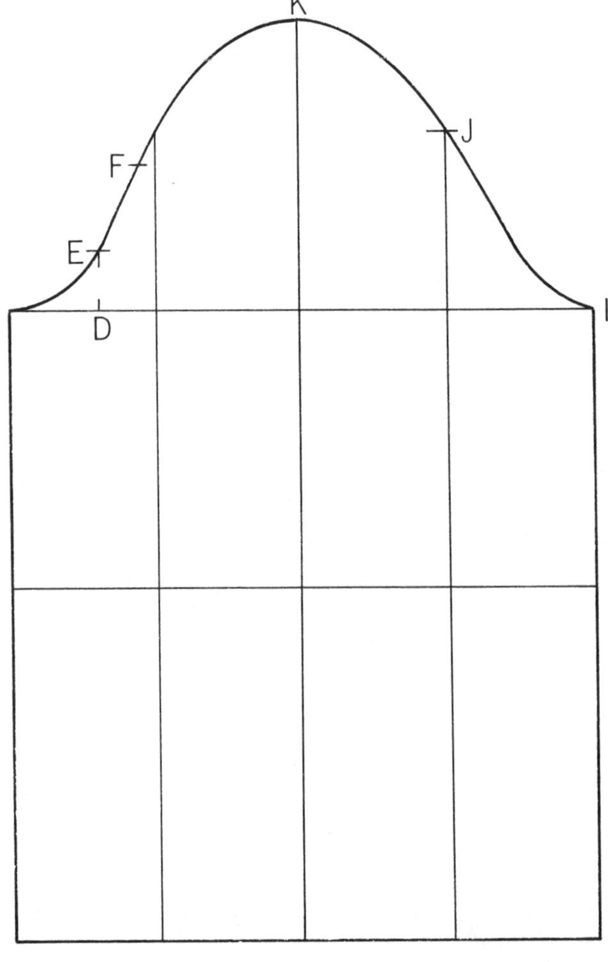

Sleeve Sloper

NOTES

PROCEDURE FOR LENGTHENING BASIC COAT SLOPER

Diagram A

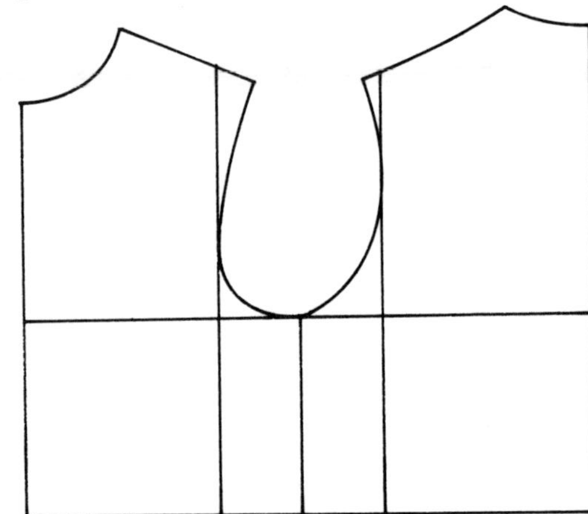

Outline basic sloper.

Diagram B

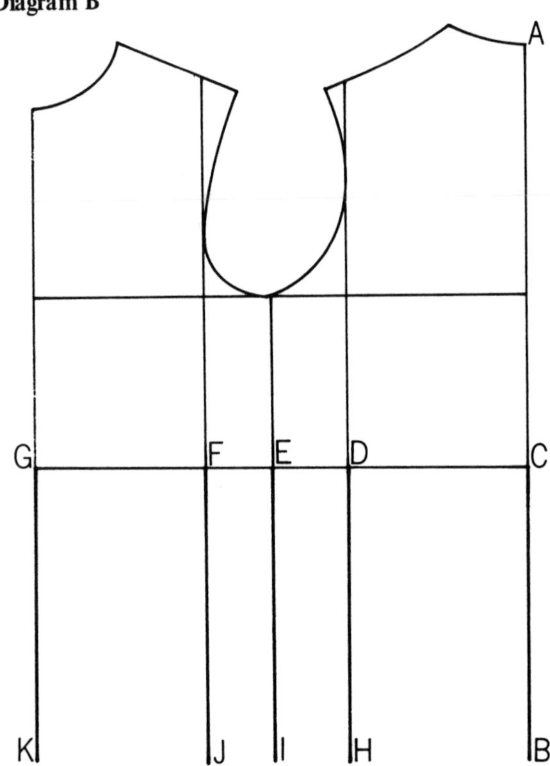

Diagram C

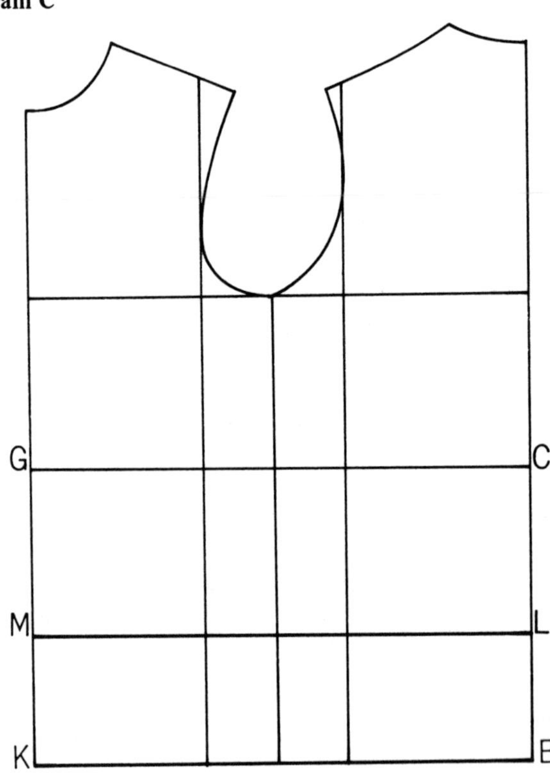

A to B = coat length according to your design.
C = waistline.
Lengthen D to H
E to I
F to J = C to B
G to K

Connect K to B = hemline.
C to L = 8" for hipline which can be used as a guideline for pocket design, etc.
Square off L to M = hipline.

COAT AND JACKET SLOPER PARTS

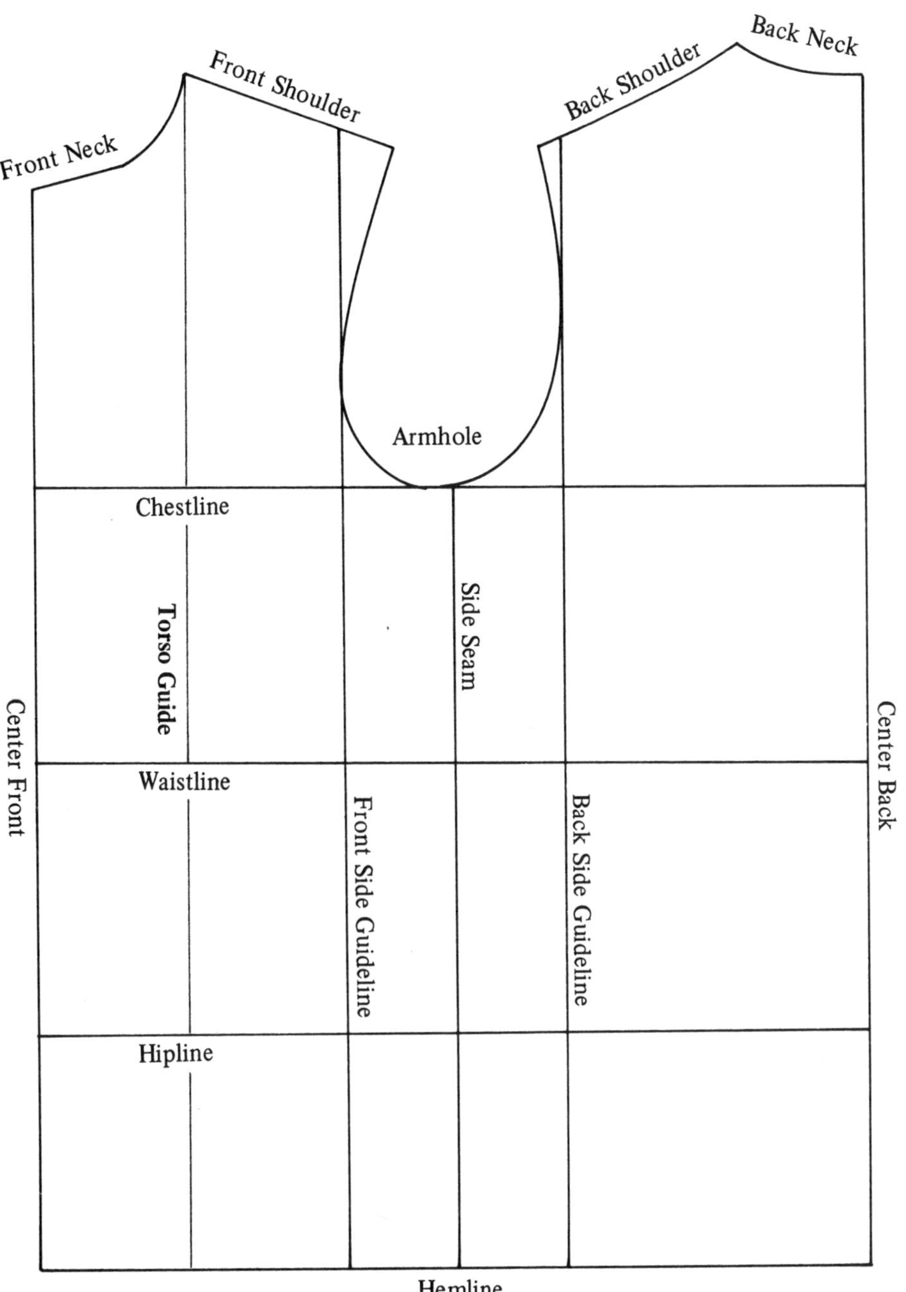

HIGH AND LOW ARMHOLES

DIAGRAM A

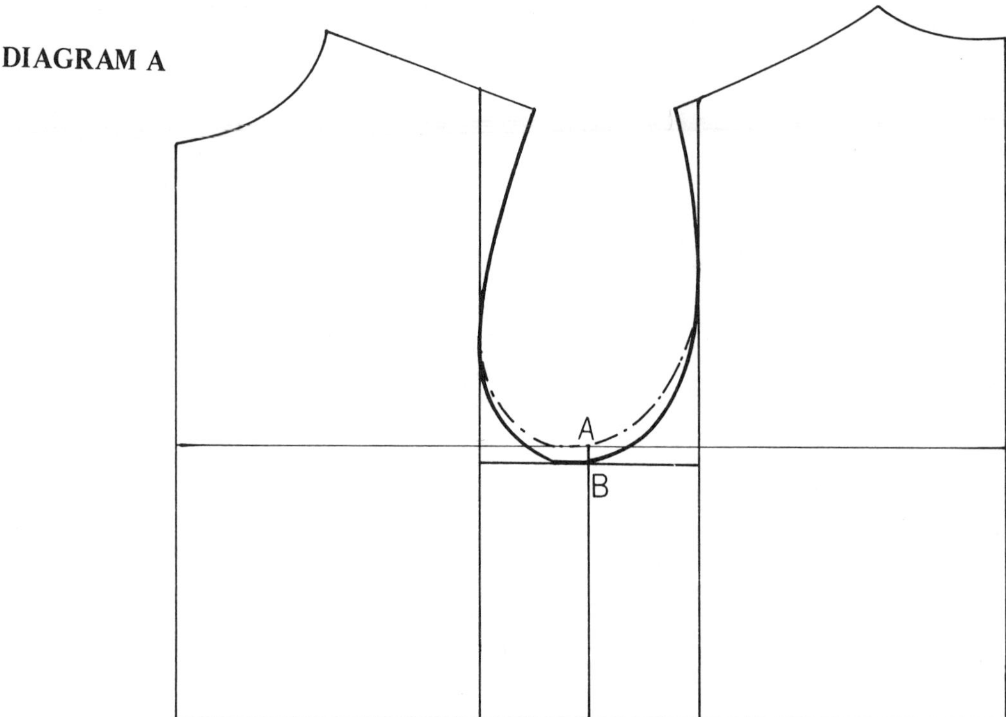

Armhole can be dropped according to design from original sloper.

Example: A to B = 1/2".

DIAGRAM B

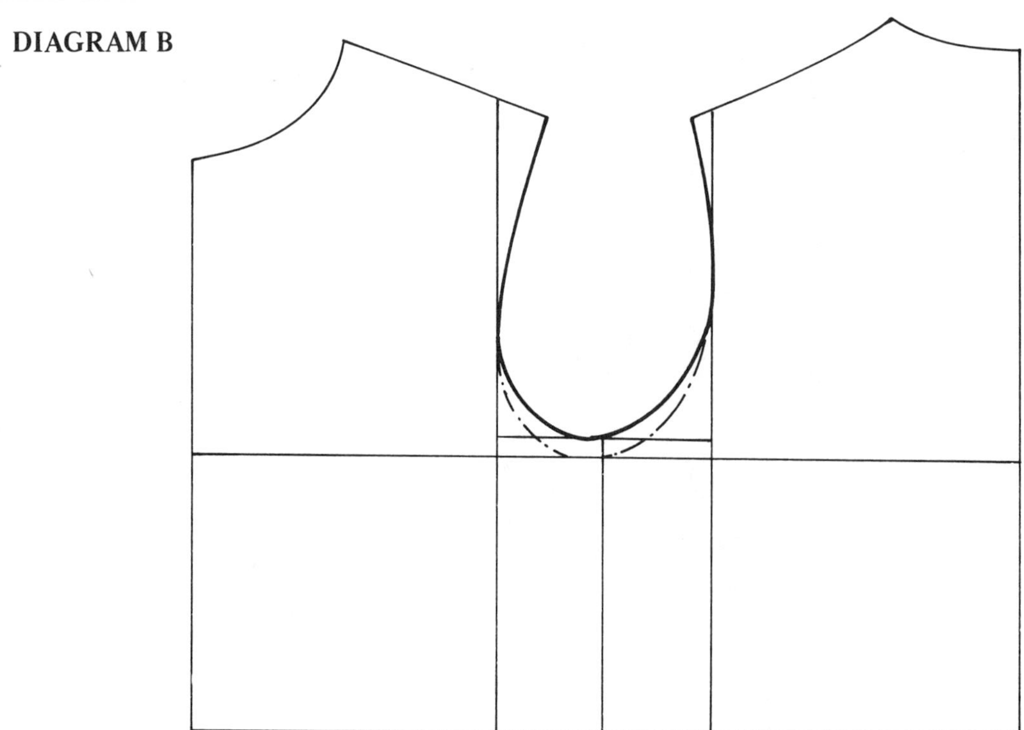

Armhole can be raised 1/2" to 1" according to design from original sloper.

SHIFTING SHOULDER LINE

DIAGRAM A

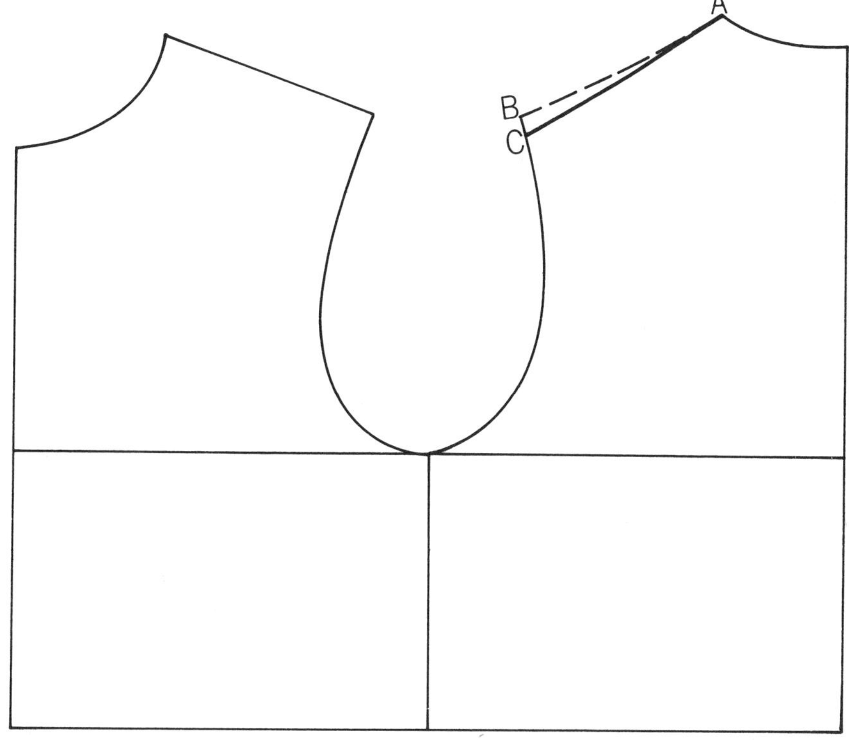

Back Shoulder
A = shoulder at neck.
B = shoulder at armhole.
B to C = 1/2".
Connect C to A with hip curve ruler and remove line A to B to C for new shoulder line A to C.

DIAGRAM B

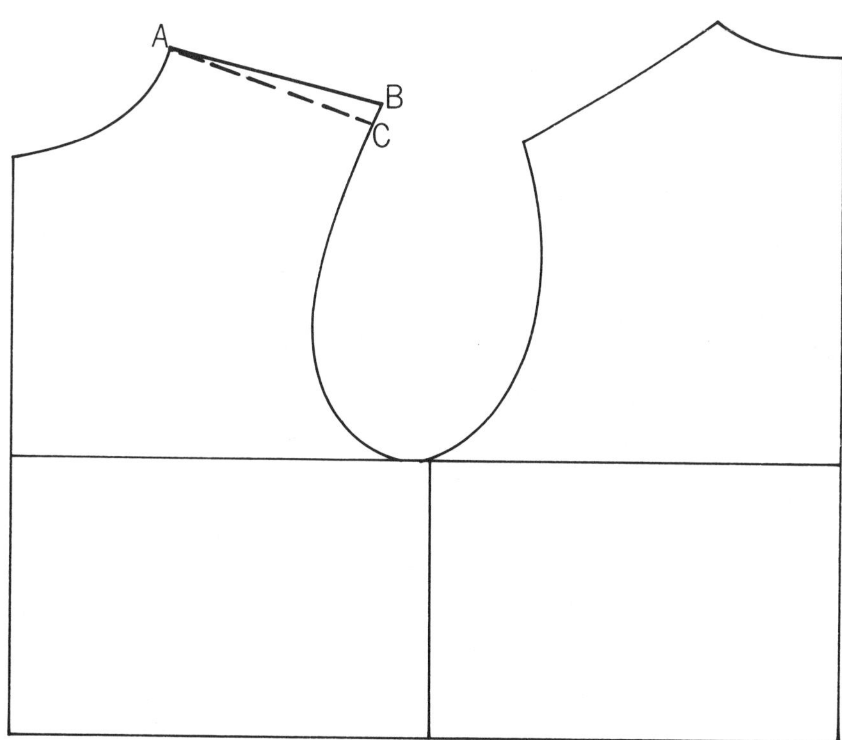

Front Shoulder
Add to the front shoulder the amount removed from the back shoulder.

SECTION IV

FUNDAMENTALS OF COAT DESIGN

FULL LENGTH BATHROBE

Outline your basic sloper.
Lengthen sloper according to your design.

Back Panel
A = side seam at armhole.
B to C = 1/2".
Connect A to C with straight line to finish back panel.

Front Panel
B to D = 1/2".
Connect A to D to finish front side seam.
E = center front at waist.
E to F = 5" for extension.
Extend neckline to G.
Square up and down from F to G to H.

Lapel
F to I = 1".
J = intersection of neck and shoulder.
J to K = Collar stand = 1-1/2" - 1/4".
Connect I to K for roll line.
L = roll line at neck.
M = 1/2 of G to L.
M to N = 2-1/2".
Connect N to M.

Collar. See page 188.
Sleeve. See page 110.

Belt
Length – 75" to 80".
Width – 2-1/4".

DIAGRAM–Full Length Bathrobe

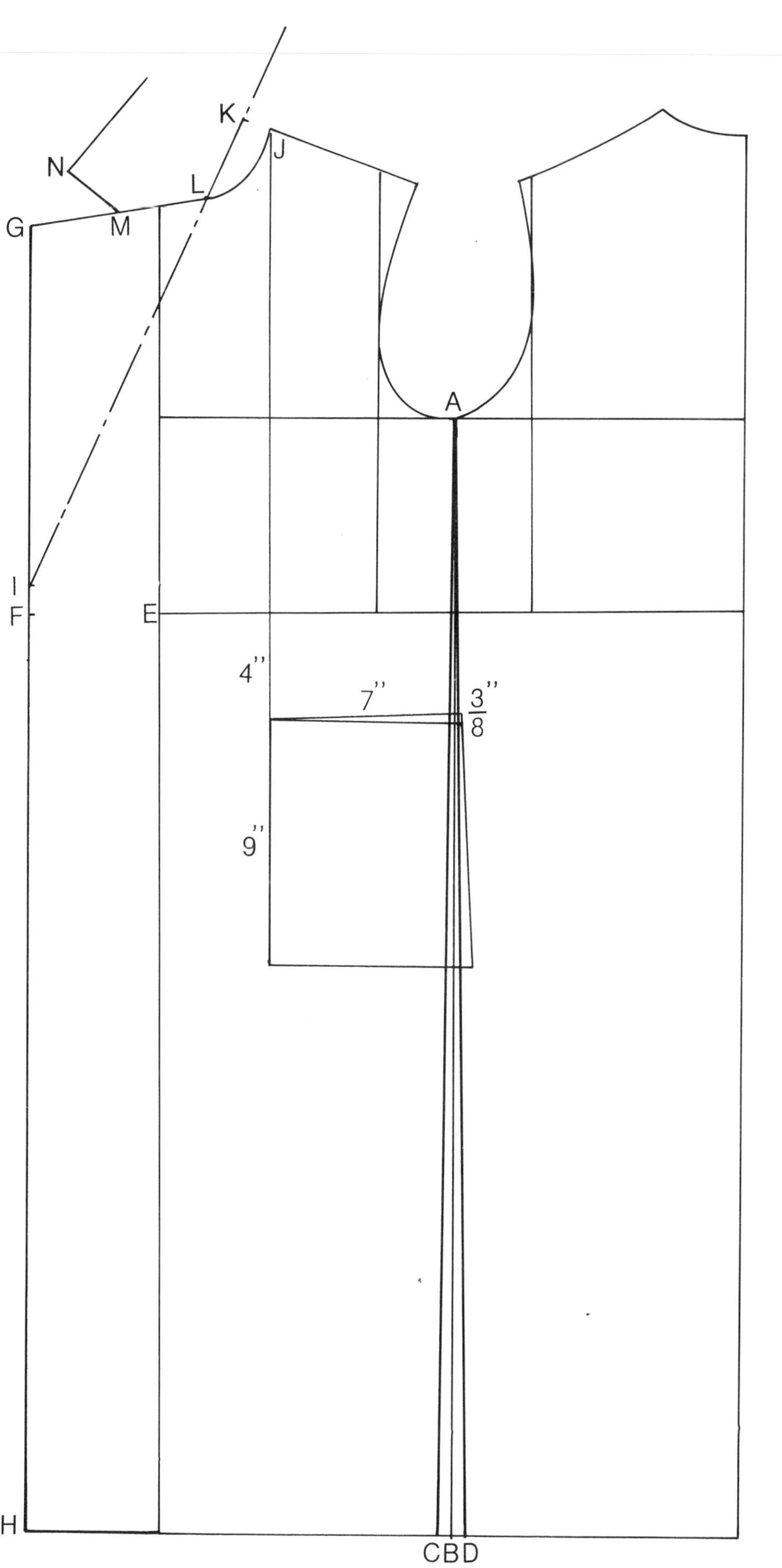

SHAWL COLLAR BATHROBE

Outline your basic sloper.
Lengthen according to design.

Back Robe Panel
A = side seam at armhole.
A to B = 1".
Square down B to C.
C to D = 1/4".
Connect B to D with straight line to finish back panel.

Front Robe Panel
C to E = 1/4".
Connect B to E with straight line to finish side seam.
F = center front at waist.
F to G = 1".
G to H = 4" for extension.
Square down from H to I.
I to J = 3/4".
Square off J to K.
Connect K to E with hip curve to finish hem line.
L = intersection of shoulder and neck.
L to M = 1-1/8".
Connect M to H and extend the line upward.
M to N = back neck measurement.
N to O = 1-1/8" plus 1/2" shift = 1-5/8".
Connect O to P.
P = deepest section of neck.
Q = new neckline at shoulder.
Measure Q to O = back neck measurement.
Square off from O to R = 1-1/8" stand plus 1-5/8" for collar fall.
Square off S to T = 2-3/4" through neck point.
U = 1/3 of S to H.
U to V = 3".
Connect T to V with hip curve ruler.
Connect V to H with hip curve ruler.
Connect R to T with hip curve ruler straight line toward R.

Pocket
See diagram.

Belt
Width – 2".
Length – 60" to 70".

DIAGRAM—Shawl Collar Bathrobe

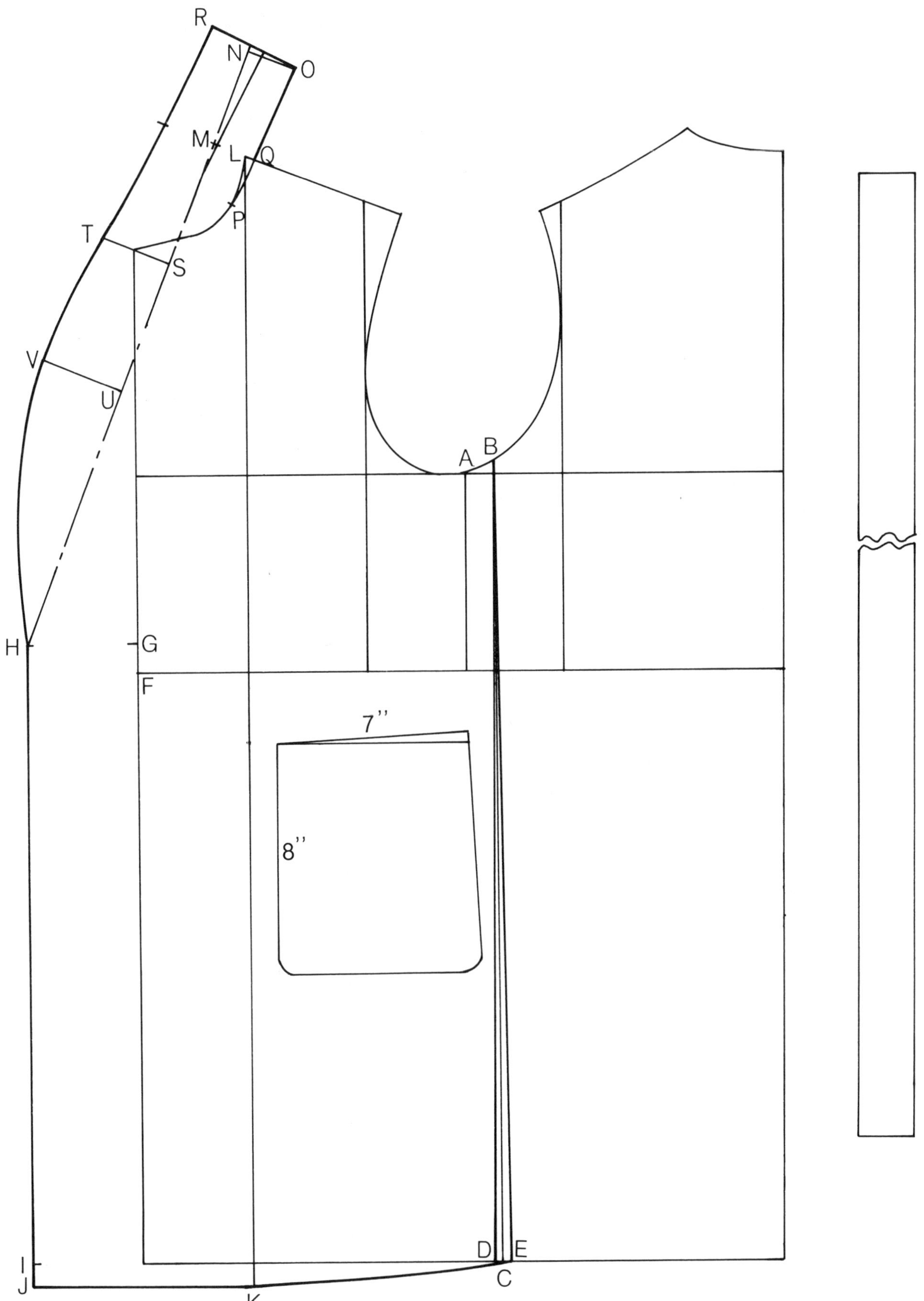

BOX COAT

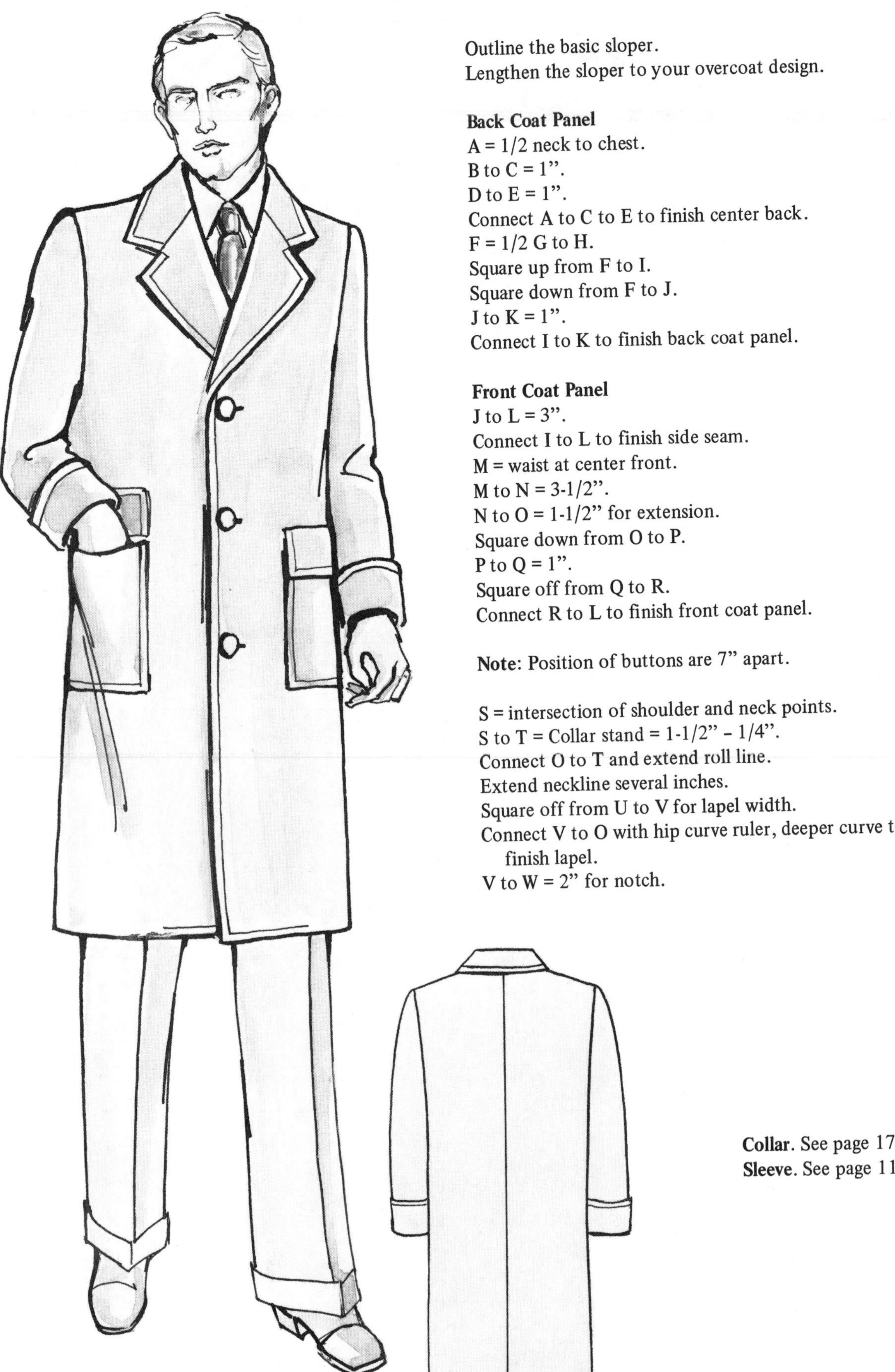

Outline the basic sloper.
Lengthen the sloper to your overcoat design.

Back Coat Panel
A = 1/2 neck to chest.
B to C = 1”.
D to E = 1”.
Connect A to C to E to finish center back.
F = 1/2 G to H.
Square up from F to I.
Square down from F to J.
J to K = 1”.
Connect I to K to finish back coat panel.

Front Coat Panel
J to L = 3”.
Connect I to L to finish side seam.
M = waist at center front.
M to N = 3-1/2”.
N to O = 1-1/2” for extension.
Square down from O to P.
P to Q = 1”.
Square off from Q to R.
Connect R to L to finish front coat panel.

Note: Position of buttons are 7” apart.

S = intersection of shoulder and neck points.
S to T = Collar stand = 1-1/2” - 1/4”.
Connect O to T and extend roll line.
Extend neckline several inches.
Square off from U to V for lapel width.
Connect V to O with hip curve ruler, deeper curve toward O to finish lapel.
V to W = 2” for notch.

Collar. See page 178.
Sleeve. See page 110.

DIAGRAM—Box Coat

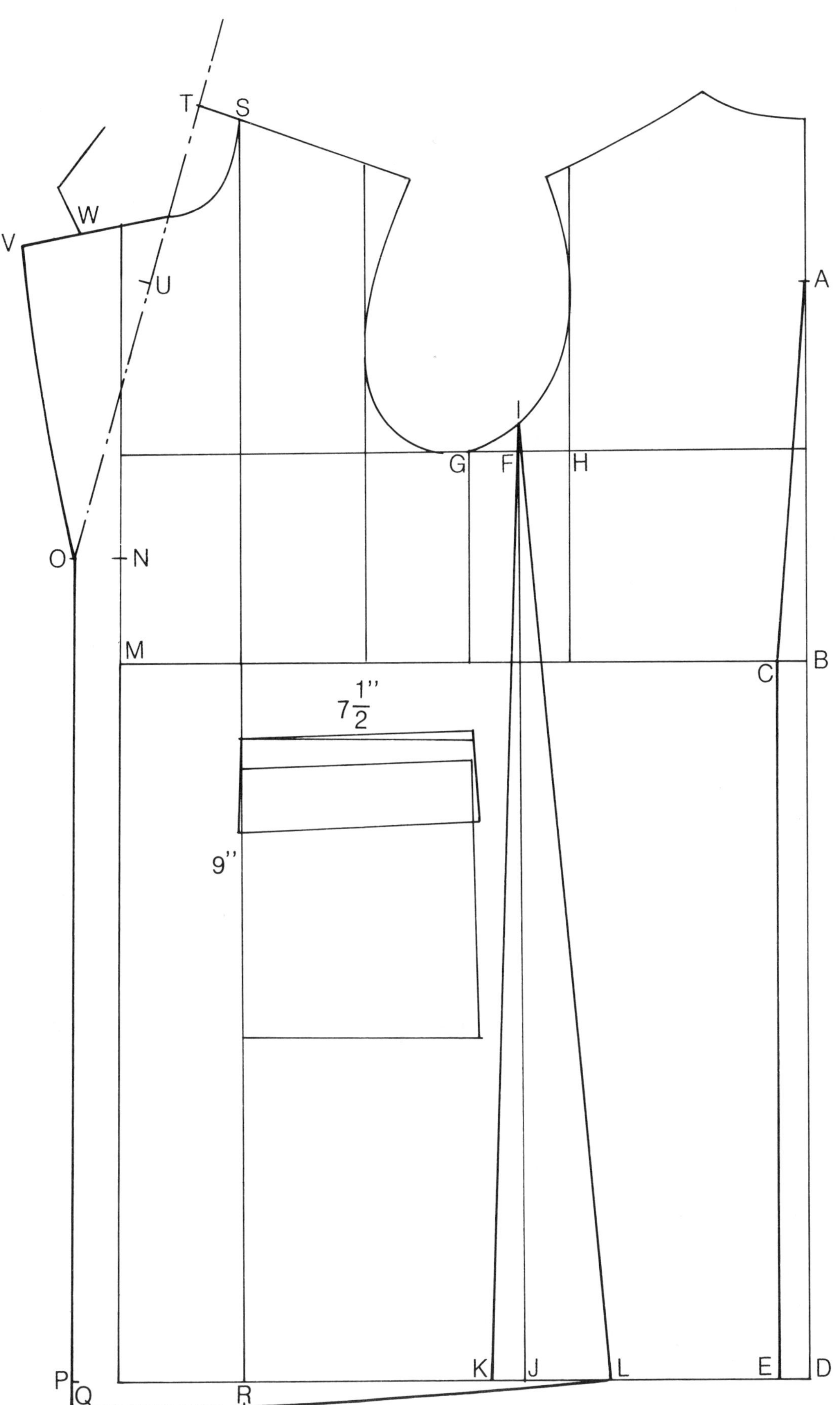

YOKED TOPCOAT

Outline basic sloper to the desired length.

Back Coat Panel
A = 1/2 of neck and chest lines.
B to C = 1".
D to E = 1".
F = 1/2 of G to H.
Square up to I and square down to J.
J to K = 1".
Connect I to K with straight line to finish back coat panel.

Front Coat Panel
J to L = 1-1/2" to finish side seam.
M = chest at center front.
M to N = 1" extension.
Square down N to O.
O to P = 3/4".
Square off from P to Q.
Connect Q to L with hip curve ruler to finish hemline.
R = neck point.
S to R = 1/2".
Shift center front 3/8" to T.
Connect T to M to establish new center front.
T to U = 1" extension.
Blend new neckline into T.
Square off from T to U to finish new neckline.
T to V = 1".
V = stitching line.
U to V = 2" (see diagram for stitching line).

Back Coat Yoke
1 = 1/3 of 2 to 3.
Square off from 1 to armhole = 4.
4 to 5 = 3/4".
5 to 6 = 1/4" to be removed.
7 = 1/2 of 1 to 4.
Connect 7 to 5 with hip curve ruler.
Connect 7 to 6 with hip curve ruler to finish the back yoke.

Front Coat Yoke
8 = 1/2 of T to 9.
10 = 1/2 of 11 to 12 – 1".
Connect 8 to 10 with straight guide line.
13 = 1/2 of 8 to 10.
10 to 14 = 3/4".
14 to 15 = 1/4.
Connect 14 to 13 with sleigh curve ruler.
Connect 13 to 15 with sleigh curve ruler to finish front coat yoke.

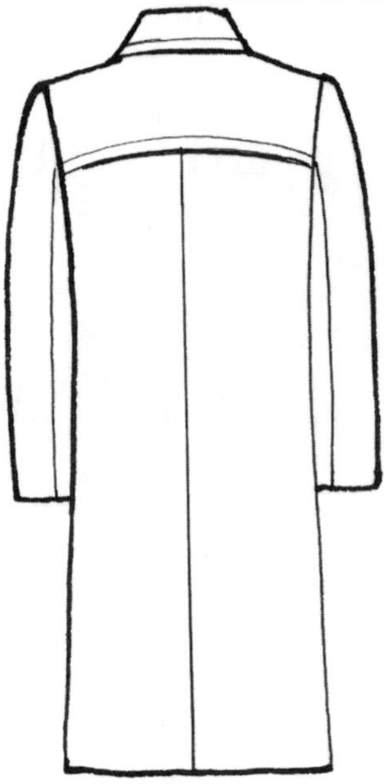

Collar
Square in both directions from a (see diagram).
a to b = back neck measurement plus front neck 9 to V.
a to c = 1/2".
c to d = 1-1/4".
d to e = 2".
Square off from e to f.
Square up from b to f.
f to g = 1".
Connect g to b.
Curve line in at g according to the design.
Square off from d to h = 2".
b to i = 1/4".
Connect h to i with sleigh curve ruler.
Connect c to b with sleigh curve ruler to finish collar (see diagram).

Pocket
(see diagram).

Sleeve. See page 110.

DIAGRAM—Yoked Topcoat

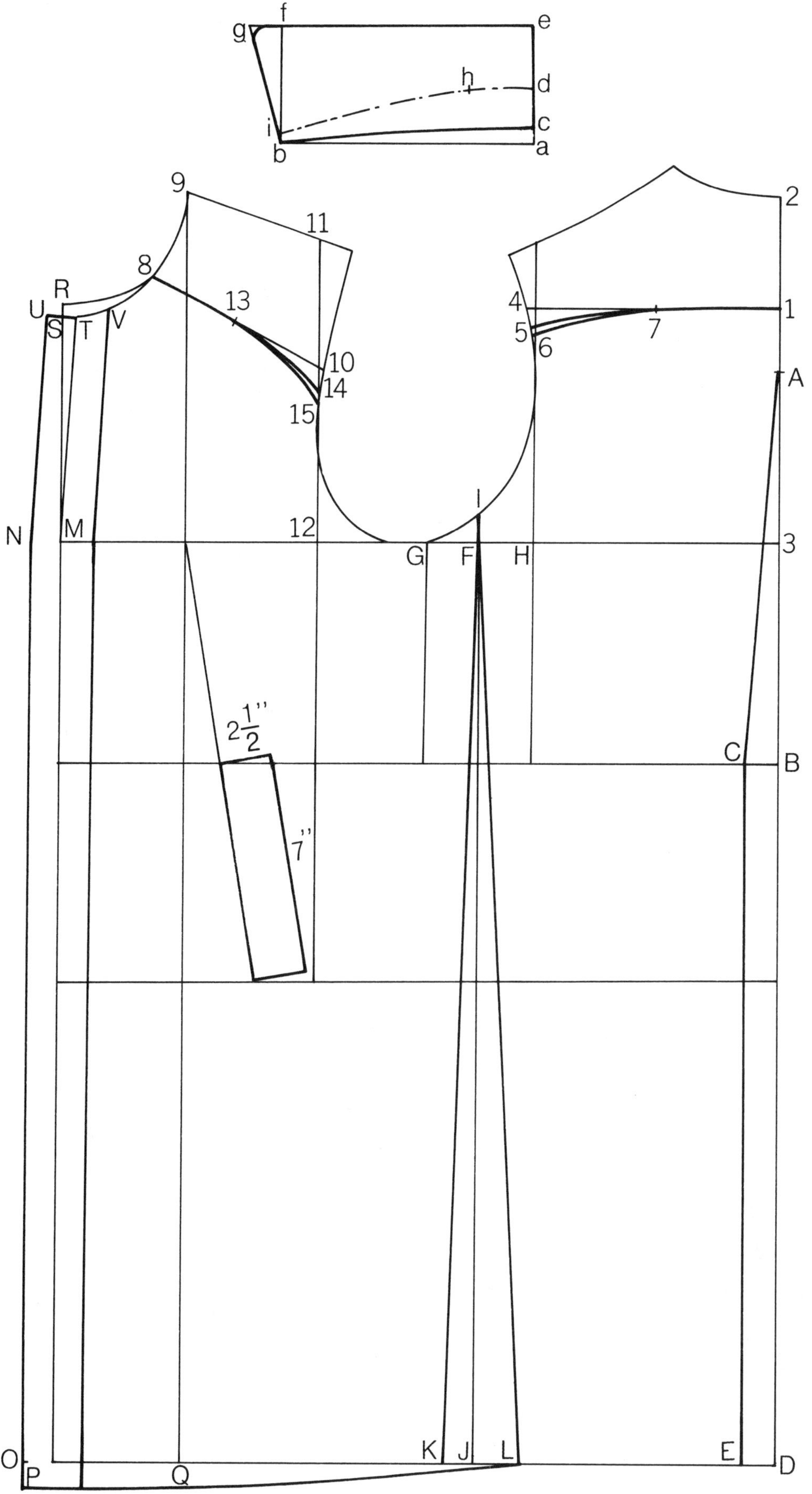

CHESTERFIELD COAT

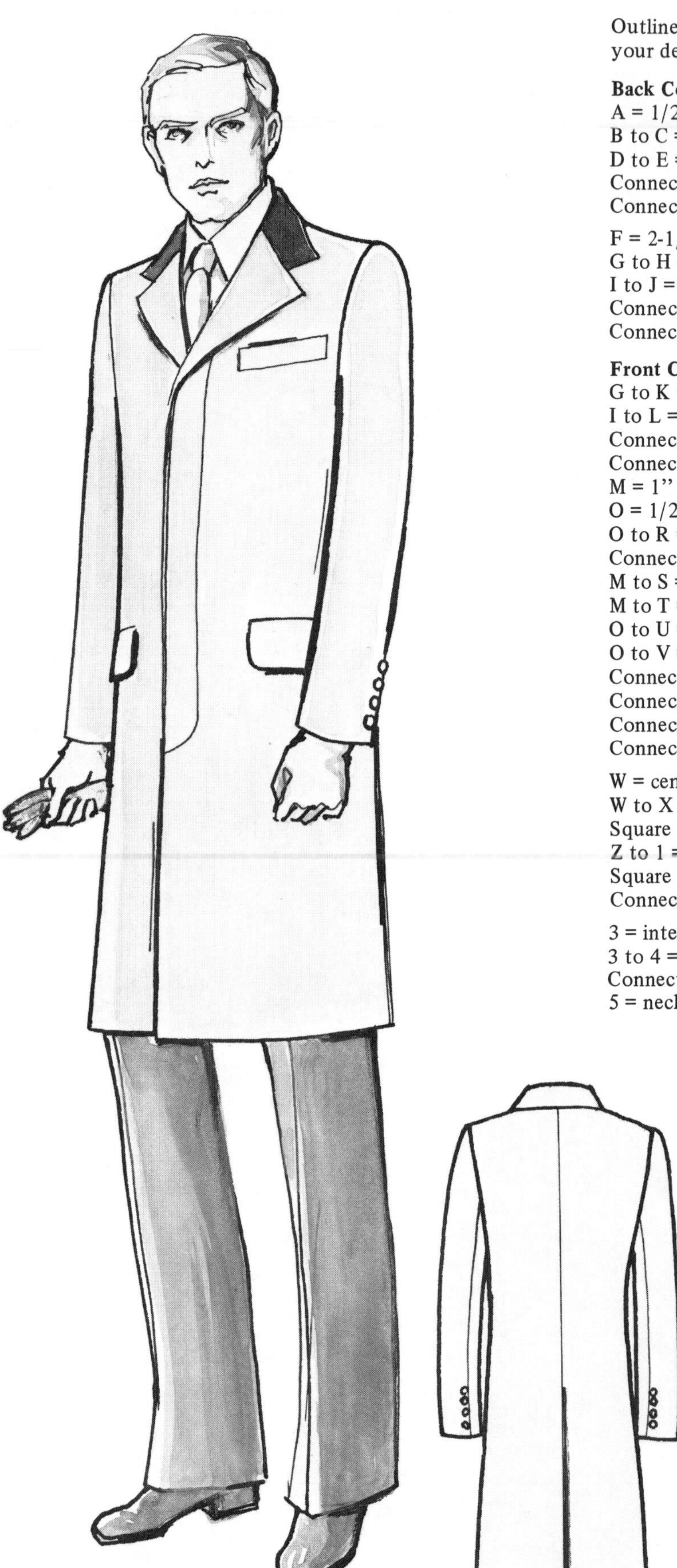

Outline your basic sloper and lengthen according to your design.

Back Coat Panel
A = 1/2 of neck to chest.
B to C = 1".
D to E = 1".
Connect A to C with straight line.
Connect C to E with straight line to finish center back.

F = 2-1/2" above chestline.
G to H = 1/2".
I to J = 1".
Connect F to H with hip curve ruler.
Connect H to J with straight line to finish back coat panel.

Front Coat Panel
G to K = 1/2"
I to L = 1-1/2".
Connect F to K with hip curve ruler.
Connect K to L with straight line to finish side seam.
M = 1" from N.
O = 1/2 of P to Q.
O to R = 3-1/2"
Connect M to O to R with straight line as a guide.
M to S = 1/4".
M to T = 1/4".
O to U = 3/8".
O to V = 3/8".
Connect S to U with hip curve ruler.
Connect U to R with straight line.
Connect T to V with hip curve ruler.
Connect V to R with straight line to finish dart.

W = center front at chest.
W to X = 1-1/4" for extension.
Square down from X to Z.
Z to 1 = 3/4".
Square off from 1 to 2.
Connect 2 to L with hip curve ruler to finish hem.

3 = intersection of neck and shoulder points.
3 to 4 = Collar Stand = 1-1/2" - 1/4".
Connect X to 4 with straight line and extend line.
5 = neckpoint.
5 to 6 = 1/4".
7 = roll line at neck.
Connect 7 to 6 and extend the line toward 9.
Square off 8 to 9 = 4" for lapel width.
Connect 9 to X with hip curve ruler, deeper curve toward X to finish front coat panel.

Collar. See page 178.
Sleeve. See page 110.

DIAGRAM—Chesterfield Coat

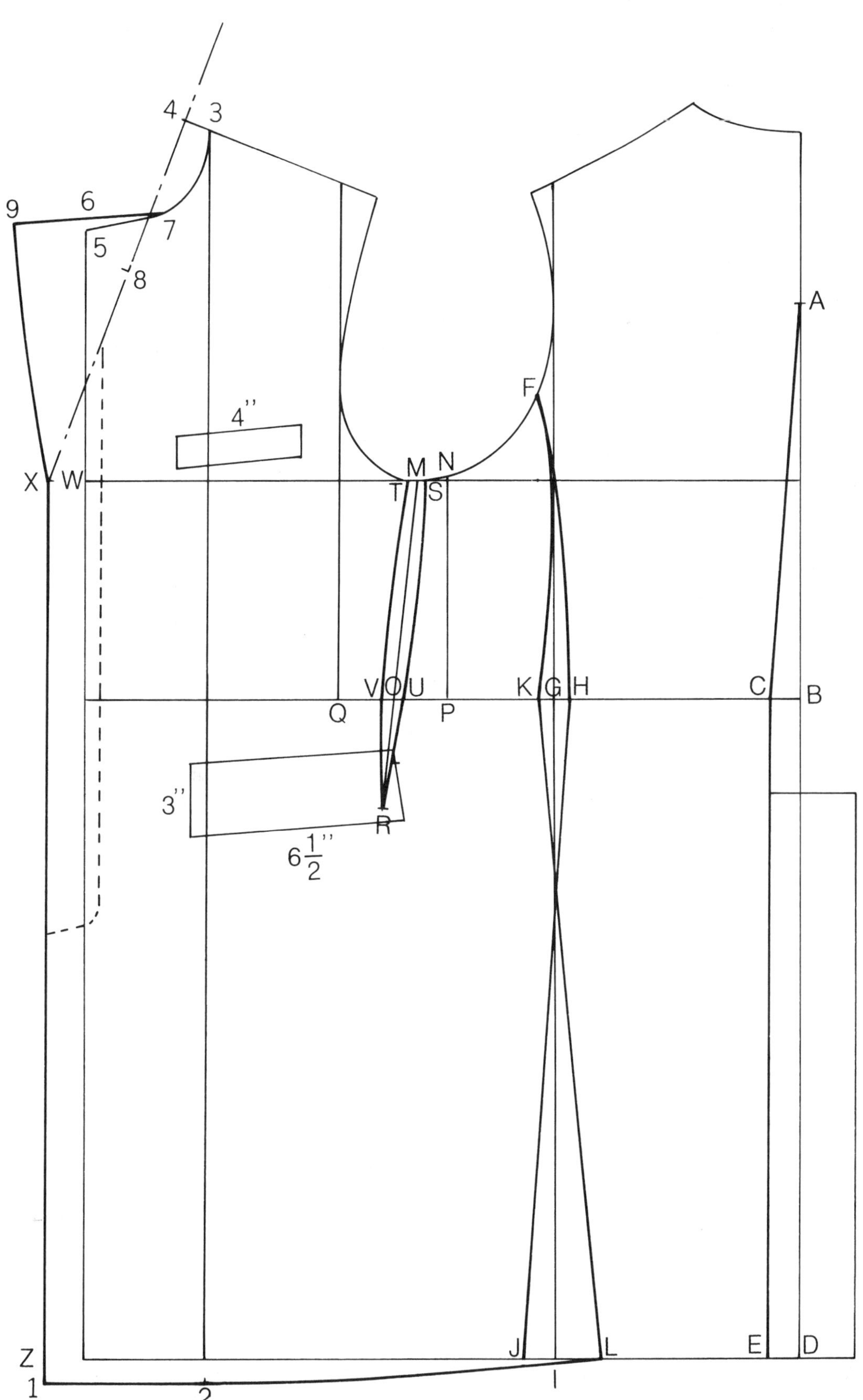

BRITISH GUARD

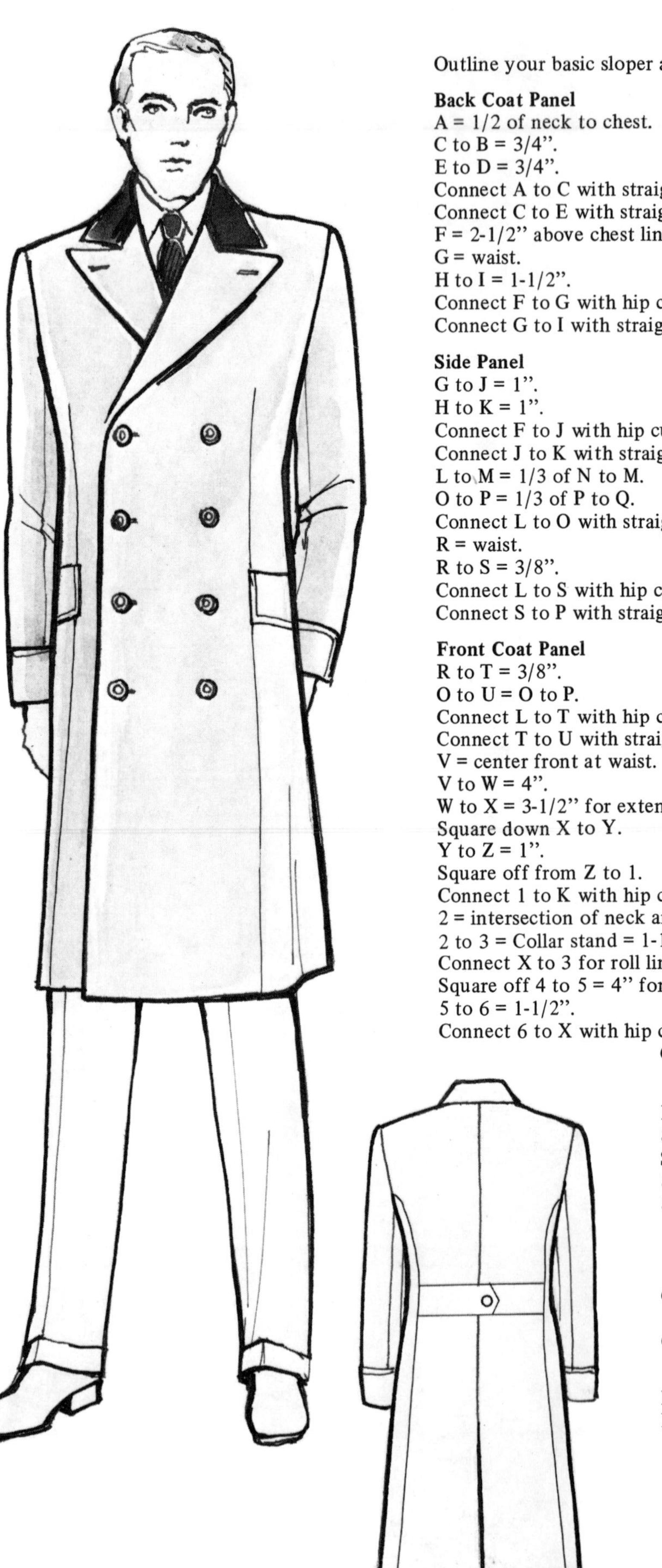

Outline your basic sloper and lengthen according to your design.

Back Coat Panel
A = 1/2 of neck to chest.
C to B = 3/4".
E to D = 3/4".
Connect A to C with straight line.
Connect C to E with straight line to finish center back.
F = 2-1/2" above chest line.
G = waist.
H to I = 1-1/2".
Connect F to G with hip curve ruler.
Connect G to I with straight line to finish back coat panel

Side Panel
G to J = 1".
H to K = 1".
Connect F to J with hip curve ruler.
Connect J to K with straight line to finish back side seam.
L to M = 1/3 of N to M.
O to P = 1/3 of P to Q.
Connect L to O with straight line as a guide.
R = waist.
R to S = 3/8".
Connect L to S with hip curve ruler.
Connect S to P with straight line to finish side panel.

Front Coat Panel
R to T = 3/8".
O to U = O to P.
Connect L to T with hip curve ruler.
Connect T to U with straight line to finish side seam.
V = center front at waist.
V to W = 4".
W to X = 3-1/2" for extension.
Square down X to Y.
Y to Z = 1".
Square off from Z to 1.
Connect 1 to K with hip curve ruler to finish hem line.
2 = intersection of neck and shoulder.
2 to 3 = Collar stand = 1-1/2" - 1/4".
Connect X to 3 for roll line.
Square off 4 to 5 = 4" for lapel width.
5 to 6 = 1-1/2".
Connect 6 to X with hip curve ruler deeper curve toward X.
Connect 6 to 7 with straight line to finish lapel.

Front Dart
8 = 1" from 9.
Square up and down from 8.
8 to 10 = 3/8".
8 to 11 = 3/8".
12 = chest.
1 to 13 = 3/8".
1 to 14 = 3/8".
Connect 12 to 10 and 10 to 13 with straight line.
Connect 12 to 11 and 11 to 14 with straight line to finish front darts.

Pocket and Belt
For size, position, and angle of the pocket and belt see diagram.

Collar. See page 178.
Sleeve. See page 110.

DIAGRAM–British Guard

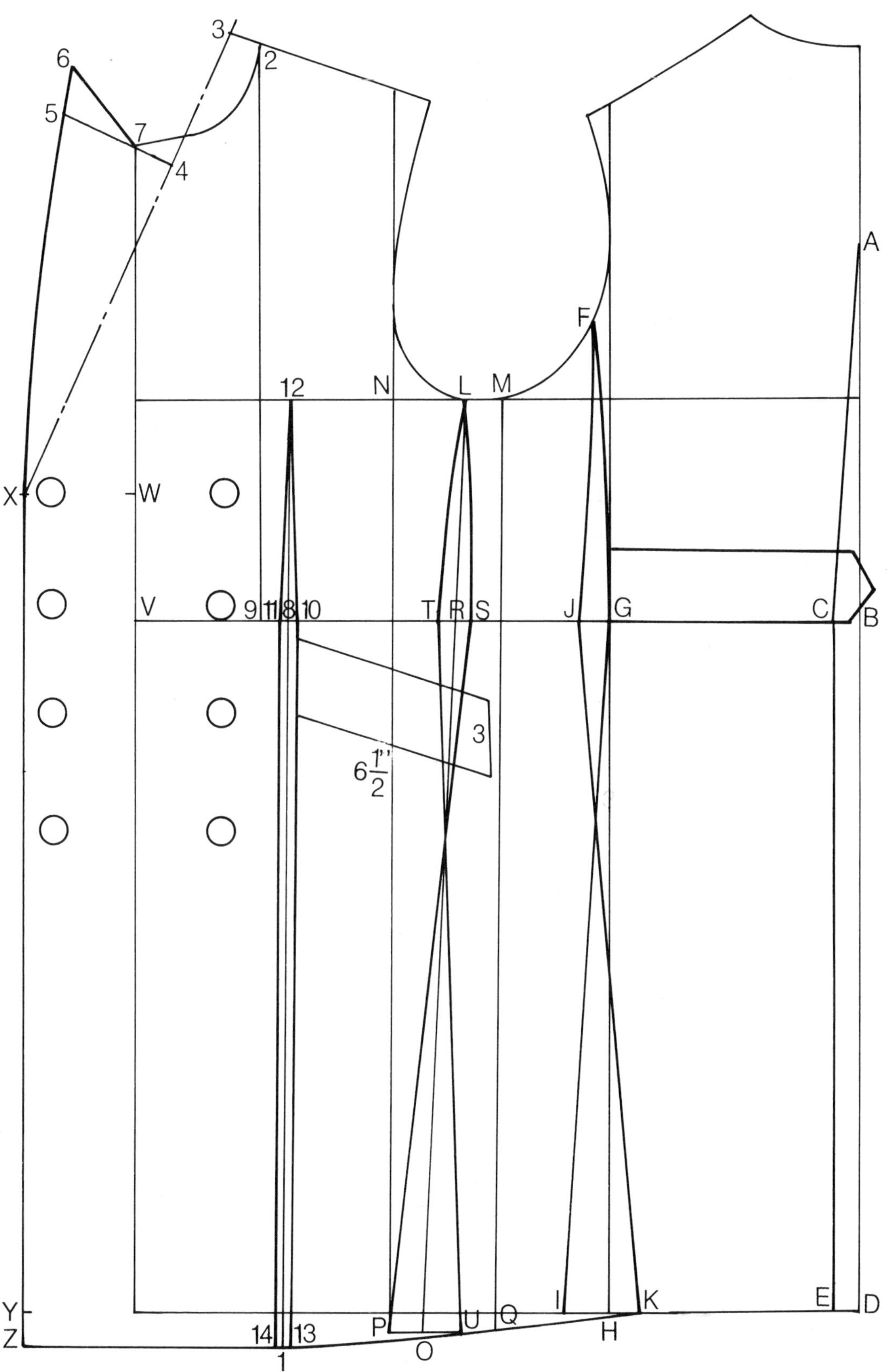

BRITISH WRAP

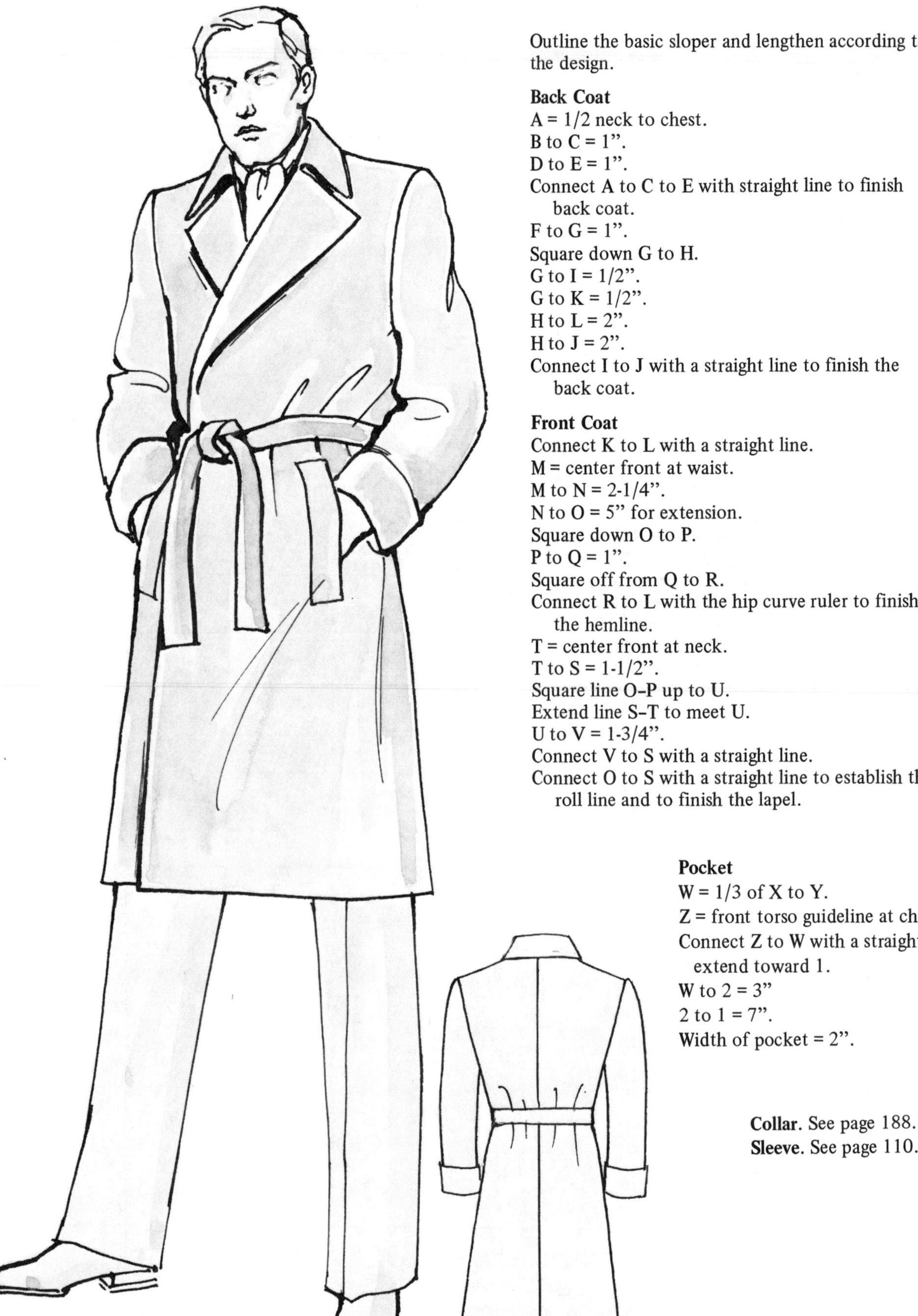

Outline the basic sloper and lengthen according to the design.

Back Coat
A = 1/2 neck to chest.
B to C = 1".
D to E = 1".
Connect A to C to E with straight line to finish back coat.
F to G = 1".
Square down G to H.
G to I = 1/2".
G to K = 1/2".
H to L = 2".
H to J = 2".
Connect I to J with a straight line to finish the back coat.

Front Coat
Connect K to L with a straight line.
M = center front at waist.
M to N = 2-1/4".
N to O = 5" for extension.
Square down O to P.
P to Q = 1".
Square off from Q to R.
Connect R to L with the hip curve ruler to finish the hemline.
T = center front at neck.
T to S = 1-1/2".
Square line O–P up to U.
Extend line S–T to meet U.
U to V = 1-3/4".
Connect V to S with a straight line.
Connect O to S with a straight line to establish the roll line and to finish the lapel.

Pocket
W = 1/3 of X to Y.
Z = front torso guideline at chest.
Connect Z to W with a straight line, extend toward 1.
W to 2 = 3"
2 to 1 = 7".
Width of pocket = 2".

Collar. See page 188.
Sleeve. See page 110.

DIAGRAM—British Wrap

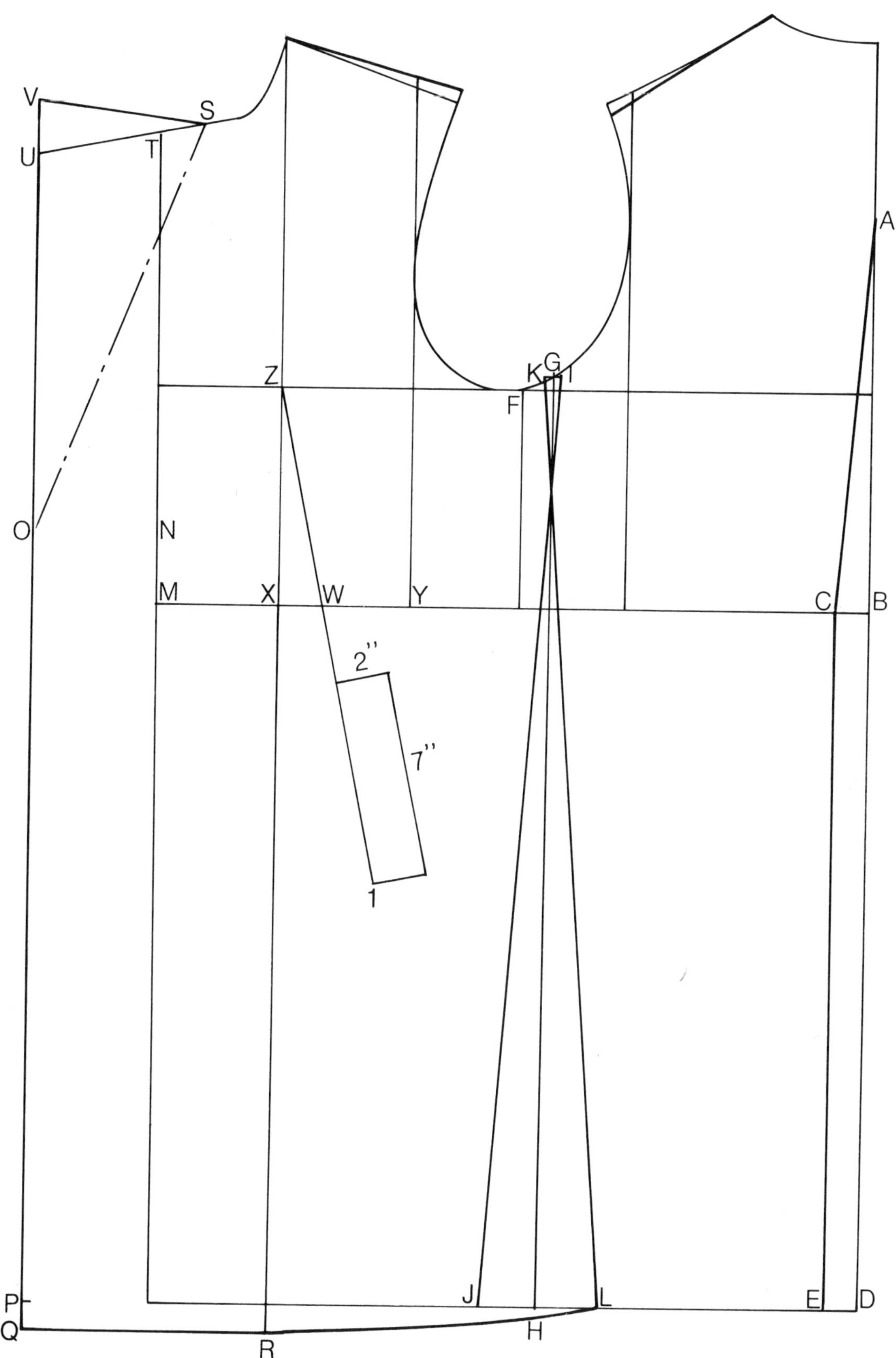

BRITISH WARMER

Outline your basic sloper and lengthen according to your design.

Back Coat Panel
A = 1/2 of neck to chest.
C to B = 1".
E to D = 1".
Connect A to C with straight line.
Connect C to E with straight line to finish center back.
F = 2-1/2" above chestline.
G = back side seam guideline at waist.
H = hem.
G to I = 1" raised waist.
I to J = 1/2".
H to K = 1-3/4".
Connect F to J with hip curve ruler.
Connect J to K with straight line to finish back coat panel.

Front Coat Panel
I to L = 1/2".
H to M = 1-3/4".
Connect F to L with hip curve ruler.
Connect L to M with straight line to finish side seam.

Side Darts
N to O = 1/3 of P to O.
Q= 1/2 of R to S.
Connect N to Q and extend the line to T.
Q to T = 4-1/4".
N to U = 1/4".
N to V = 1/4".
Q to W = 3/8".
Q to X = 3/8".
Connect V to X to T with hip curve ruler.
Connect U to W to T with hip curve ruler to finish side darts.
Y = front guideline at new waistline.
Y to Z = 4-1/2".
Y to 1 = 1/4".
Y to 2 = 1/4".
3 = chest.
Connect 3 to 1 to Z with straight line.
Connect 3 to 2 to Z with straight line to finish front darts.
4 = center front at waist.
4 to 5 = 3-1/4".
5 to 6 = 3" for extension.
Square down 6 to 7.
7 to 8 = 3/4".
Square off 8 to 9.
Connect 9 to M with hip curve ruler to finish hemline.
10 = intersection of neck and shoulder.
10 to 11 = Collar stand = 1-1/2" - 1/4".
Connect 6 to 11 for roll line.
Square off 12 to 13 = 4" for lapel width.
13 to 14 = 2-1/2".
13 to 15 = 2-1/2".
Connect 14 to 15 to finish lapel.

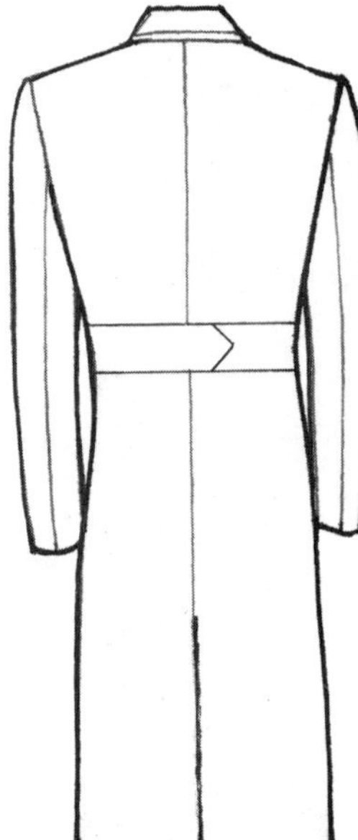

Collar. See page 178.
Sleeve. See page 110.

Pocket
See diagram.

DIAGRAM–British Warmer

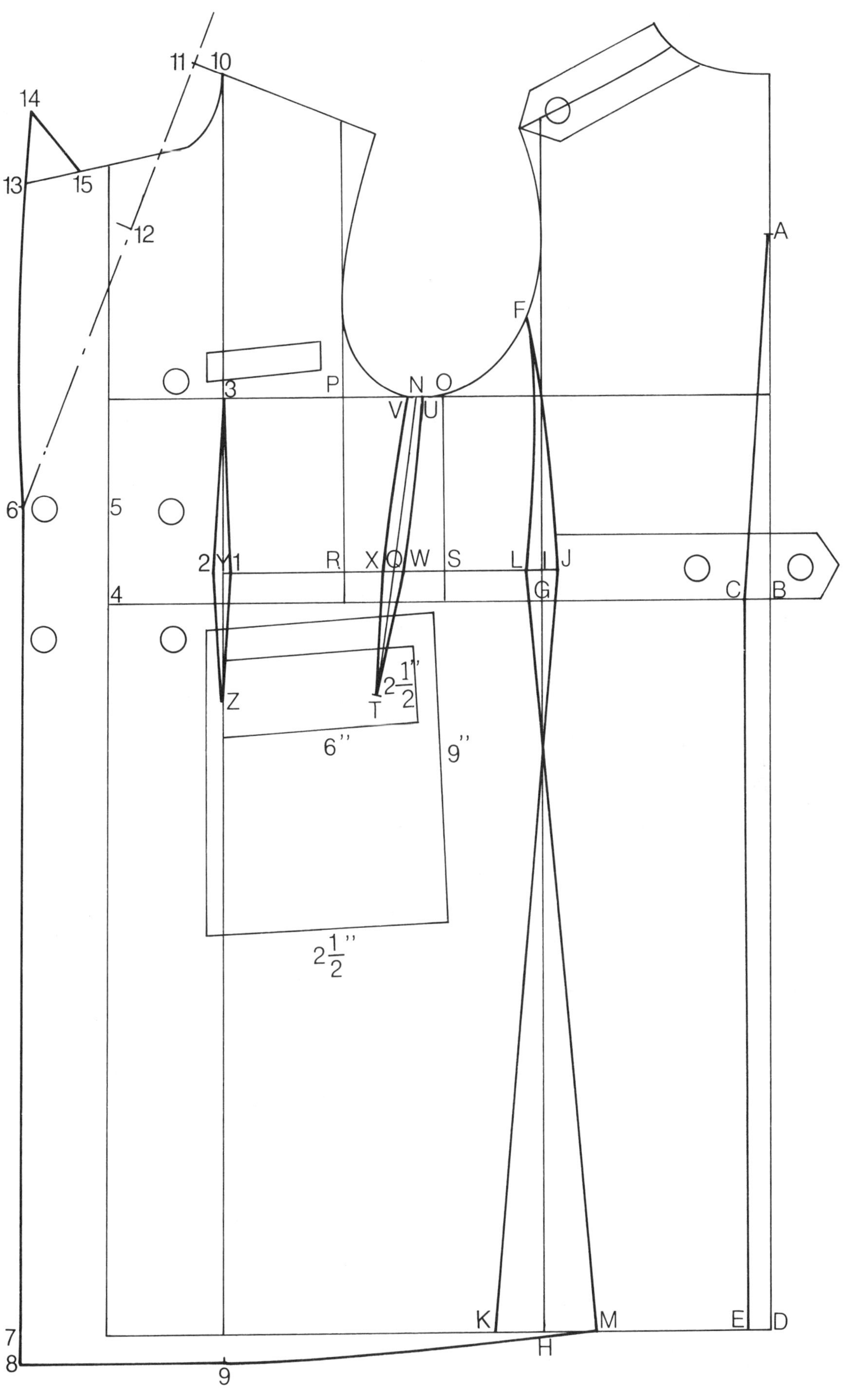

REGENCY COAT

Outline basic coat sloper with the shoulder line shifted 1/2" toward back.

Back Coat Panel
A = 1/2 of neck to chest.
B to C = 3/4".
D to E = 3/4".
Connect A to C to E to finish center back.
Square up F to G = 2".
H = waist.
H to I = 1/2".
J = hem.
J to K = 1-1/2".
Connect G to I with hip curve ruler.
Connect I to K with straight line to finish back panel.

Side Coat Panel
H to L = 1/2".
J to M = 1-1/2".
Connect G to L with hip curve ruler.
Connect L to M with straight line.
N = 1/3 of O to P.
Q = 1/2 of R to S at hem.
T = waist.
N to U = 1/4".
T to V = 1/2".
Connect U to V with hip curve ruler.
Connect V to R with straight line to finish side panel.

Front Coat Panel
N to W = 1/4".
T to X = 1/2".
Connect W to X with hip curve ruler.
Connect X to S with straight line to finish side seam.
Y = center front at waist.
Y to Z = 7".
Z to 1 = 3-1/2" for double-breasted extension.
Square down 1 to 2.
2 to 3 = 1".
Square off from 3 to 4.
4 = 1/2 of 3 to S.
Connect 4 to M with hip curve ruler to finish hem.
5 = neck point.
6 = 1/2 of 5 to 7.
Extend line at 1 upward.
Square off from 6 to 8.
8 to 9 = 2".
10 to 11 = 3/8".
Curve from 6 to 9 to 11 to 1 according to the design.

Front Waist Dart
Y to 12 = 4-3/4".
12 to 13 = 4-1/2".
14 at chest line.
12 to 15 = 1/4".
12 to 16 = 1/4".
Connect 14 to 15 to 13.
Connect 14 to 16 to 13 to finish waist dart.

Pocket
Width of welt pocket = 1-1/2" to 1-3/4".
For position of pocket see diagram.
Length of pocket = 6-1/2" to 7".

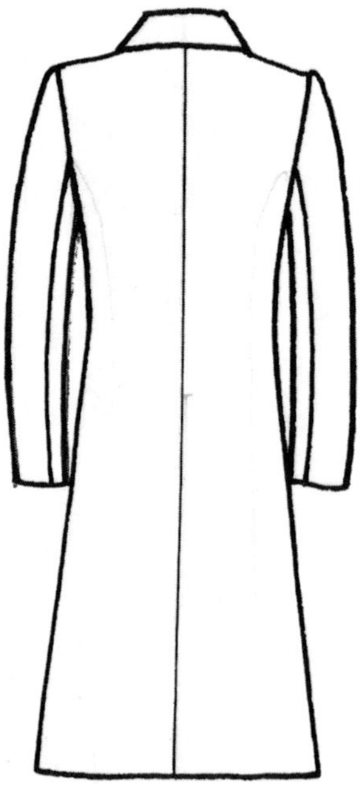

Collar. See page 192.
Sleeve. See page 110.

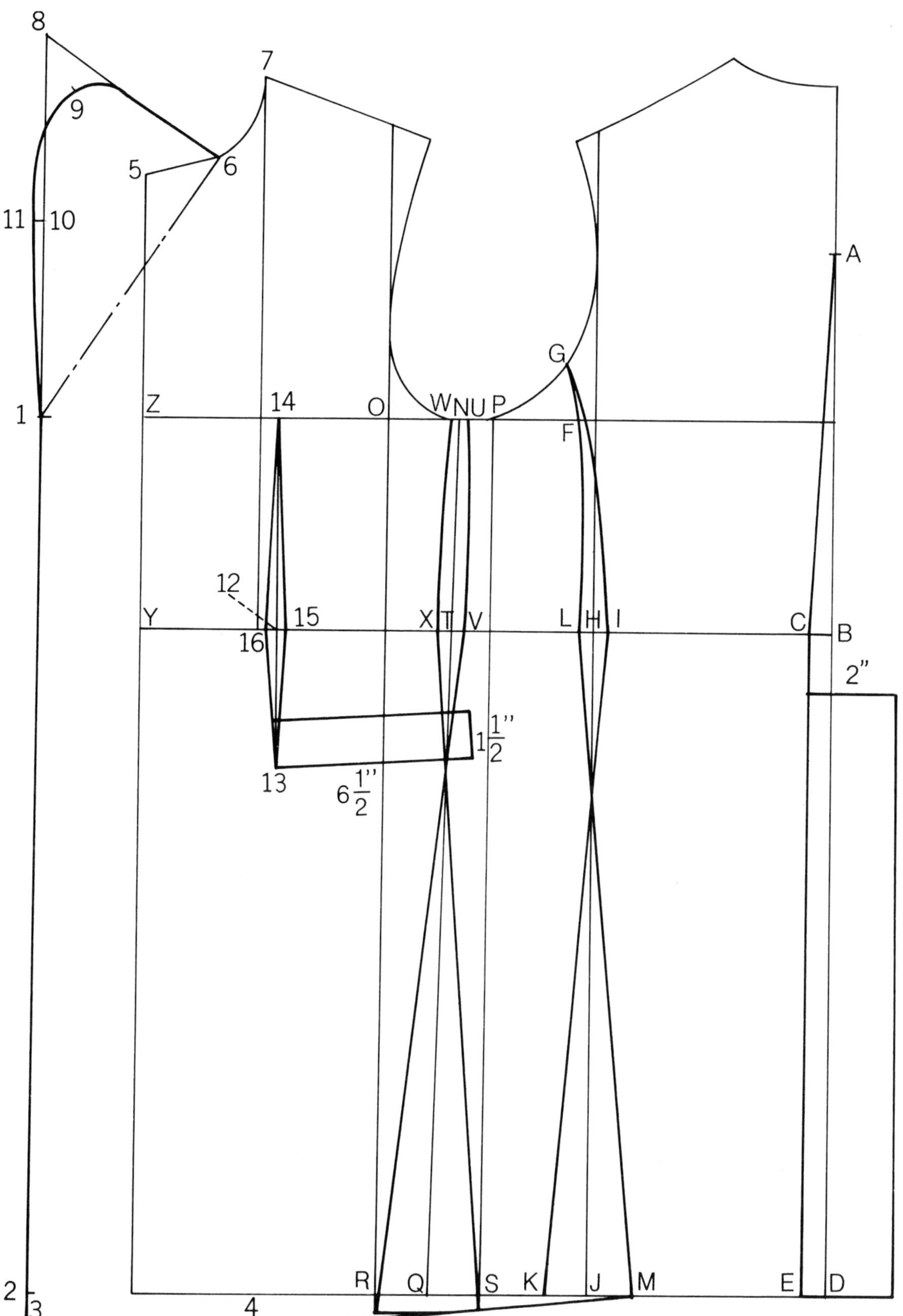
8
7
9
5
6
11
10
A
G
1
Z
14
O
W
N
U
P
F
12
Y
15
X
T
V
L
H
I
C
B
16
2"
1 1/2"
13
6 1/2"
R
Q
S
K
J
M
E
D
2
3
4

PADDOCK COAT

Outline basic coat sloper with shoulder line shifted 1/2" toward back.

Back Coat Panel
A = 1/2 of neck to chest line.
B to C = 1".
D to E = 1" to finish center back.
Square up from F to G = 3".
H = waist.
H to I = 1-1/4".
J = hem.
Connect G to I with hip curve ruler.
Connect I to J with straight line to finish back coat panel.

Front Coat Panel
H to K = 1/4".
J to L = 2".
Connect G to K with hip curve ruler.
Connect K to L with straight line.

Front Side Darts
M to N = 1/2".
O = 1/2 of M to N.
P = 1/2 of Q to R.
Connect O to P with straight guide line.
S = waist.
S to T = 1/2".
S to U = 1/2".
S to V = 4-1/2".
Connect M to T to V with hip curve ruler.
Connect N to U to V with hip curve ruler to finish side dart.

Front Waist Dart
W to X = 3/4".
Square down X to Y.
Y = 3" below waist.
Deepest section of front waist dart will be 1" above the waist = Z.
Take 1/4" both sides of Z to finish front waist dart. (see diagram)
1 = center front at waist.
1 to 2 = 4".
2 to 3 = extension for 1-1/2".
Square down to 4.
4 to 5 = 1".
Square off 5 to 6.
Connect 6 to L to finish coat hem.

Lapel
Extend shoulder line to 7.
7 to 8 = Collar stand – 1/4".
Connect 3 to 7 for roll line.
Extend neck line.
Square off from 10 to 9 = lapel width.
Connect 9 to 3 with hip curve ruler, with deepest part of curve toward 3.

Front Closing
Width of front fly = 2".
3 to 11 = 13". (see diagram)

Pocket
(see diagram)

Center Back Vent
Width = 4-3/4". (see diagram)

Collar. See page 178.
Sleeve. See page 110.

DIAGRAM–Paddock Coat

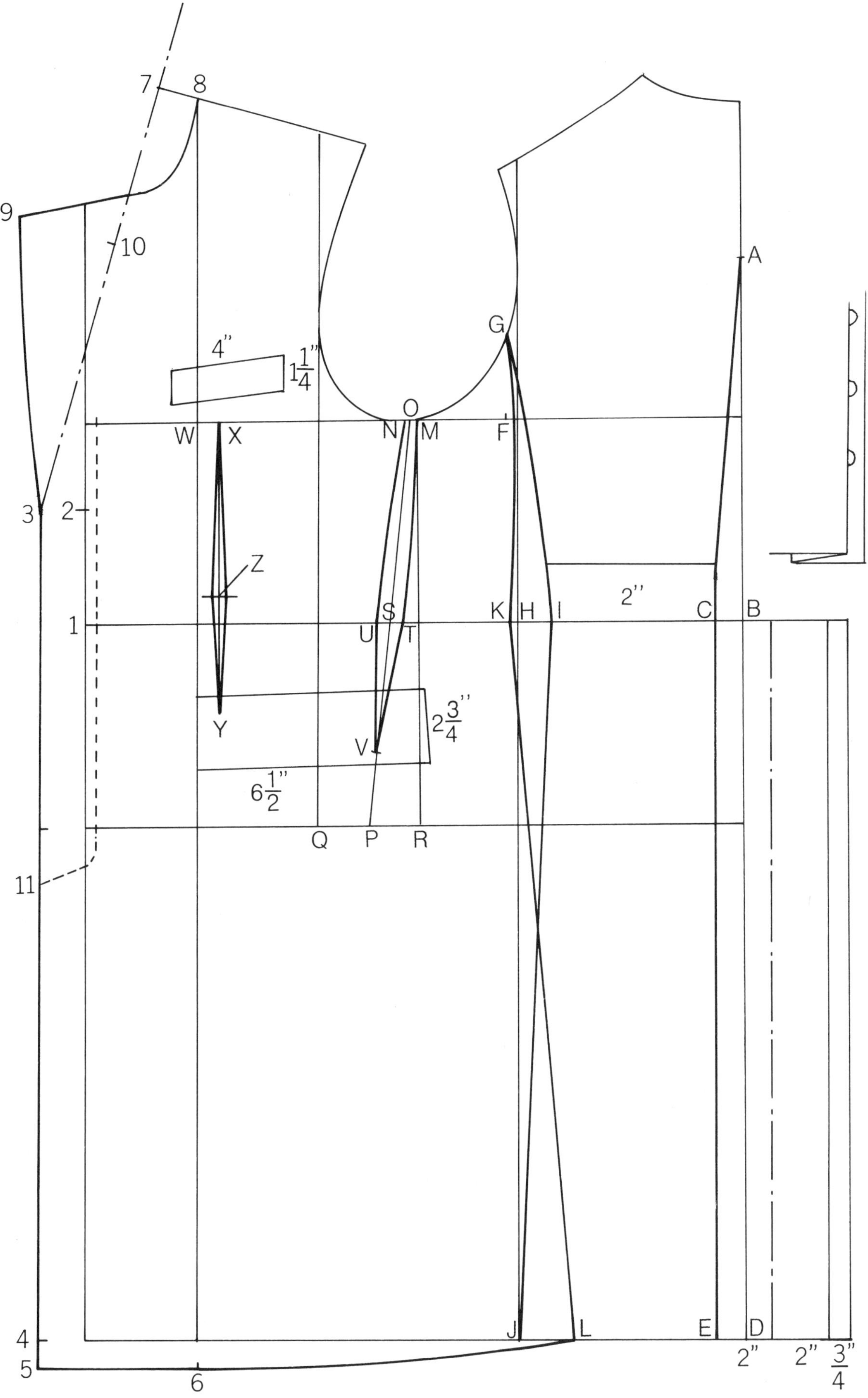

REDINGOTE

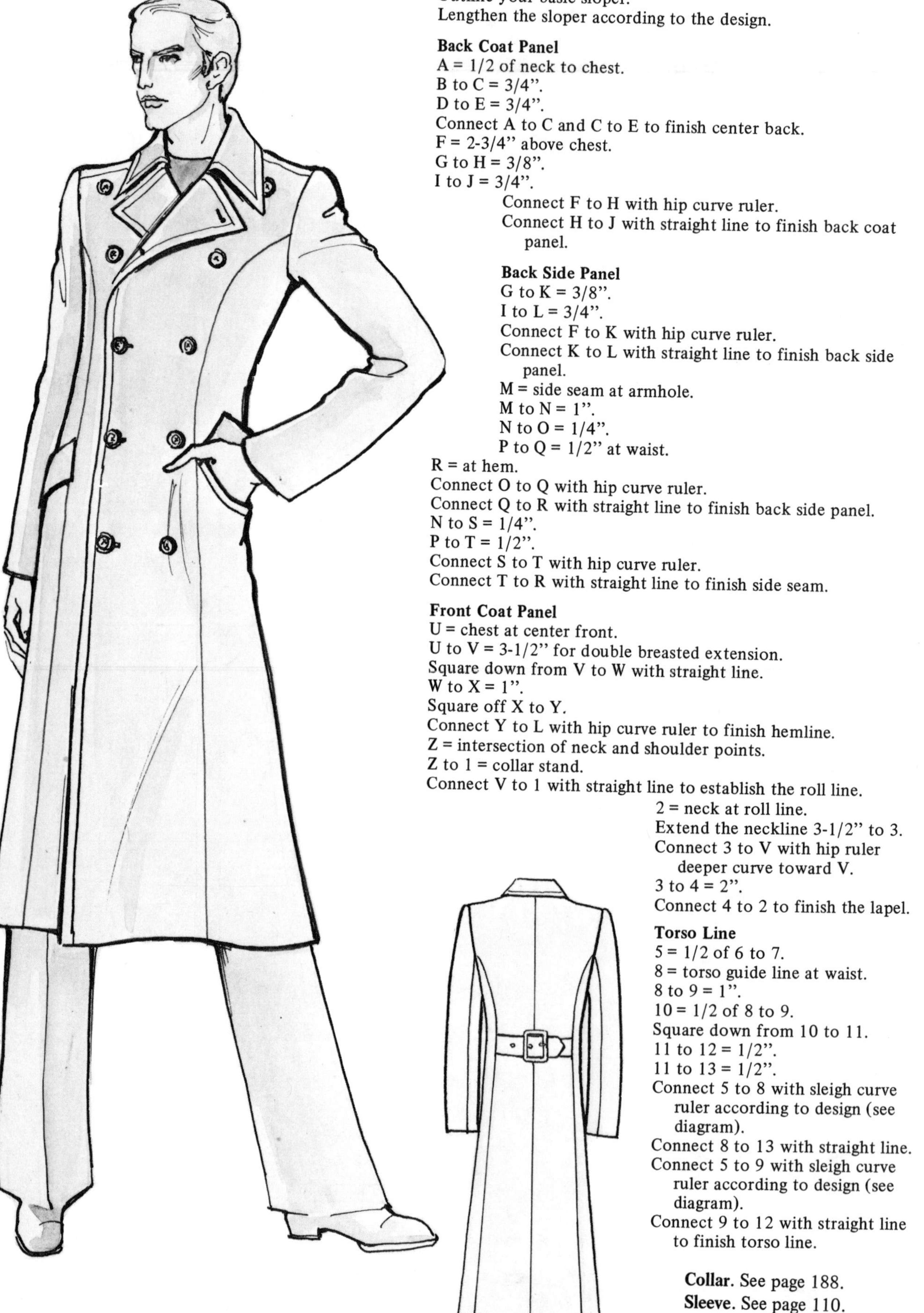

Outline your basic sloper.
Lengthen the sloper according to the design.

Back Coat Panel
A = 1/2 of neck to chest.
B to C = 3/4".
D to E = 3/4".
Connect A to C and C to E to finish center back.
F = 2-3/4" above chest.
G to H = 3/8".
I to J = 3/4".
Connect F to H with hip curve ruler.
Connect H to J with straight line to finish back coat panel.

Back Side Panel
G to K = 3/8".
I to L = 3/4".
Connect F to K with hip curve ruler.
Connect K to L with straight line to finish back side panel.
M = side seam at armhole.
M to N = 1".
N to O = 1/4".
P to Q = 1/2" at waist.
R = at hem.
Connect O to Q with hip curve ruler.
Connect Q to R with straight line to finish back side panel.
N to S = 1/4".
P to T = 1/2".
Connect S to T with hip curve ruler.
Connect T to R with straight line to finish side seam.

Front Coat Panel
U = chest at center front.
U to V = 3-1/2" for double breasted extension.
Square down from V to W with straight line.
W to X = 1".
Square off X to Y.
Connect Y to L with hip curve ruler to finish hemline.
Z = intersection of neck and shoulder points.
Z to 1 = collar stand.
Connect V to 1 with straight line to establish the roll line.
2 = neck at roll line.
Extend the neckline 3-1/2" to 3.
Connect 3 to V with hip ruler deeper curve toward V.
3 to 4 = 2".
Connect 4 to 2 to finish the lapel.

Torso Line
5 = 1/2 of 6 to 7.
8 = torso guide line at waist.
8 to 9 = 1".
10 = 1/2 of 8 to 9.
Square down from 10 to 11.
11 to 12 = 1/2".
11 to 13 = 1/2".
Connect 5 to 8 with sleigh curve ruler according to design (see diagram).
Connect 8 to 13 with straight line.
Connect 5 to 9 with sleigh curve ruler according to design (see diagram).
Connect 9 to 12 with straight line to finish torso line.

Collar. See page 188.
Sleeve. See page 110.

DIAGRAM—Redingote

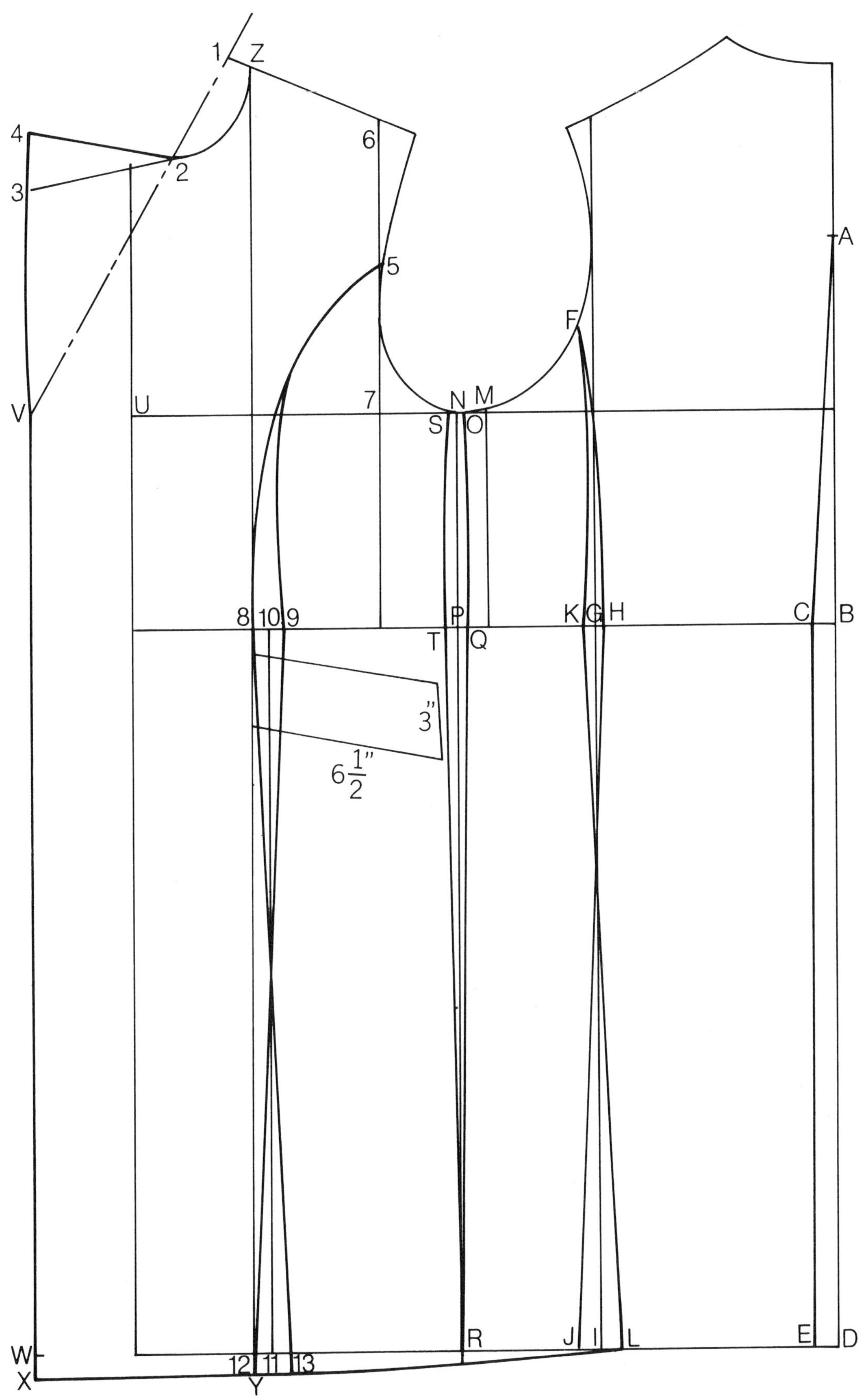

DUFFLE COAT

Outline basic sloper; lengthen sloper according to your design.

Back Coat Panel
A = side seam at armhole.
A to B = 1-1/4".
Square up from B to C.
Square down from B to D.
D to E = 1-1/2".
Connect C to E with straight line to finish back coat panel.

Front Coat Panel
D to F = 1-1/2".
Connect C to F with straight line to finish side seam.
G = center front at chest.
G to H = 1-1/2" for extension.
Square down from H to I.
I to J = 1/2".
Square off from J to K.
Connect K to F with hip curve ruler to finish hem.
L = neck point.
L to M = 3/8".
Square off M to N for 1/2".
Connect M to G for new center front.
Connect N to H with straight line.
Curve line at neck to finish the front coat panel. (see diagram)

Back Yoke
Yoke line = 2" above chest line.

Front Yoke
Yoke line = 1" above chest line.

Pocket
(see diagram)
length = approximately 8".
width = approximately 7".

Hood. See page 75.
Sleeve. See page 110.

Note: For additional details see diagram.

DIAGRAM–Duffle Coat

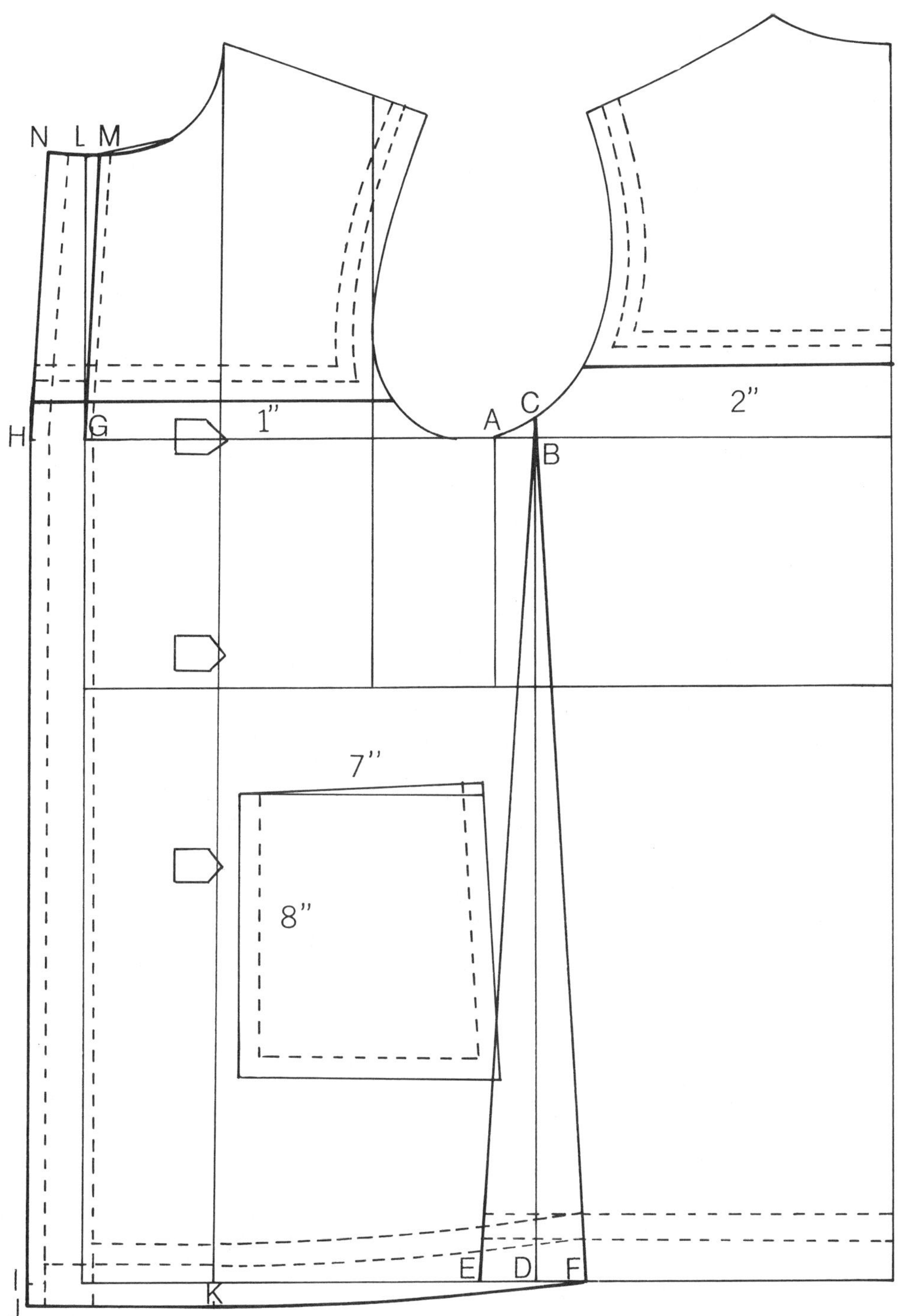

SADDLE-YOKED CAR COAT

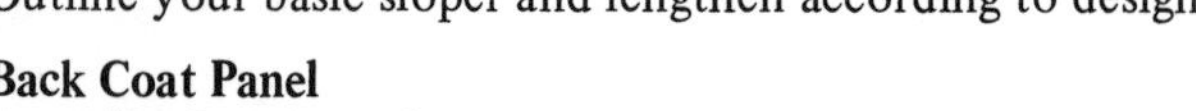

Outline your basic sloper and lengthen according to design.

Back Coat Panel
A = 1/2 of neck to chest.
B to C = 3/4".
D to E = 3/4".
Connect A to C to E to finish center back.
F = 1" squared up from chest line.
Square down F to G.
H to I = 3/8".
G to J = 1/2".
Connect F to I with straight line.
Connect I to J with straight line to finish the back coat panel.

Front Coat Panel
H to K = 3/8".
G to L = 1/2".
Connect F to K with straight line.
Connect K to L with straight line.
M = center front at chest line.
M to N = 2".
N to O = 1-1/4" for extension.
Square down from O to P.
P to Q = 1".
Square off from Q to R.
Connect R to L with hip curve ruler to finish the hem.
S = intersection of neck and shoulder points.
S to T = 1-1/8" collar stand.
Connect O to T to establish the roll line.

Back Yoke
U = 1/2 of back neck measurement.
W to V = 1/2".
X = 1" above V.
Connect U to X with straight line.
Blend X into the back armhole with a sleigh curve ruler to finish the back yoke.

Front Yoke
Y to S = 2".
1 = 1" above Z.
Connect Y to 1 with straight line.
Blend 1 into the front armhole with a sleigh curve ruler to finish the front yoke.

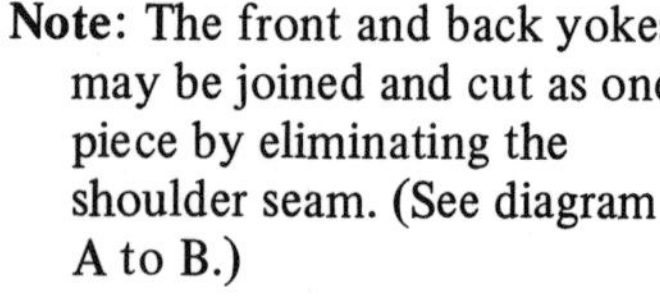

Note: The front and back yokes may be joined and cut as one piece by eliminating the shoulder seam. (See diagram A to B.)

Pocket
For size, angle, and position of the pocket, see diagram.

Collar. See page 171.
Sleeve. See page 118.

DIAGRAM–Saddle-Yoked Car Coat

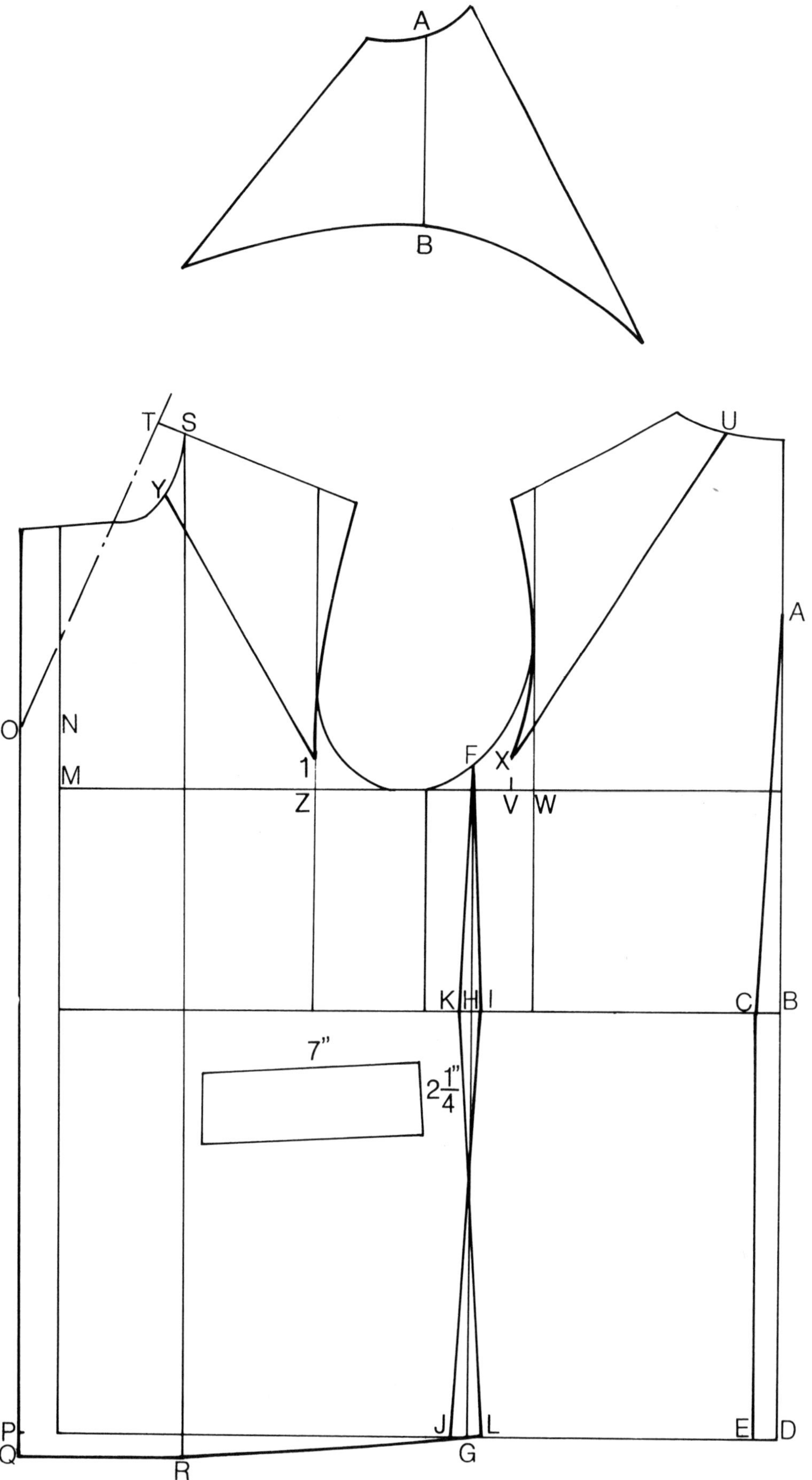

PEA COAT

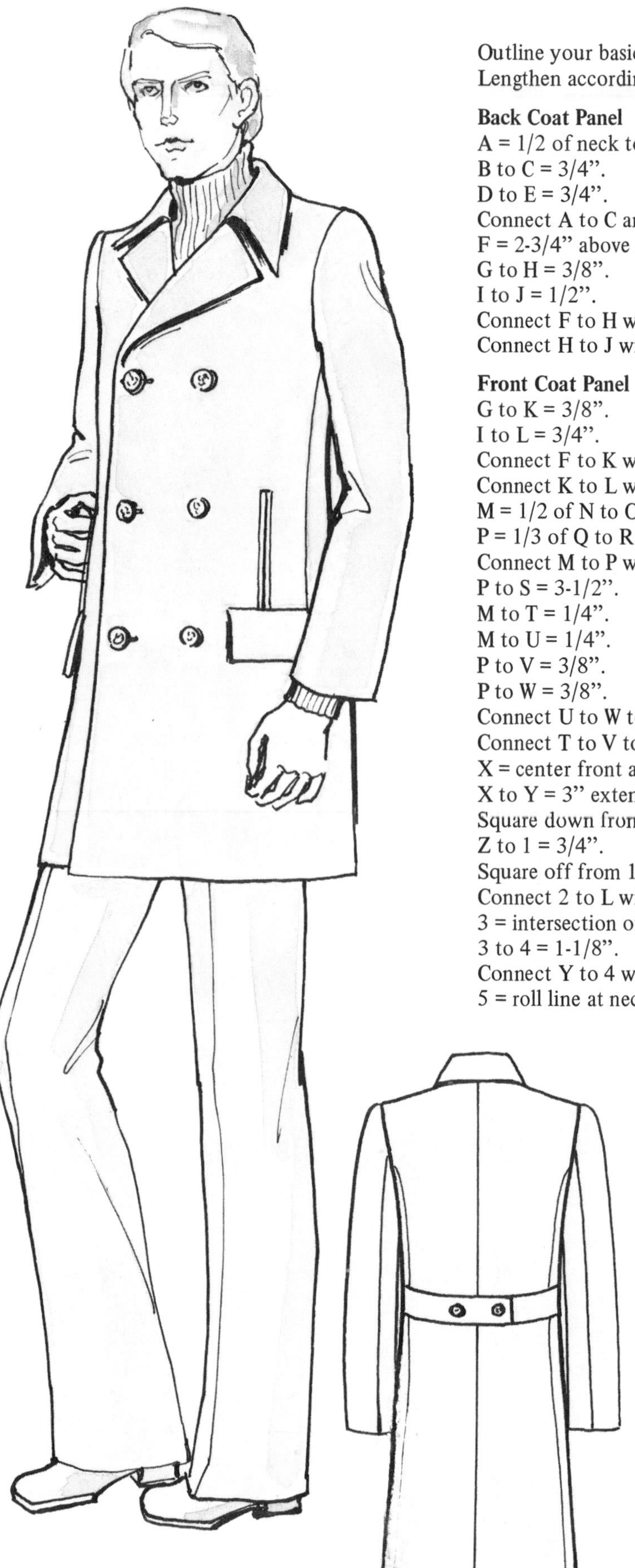

Outline your basic sloper.
Lengthen according to the design.

Back Coat Panel
A = 1/2 of neck to chest.
B to C = 3/4".
D to E = 3/4".
Connect A to C and C to E with straight line to finish center back.
F = 2-3/4" above chest line at armhole.
G to H = 3/8".
I to J = 1/2".
Connect F to H with hip curve.
Connect H to J with straight line to finish back coat panel.

Front Coat Panel
G to K = 3/8".
I to L = 3/4".
Connect F to K with shallowest part of hip curve ruler.
Connect K to L with straight line to finish side seam.
M = 1/2 of N to O.
P = 1/3 of Q to R.
Connect M to P with straight line and extend toward S.
P to S = 3-1/2".
M to T = 1/4".
M to U = 1/4".
P to V = 3/8".
P to W = 3/8".
Connect U to W to S with hip curve.
Connect T to V to S with hip curve to finish dart.
X = center front at chest.
X to Y = 3" extension.
Square down from Y to Z.
Z to 1 = 3/4".
Square off from 1 to 2.
Connect 2 to L with hip curve ruler to finish hem line.
3 = intersection of neck and shoulder.
3 to 4 = 1-1/8".
Connect Y to 4 with straight line and extend line upward.
5 = roll line at neck.
6 to 7 = 3/4".
Connect 5 to 7 and extend the line.
Square off from 8 to 9 = 4" lapel width.
Connect 9 to Y with hip curve ruler using deeper curve toward Y to finish lapel.

Collar. See page 188.
Sleeve. See page 110.

DIAGRAM–Pea Coat

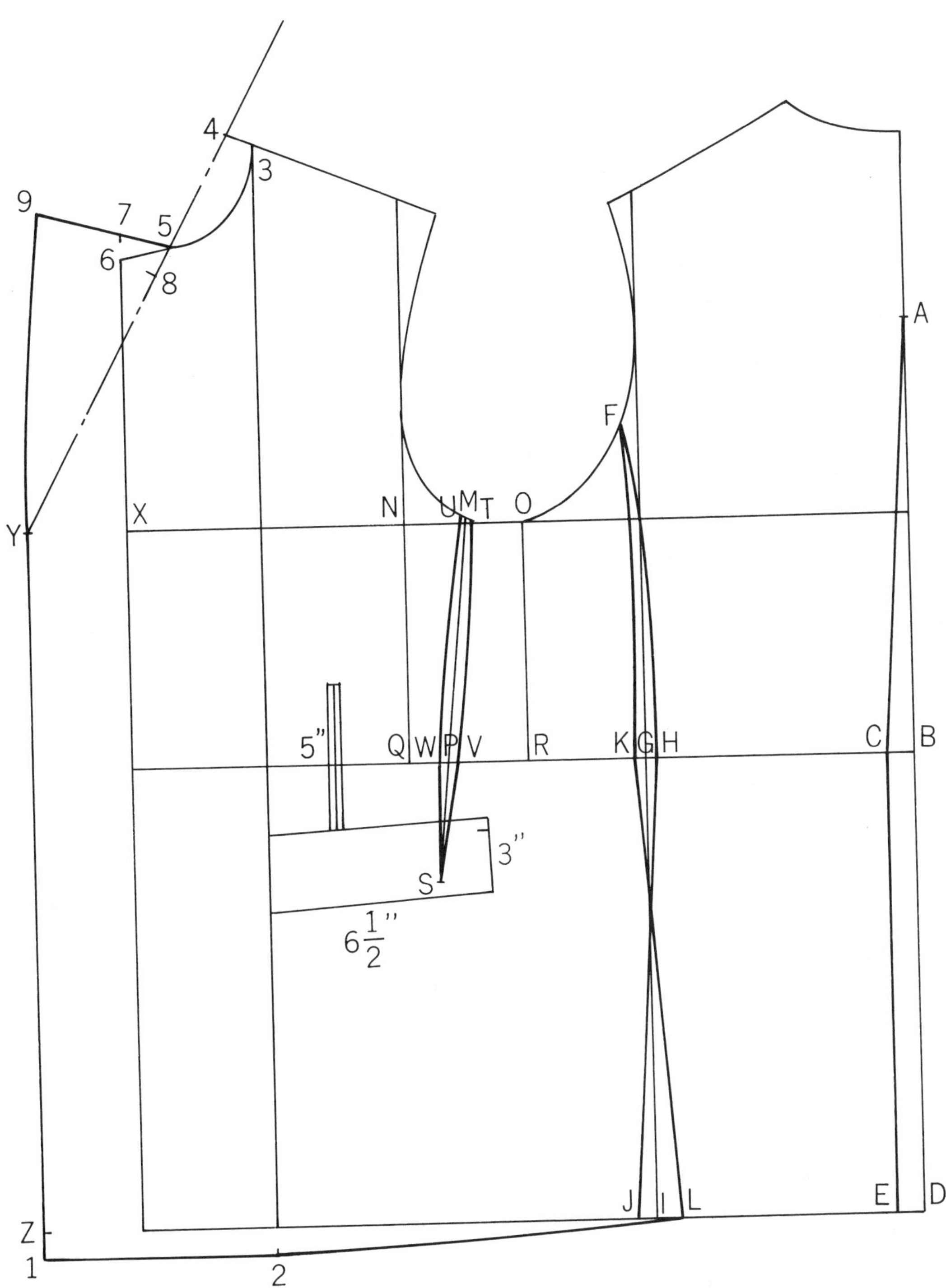

HOODED COAT WITH DROPPED SHOULDER

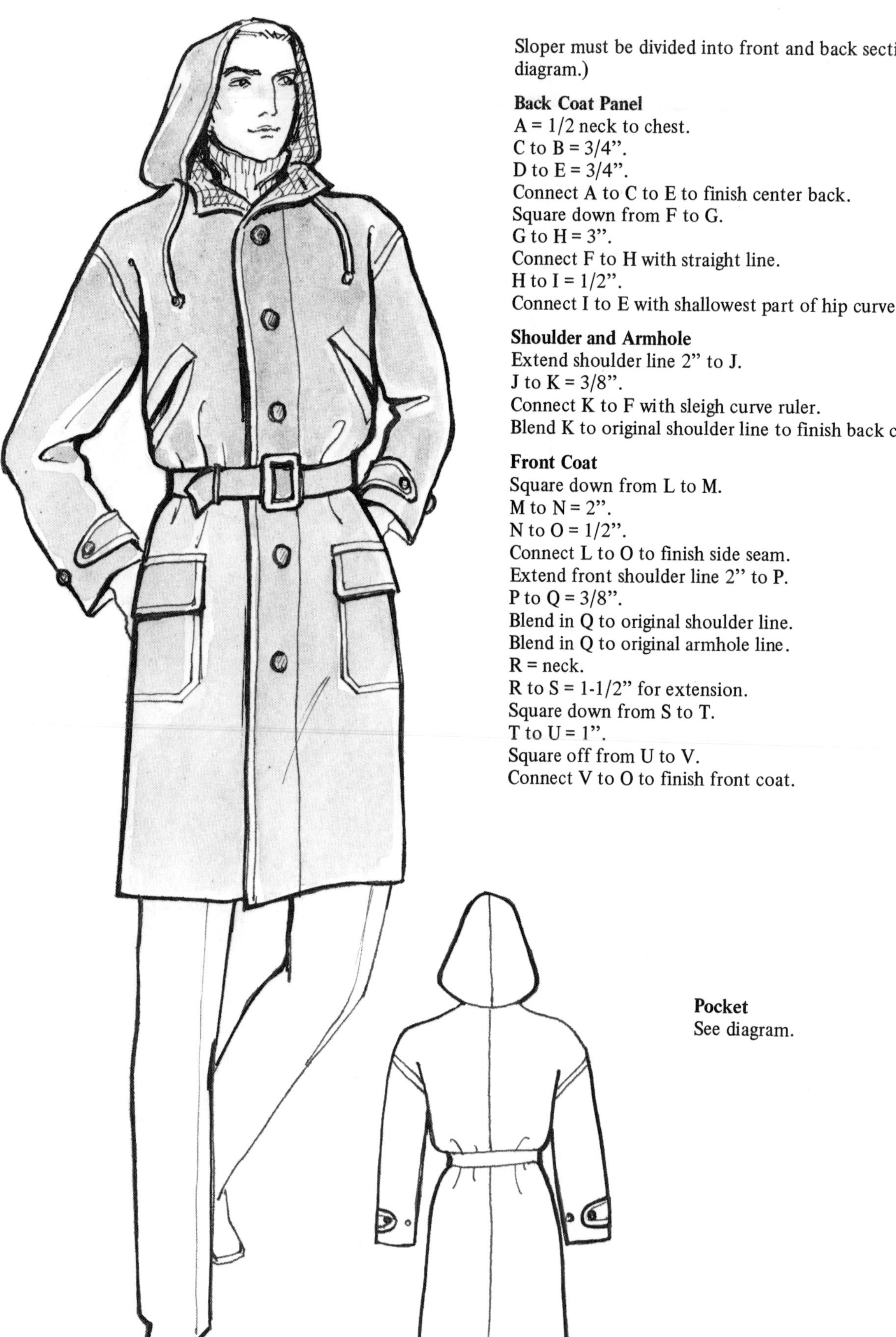

Sloper must be divided into front and back sections. (See diagram.)

Back Coat Panel
A = 1/2 neck to chest.
C to B = 3/4".
D to E = 3/4".
Connect A to C to E to finish center back.
Square down from F to G.
G to H = 3".
Connect F to H with straight line.
H to I = 1/2".
Connect I to E with shallowest part of hip curve ruler.

Shoulder and Armhole
Extend shoulder line 2" to J.
J to K = 3/8".
Connect K to F with sleigh curve ruler.
Blend K to original shoulder line to finish back coat panel.

Front Coat
Square down from L to M.
M to N = 2".
N to O = 1/2".
Connect L to O to finish side seam.
Extend front shoulder line 2" to P.
P to Q = 3/8".
Blend in Q to original shoulder line.
Blend in Q to original armhole line.
R = neck.
R to S = 1-1/2" for extension.
Square down from S to T.
T to U = 1".
Square off from U to V.
Connect V to O to finish front coat.

Pocket
See diagram.

DIAGRAM–Hooded Coat with Dropped Shoulder

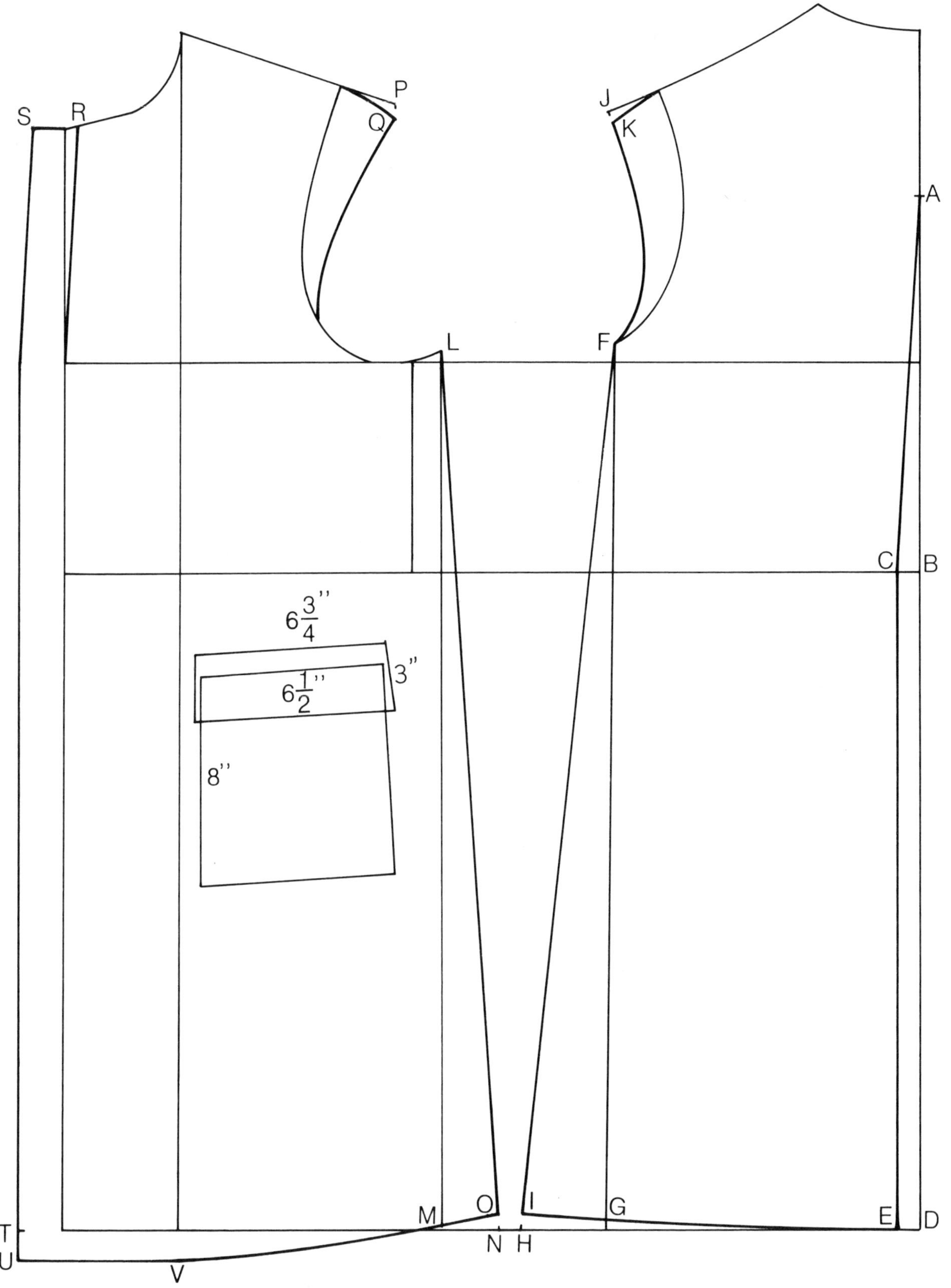

DIAGRAM—Hooded Coat with Dropped Shoulder

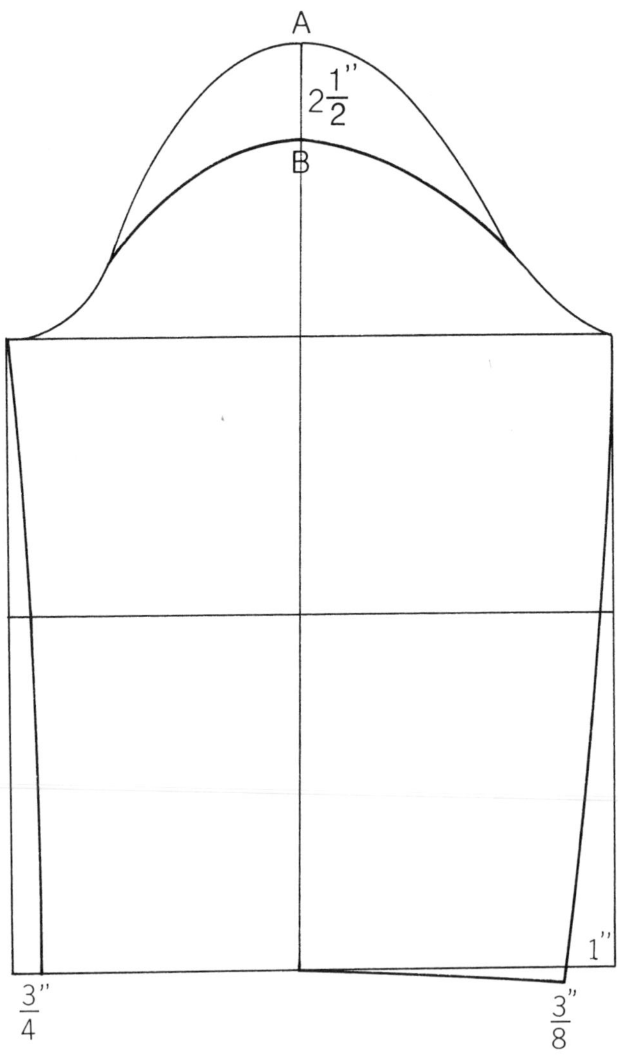

Extended shoulder areas shown on coat sketch, Q and K must be eliminated from basic sleeve cap. Amount eliminated is in accord with designer's styling. See diagram A to B. Blend new sleeve cap curve into sleeve cap under arm curves, front and back, as shown.

HOODS

DIAGRAM–Hoods

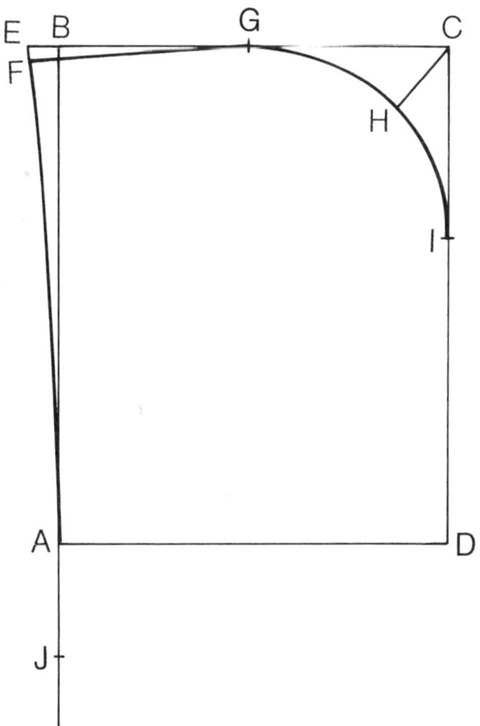

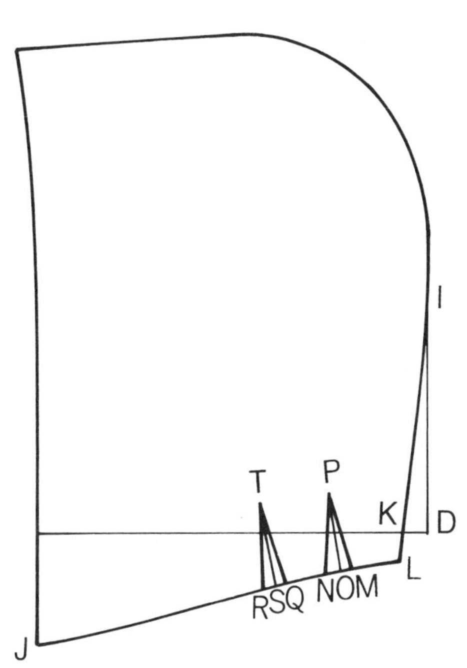

HOOD A

Diagram A

Draw a line A to B = 13".
B to C = 10-1/2".
Square down from C to D.
Square out from A to D.
B to E = 3/4".
E to F = 3/8".
G = 1/2 B to C.
Connect F to A with hip curve ruler using the shallow curve.
Connect F to G with straight line.
H = 2" from C on 45° angle.
Connect G to H to I with sleigh curve ruler.
A to J = 3"

HOOD A

Diagram B

D to K = 1/2".
K to L = 3/4".
Connect I to L with hip curve ruler.
Connect J to L with hip curve ruler. (See diagram.)
L to M = 1-1/4".
M to N = 3/4".
O = 1/2 of M to N.
Square up from O to P = 3".
Connect M to P and N to P with straight line.
N to Q = 1-1/8".
Q to R = 5/8".
S = 1/2 of Q to R.
Square up from S to T = 2-1/2".
Connect R to T and Q to T with straight line to finish hood.

DIAGRAM–Hoods

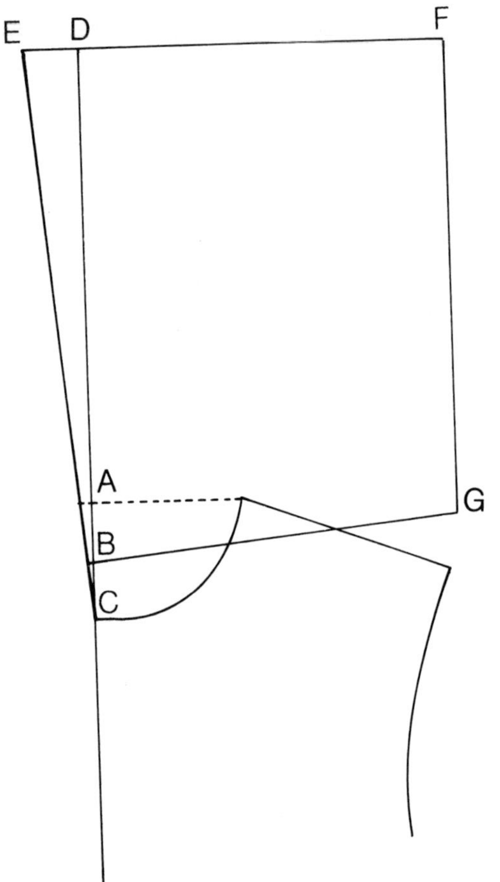

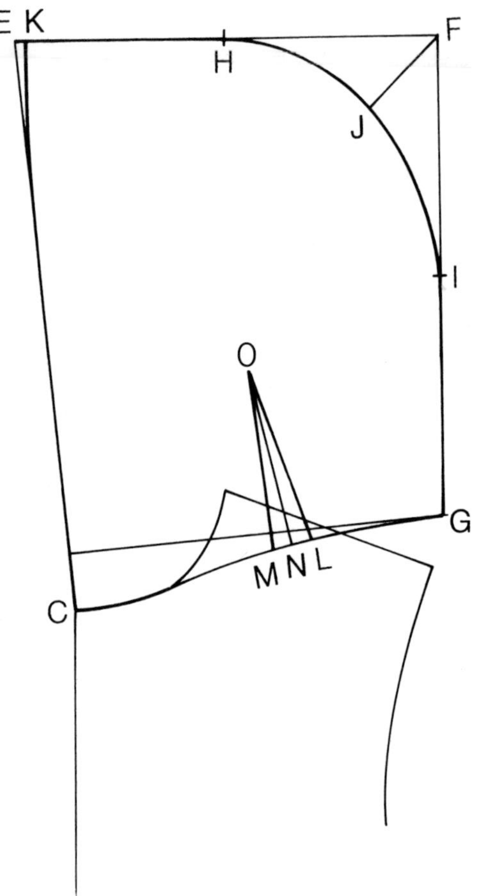

HOOD B

Diagram A

Outline the front of the basic coat sloper.
Extend center front line upward.
Square off from A to neck and shoulder intersection.
B = 1/2 of A to C.
A to D = 12".
D to E = 1-1/2".
Connect E to C with straight line.
D to F = 10".
Square out from line E-C.
Square down from F to G.

HOOD B

Diagram B

H = 1/2 of E to F.
I = 1/2 of F to G.
F to J = 2-1/2" on 45° angle.
Connect H to J to I with sleigh curve ruler.
E to K = 1/4".
Blend K into the new center front.
Connect C to G with hip curve ruler. (See diagram.)
G to L = back neck measurement from sloper.
L to M = 1".
N = 1/2 of M to L.
Square up N to O = 4-1/2".
Connect M to O and L to O with straight line to finish hood.

Note: The darts may be eased rather than sewn.

NOTES

SHIRT STYLED RAINCOAT

Outline your basic sloper.
Lengthen the sloper according to the design.

Back Coat Panel
A = side seam at waist.
A to B = 1".
Square up from B to C.
Square down from B to D.
D to E = 1".
Connect B to E with straight line to finish back side seam.

Front Coat Panel
D to F = 1-1/4".
Connect B to F to finish front side seam.
G = center front at chest.
G to H = 1-1/2" for extension.
Square down from H to I.
I to J = 3/4".
Square off from J to K.
Connect K to F with hip curve to finish hemline.
L = neck point.
L to M = 3/8".
Connect M to G to establish new center front.
Square off M to N = 1-1/2".
Connect N to H.
O = intersection of shoulder and neck.
O to P = additional 3/8".
Connect P to M with sleigh curve for new neckline.

Back Yoke
O = intersection of shoulder and neck.
O to P = additional 3/8".
Q to R = additional 1/8".
Connect P to R with sleigh curve for new neckline.
R to S = 4".
Square off from S to T.
U = 1/2 of S to T.
T to V = 1/4" to be removed.
Connect V to U with shallow part of hip curve.

Center Back Pleat
2" depth (see Diagram).

Pocket (see Diagram)

Collar. See page 171.
Sleeve. See page 114.

DIAGRAM—Shirt Styled Raincoat

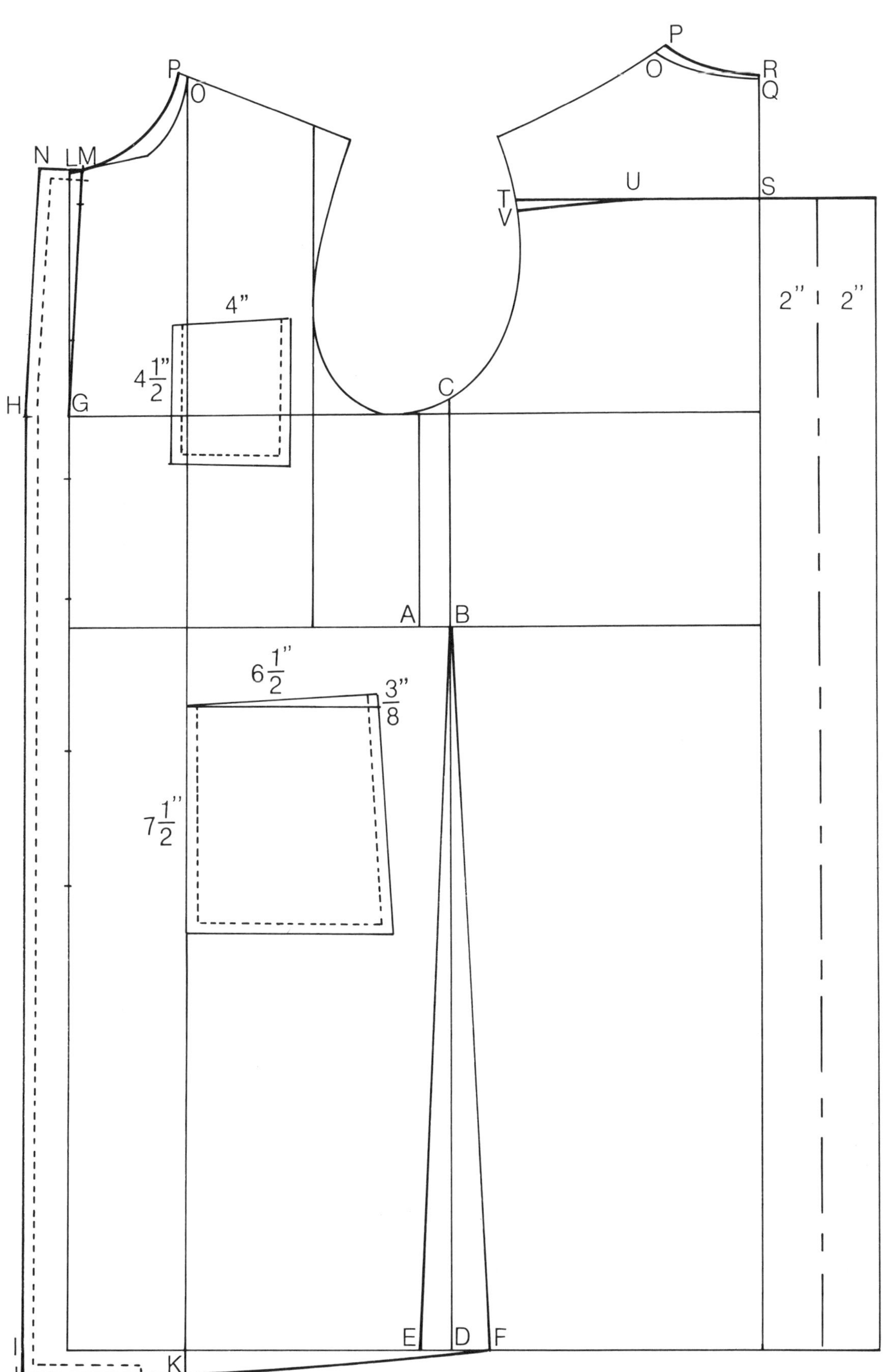

SHORT TUNNEL-BELTED RAINCOAT

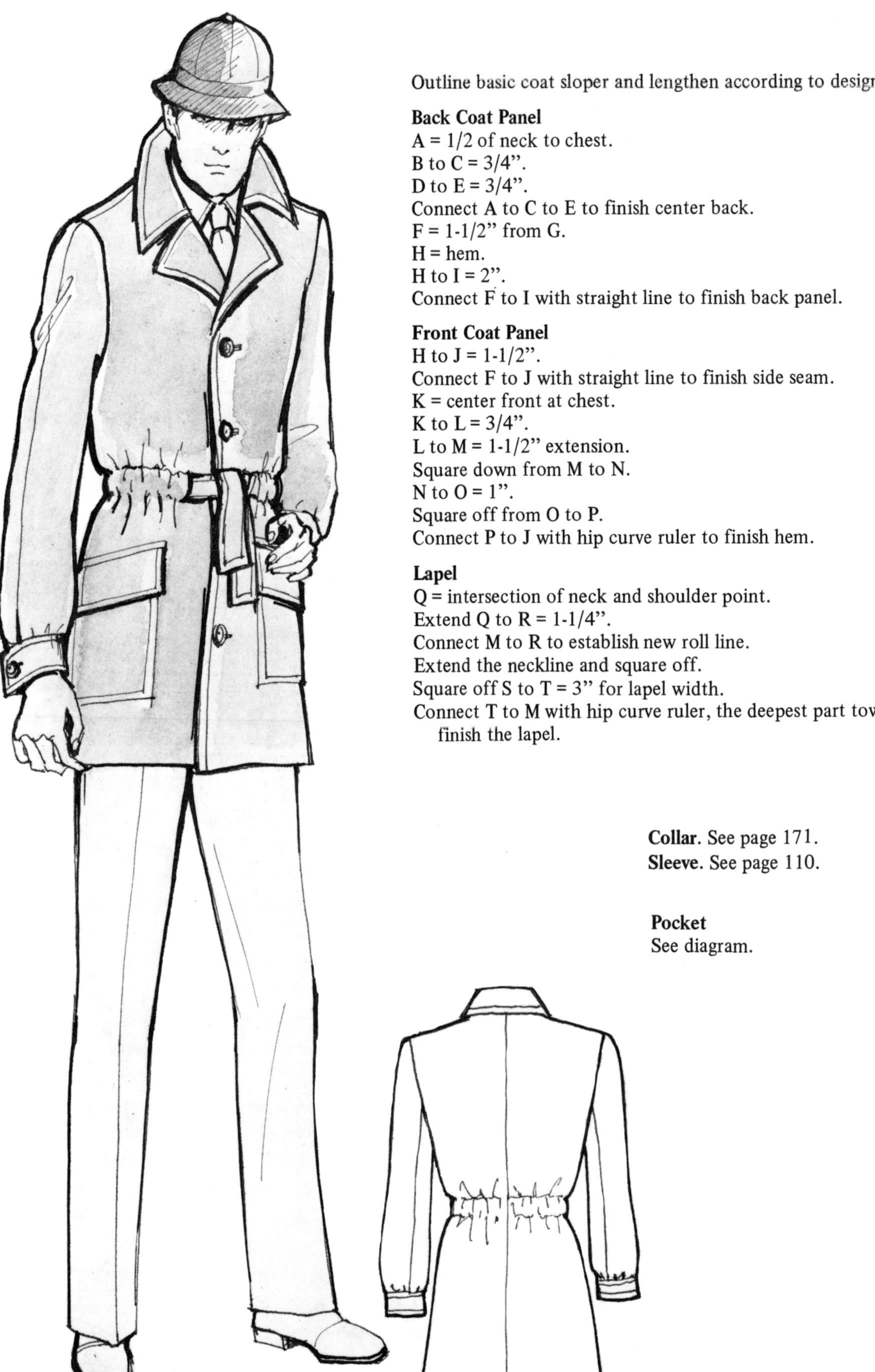

Outline basic coat sloper and lengthen according to design.

Back Coat Panel
A = 1/2 of neck to chest.
B to C = 3/4".
D to E = 3/4".
Connect A to C to E to finish center back.
F = 1-1/2" from G.
H = hem.
H to I = 2".
Connect F to I with straight line to finish back panel.

Front Coat Panel
H to J = 1-1/2".
Connect F to J with straight line to finish side seam.
K = center front at chest.
K to L = 3/4".
L to M = 1-1/2" extension.
Square down from M to N.
N to O = 1".
Square off from O to P.
Connect P to J with hip curve ruler to finish hem.

Lapel
Q = intersection of neck and shoulder point.
Extend Q to R = 1-1/4".
Connect M to R to establish new roll line.
Extend the neckline and square off.
Square off S to T = 3" for lapel width.
Connect T to M with hip curve ruler, the deepest part toward M to finish the lapel.

Collar. See page 171.
Sleeve. See page 110.

Pocket
See diagram.

DIAGRAM—Short Tunnel-Belted Raincoat

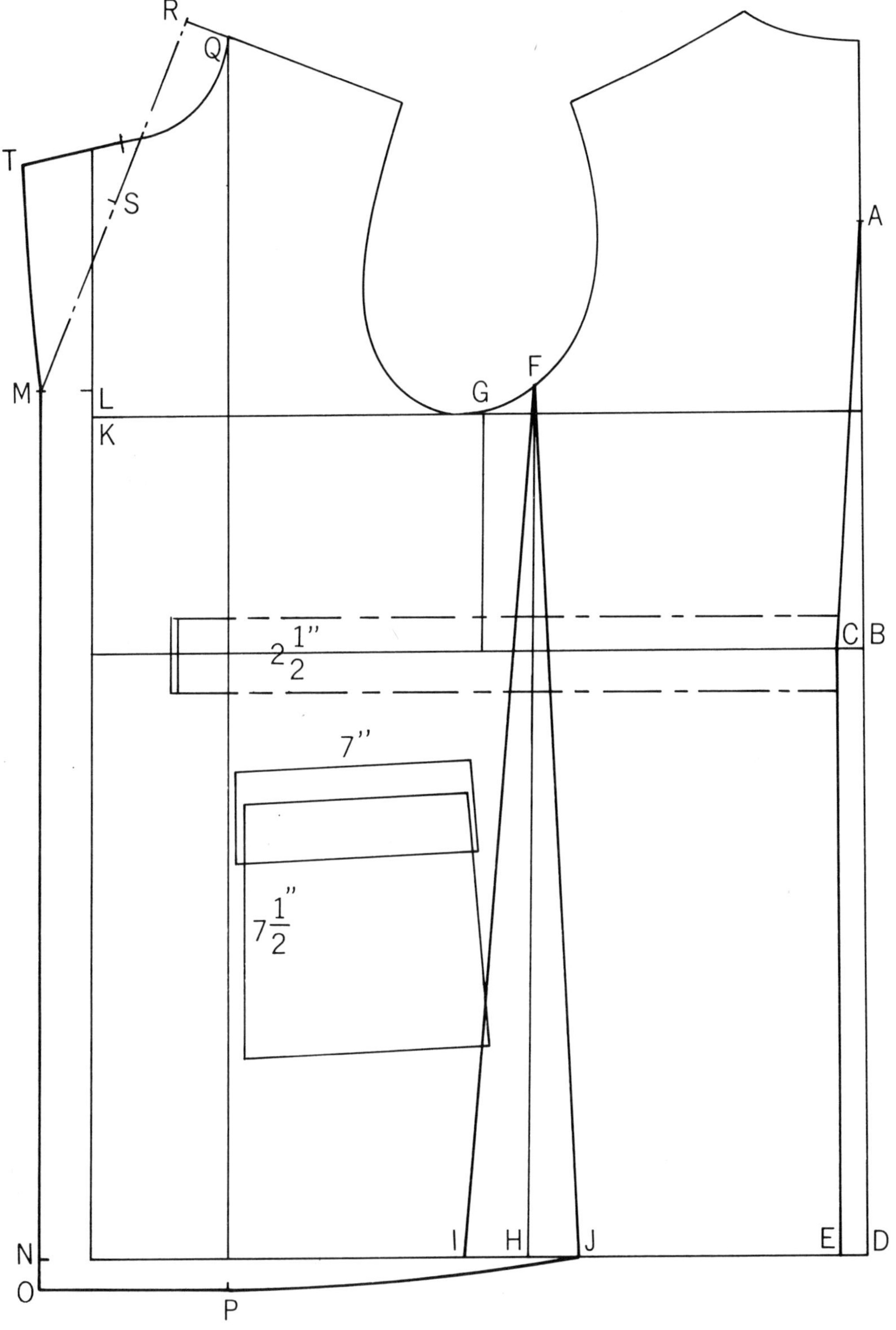

ZIPPERED FRONT RAINCOAT WITH UMBRELLA YOKE

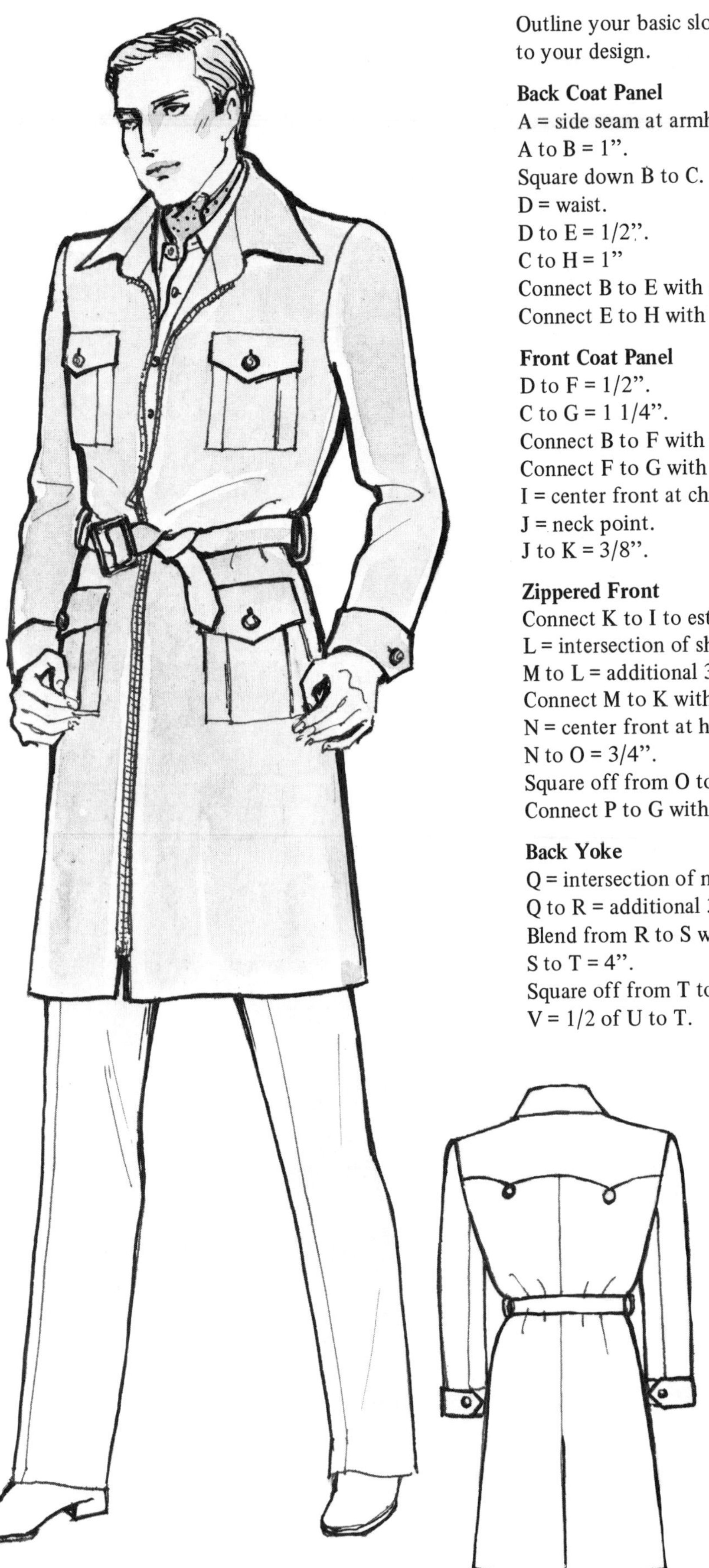

Outline your basic sloper. Lengthen your sloper according to your design.

Back Coat Panel

A = side seam at armhole.
A to B = 1”.
Square down B to C.
D = waist.
D to E = 1/2”.
C to H = 1”
Connect B to E with shallow curve line.
Connect E to H with straight line to finish back panel.

Front Coat Panel

D to F = 1/2”.
C to G = 1 1/4”.
Connect B to F with shallow curve line.
Connect F to G with straight line to finish side seam.
I = center front at chest.
J = neck point.
J to K = 3/8”.

Zippered Front

Connect K to I to establish new center front.
L = intersection of shoulder and neck.
M to L = additional 3/8”.
Connect M to K with sleigh curve to form new neckline.
N = center front at hem.
N to O = 3/4”.
Square off from O to P.
Connect P to G with hip curve ruler to finish hemline.

Back Yoke

Q = intersection of neck and shoulder.
Q to R = additional 3/8”.
Blend from R to S with sleigh curve to finish new neckline.
S to T = 4”.
Square off from T to U.
V = 1/2 of U to T.
V to X = 3/4”.
U to W = 1/4” to be removed.
Connect W to X and T to X with sleigh curve to finish back yoke.

Belt loop should be 1/2” wider than belt width. (Belt = 2” width and 60” - 70” length.)

Collar. See page 174.
Sleeve. See page 114.

DIAGRAM–Zippered Front Raincoat with Umbrella Yoke

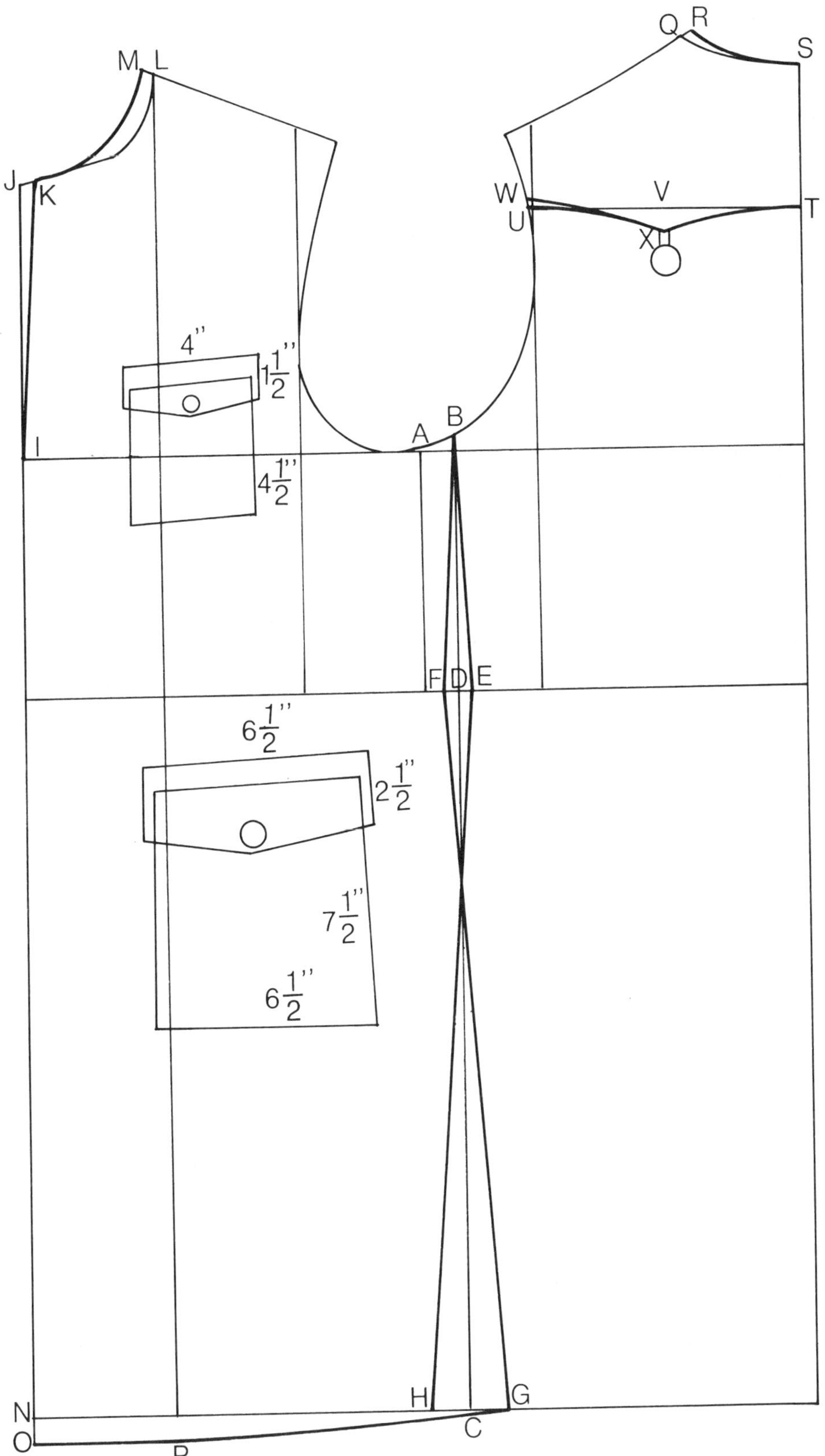

SHAWL COLLAR RANCH COAT

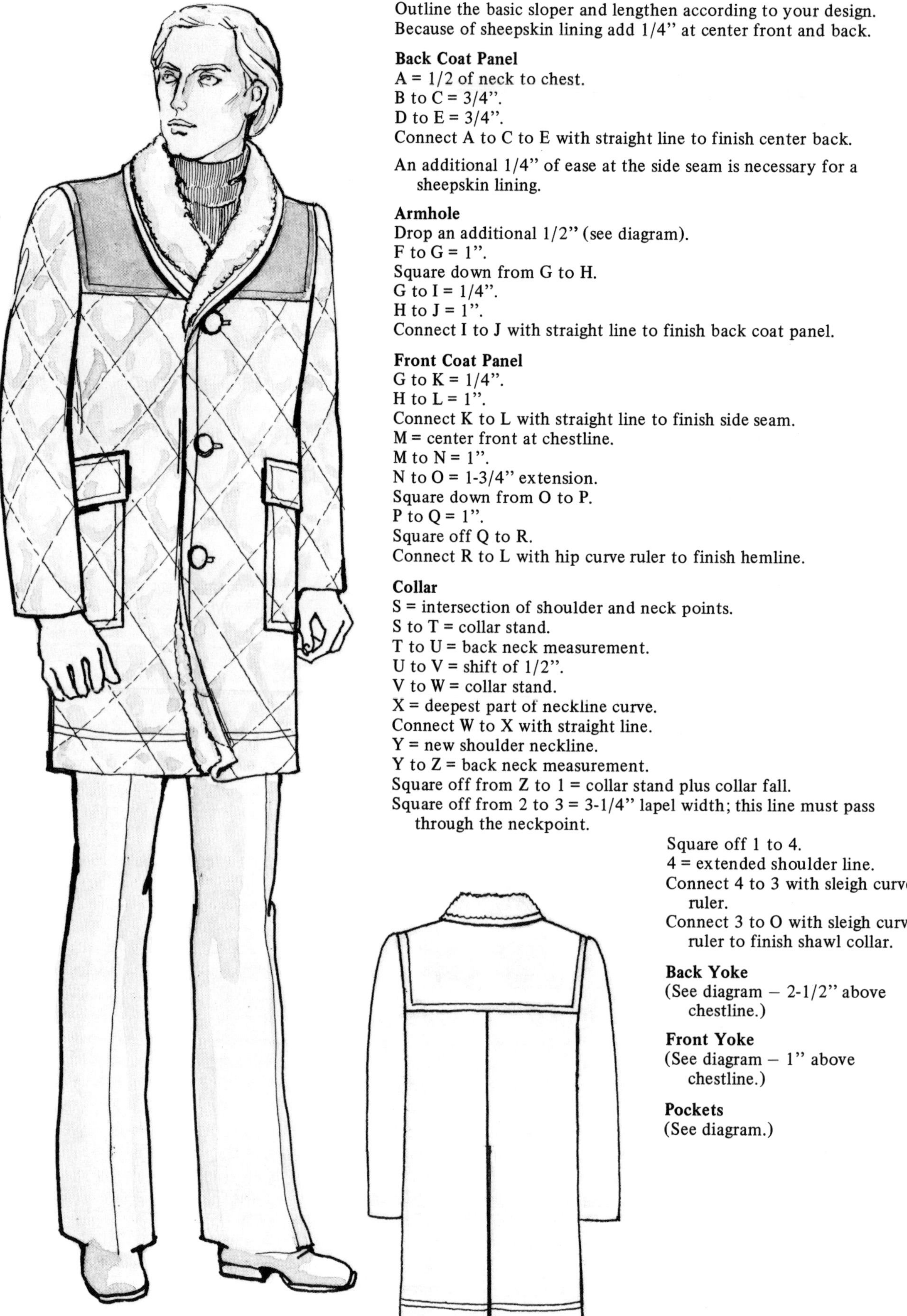

Outline the basic sloper and lengthen according to your design. Because of sheepskin lining add 1/4" at center front and back.

Back Coat Panel
A = 1/2 of neck to chest.
B to C = 3/4".
D to E = 3/4".
Connect A to C to E with straight line to finish center back.

An additional 1/4" of ease at the side seam is necessary for a sheepskin lining.

Armhole
Drop an additional 1/2" (see diagram).
F to G = 1".
Square down from G to H.
G to I = 1/4".
H to J = 1".
Connect I to J with straight line to finish back coat panel.

Front Coat Panel
G to K = 1/4".
H to L = 1".
Connect K to L with straight line to finish side seam.
M = center front at chestline.
M to N = 1".
N to O = 1-3/4" extension.
Square down from O to P.
P to Q = 1".
Square off Q to R.
Connect R to L with hip curve ruler to finish hemline.

Collar
S = intersection of shoulder and neck points.
S to T = collar stand.
T to U = back neck measurement.
U to V = shift of 1/2".
V to W = collar stand.
X = deepest part of neckline curve.
Connect W to X with straight line.
Y = new shoulder neckline.
Y to Z = back neck measurement.
Square off from Z to 1 = collar stand plus collar fall.
Square off from 2 to 3 = 3-1/4" lapel width; this line must pass through the neckpoint.
Square off 1 to 4.
4 = extended shoulder line.
Connect 4 to 3 with sleigh curve ruler.
Connect 3 to O with sleigh curve ruler to finish shawl collar.

Back Yoke
(See diagram – 2-1/2" above chestline.)

Front Yoke
(See diagram – 1" above chestline.)

Pockets
(See diagram.)

DIAGRAM–Shawl Collar Ranch Coat

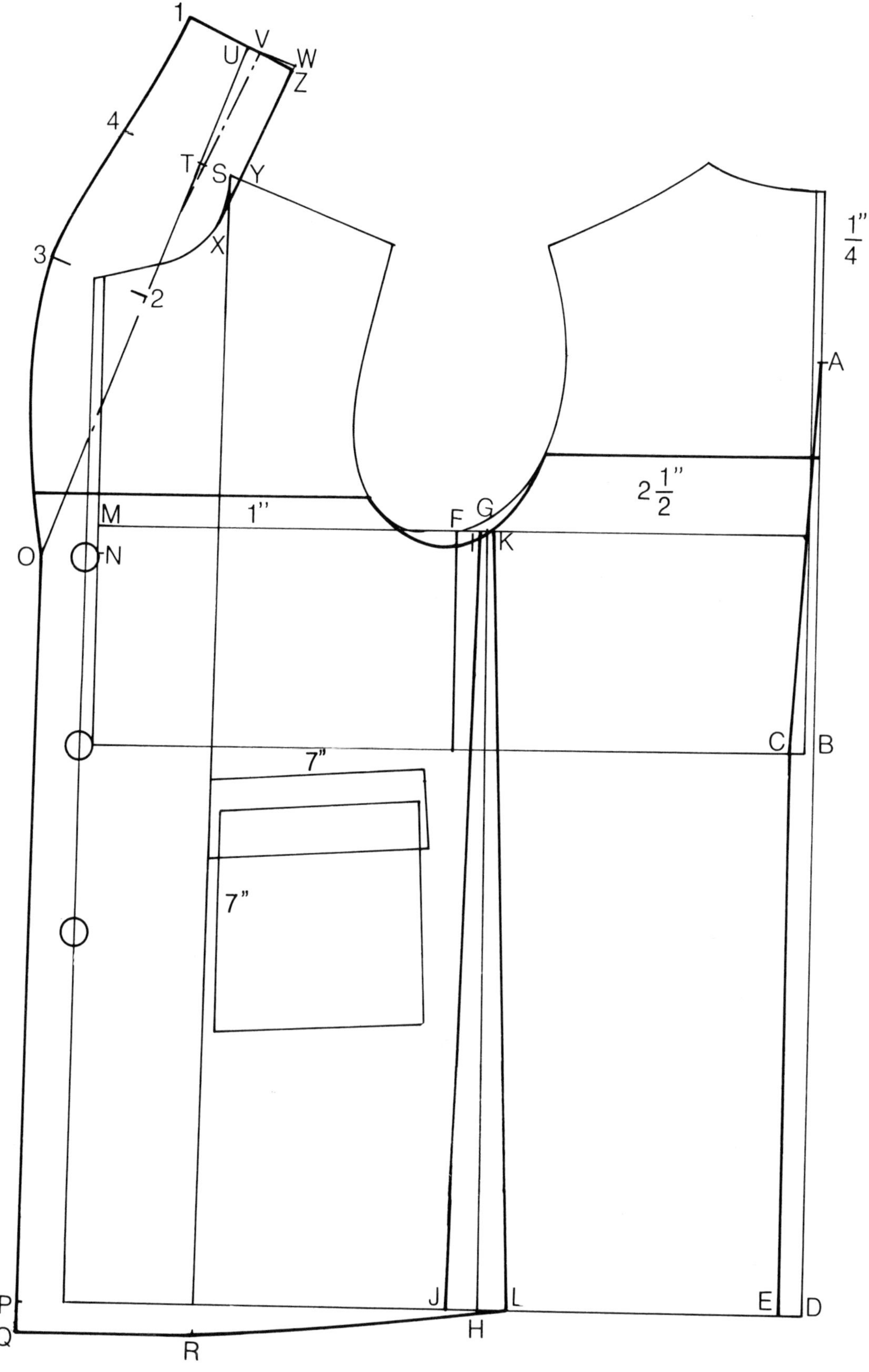

SHEEPSKIN LINED POLO COAT

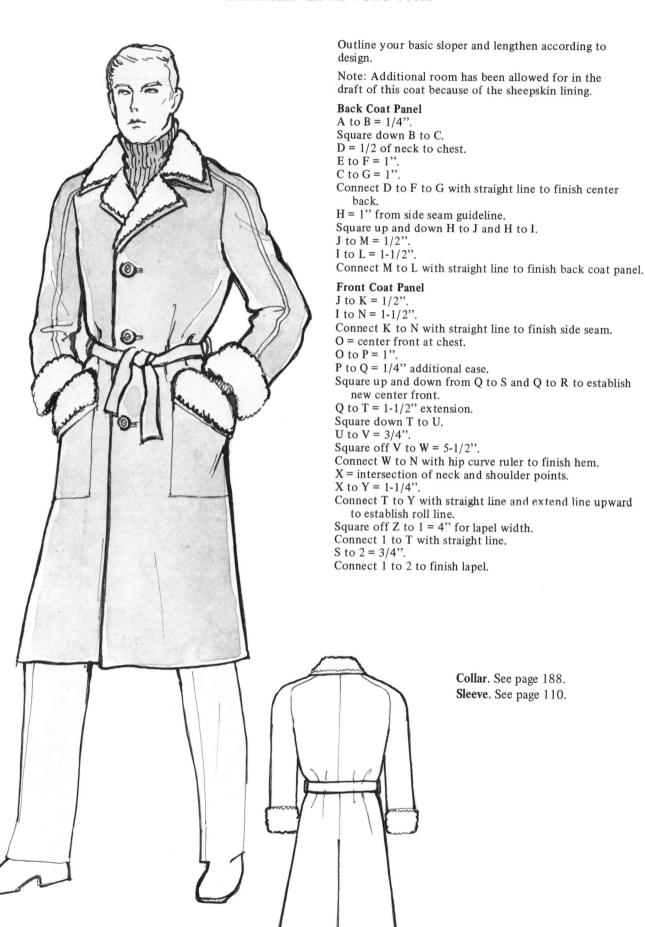

Outline your basic sloper and lengthen according to design.

Note: Additional room has been allowed for in the draft of this coat because of the sheepskin lining.

Back Coat Panel
A to B = 1/4".
Square down B to C.
D = 1/2 of neck to chest.
E to F = 1".
C to G = 1".
Connect D to F to G with straight line to finish center back.
H = 1" from side seam guideline.
Square up and down H to J and H to I.
J to M = 1/2".
I to L = 1-1/2".
Connect M to L with straight line to finish back coat panel.

Front Coat Panel
J to K = 1/2".
I to N = 1-1/2".
Connect K to N with straight line to finish side seam.
O = center front at chest.
O to P = 1".
P to Q = 1/4" additional ease.
Square up and down from Q to S and Q to R to establish new center front.
Q to T = 1-1/2" extension.
Square down T to U.
U to V = 3/4".
Square off V to W = 5-1/2".
Connect W to N with hip curve ruler to finish hem.
X = intersection of neck and shoulder points.
X to Y = 1-1/4".
Connect T to Y with straight line and extend line upward to establish roll line.
Square off Z to 1 = 4" for lapel width.
Connect 1 to T with straight line.
S to 2 = 3/4".
Connect 1 to 2 to finish lapel.

Collar. See page 188.
Sleeve. See page 110.

DIAGRAM–Sheepskin Lined Polo Coat

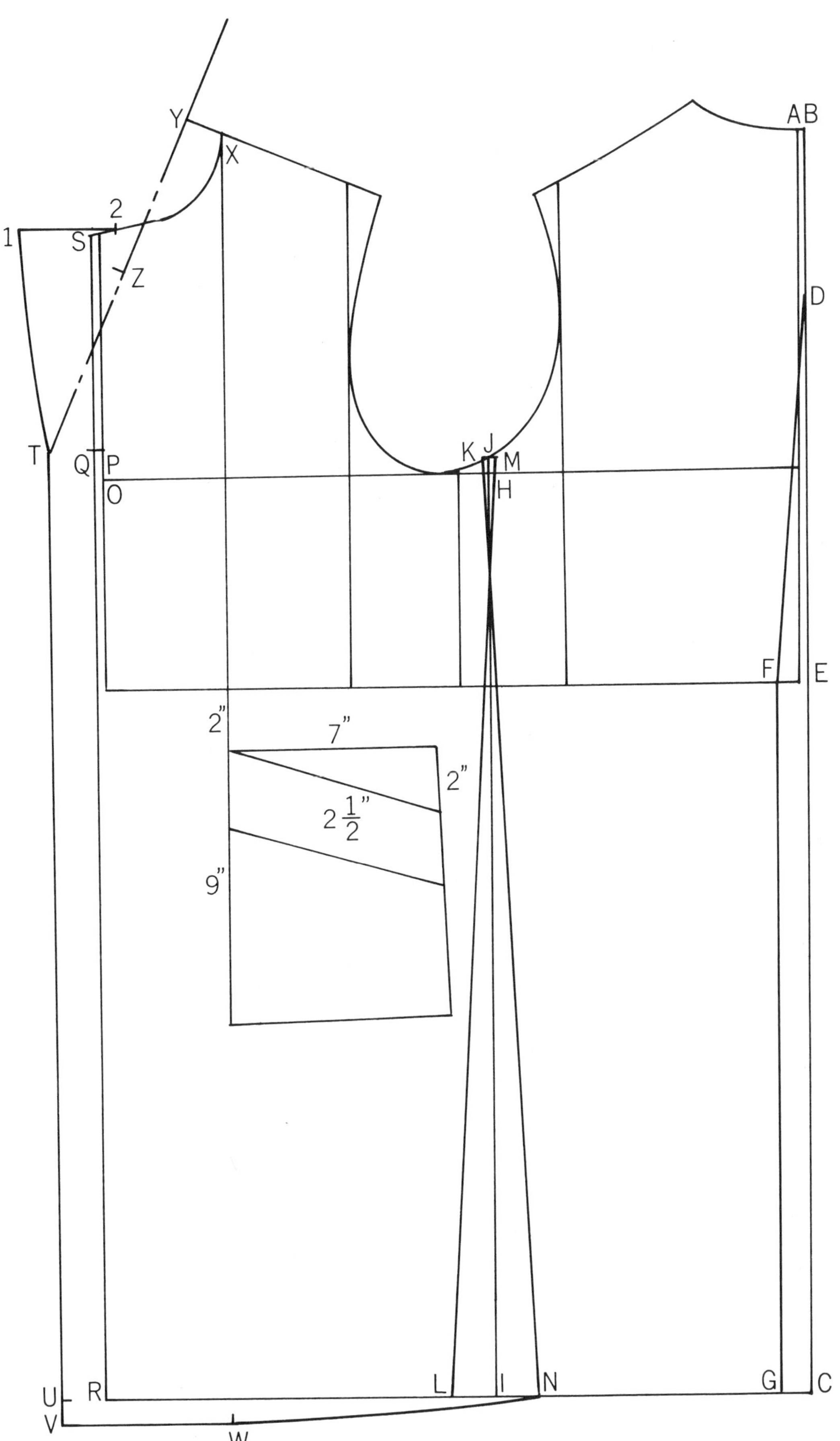

DIAGRAM–Sheepskin Lined Polo Coat Sleeve

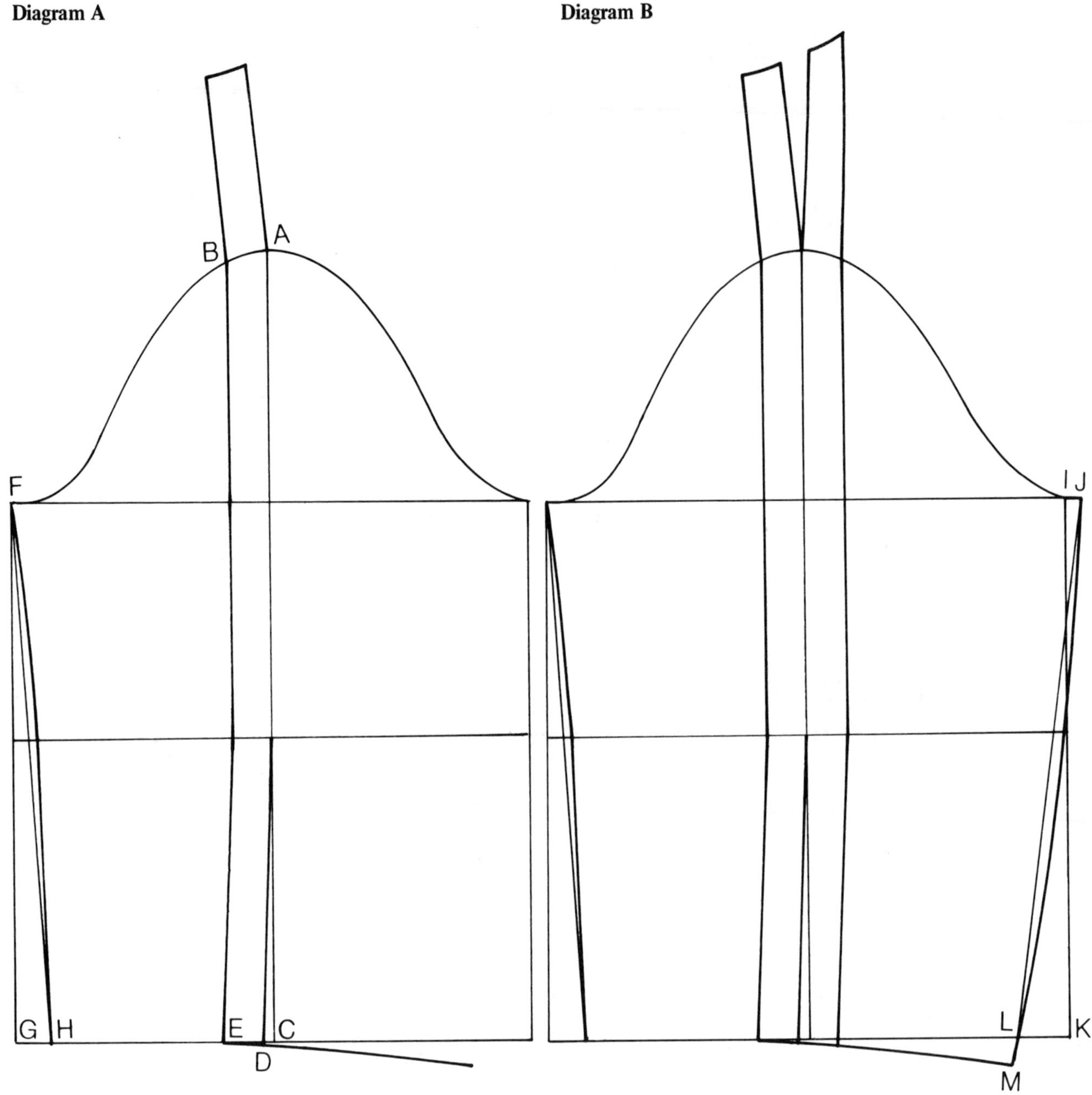

Place front shoulder saddle to sleeve cap at points A - B.
Follow center sleeve line to wrist at point C.
C to D = 3/8".
Connect D to elbow line level.
D to E = A - B front shoulder saddle width.
Connect E to elbow line level to B parallel to D - A, as shown in diagram.
G to H = 1".
Connect F - H with hip curve ruler.

Repeat placement and design lines for back shoulder saddle, as shown in diagram. From sleeve cap to wrist lines are parallel to front shoulder saddle, A - D, B - E. Saddle width according to designer's styling.
Extend back under arm sleeve cap curve, I to J = 1/2".
K to L = 1 1/4".
Connect J to L with hip curve ruler.
Extend line L to M = 1/2".
Connect E - M to finish wrist.

NOTES

FUR-COLLARED OVERCOAT

Outline your basic sloper and lengthen according to design.

Back Coat Panel
A = 1/2 of neck to chest.
B to C = 3/4".
D to E = 3/4".
Connect A to C to E to finish center back.
F = square from A to armhole.
G to H = 2-1/2".
Square down from H to I.
J to K = 3/8".
I to L = 3/4".
Connect F to H to K using both the sleigh and hip curve rulers.
Connect K to L with straight line to finish the back coat panel.

Back Coat Side Panel
J to M = 3/8".
I to N = 3/4".
Connect H to M with hip curve ruler.
Connect M to N with straight line.
O = side seam at armhole.
O to P = 1/2".
Square down P to Q.
Q to S = 1/2".
R to T = 1/2".
Connect P to R with hip curve ruler.
Connect R to S with straight line to finish back coat side panel.

Front Coat Side Panel
Q to U = 1/2".
Connect P to T with hip curve ruler.
Connect T to U with straight line to finish side seam.
V to W = 3".
X = 1/2 of Y to Z.
Square down X to 1.
X to 2 = 1/4".
1 to 3 = 1/2".
Connect V to 2 with sleigh curve ruler.
Connect 2 to 3 with straight line to finish front coat side panel.

Front Coat Panel
X to 4 = 1/4".
1 to 5 = 1/2".
Connect V to 4 with hip curve ruler.
Connect 4 to 5 with straight line to finish side seam.
6 = 2" above waistline at center front.
6 to 7 = 3" for extension.
Square down 7 to 8.
8 to 9 = 1".
Square off from 9 to 5.
Connect 5 to N with hip curve ruler to finish hem.

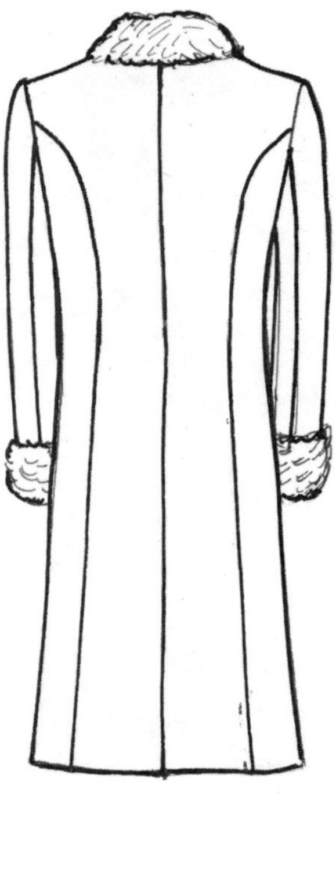

Collar
11 = intersection of neck and shoulder points.
11 to 12 = 1-1/4" collar stand.
Connect 7 to 12 with straight line and extend to establish the roll line.
12 to 13 = back neck measurement.
Square off 13 to 14 = 2-1/2" – collar stand plus 1" shift.
15 = deepest part of neckline curve.
Connect 14 to 15 with straight line.
12 to 13 = 16 to 17.
Square off from 17 to 18 = 4".
19 = intersection of roll line and center front.
Square off 19 to 20 = 3-1/2".
Connect 18 to 20 with hip curve ruler.
Connect 20 to 7 with hip curve ruler to finish shawl collar.

Pocket
For angle, size and position of pocket see diagram.

DIAGRAM–Fur-Collared Overcoat

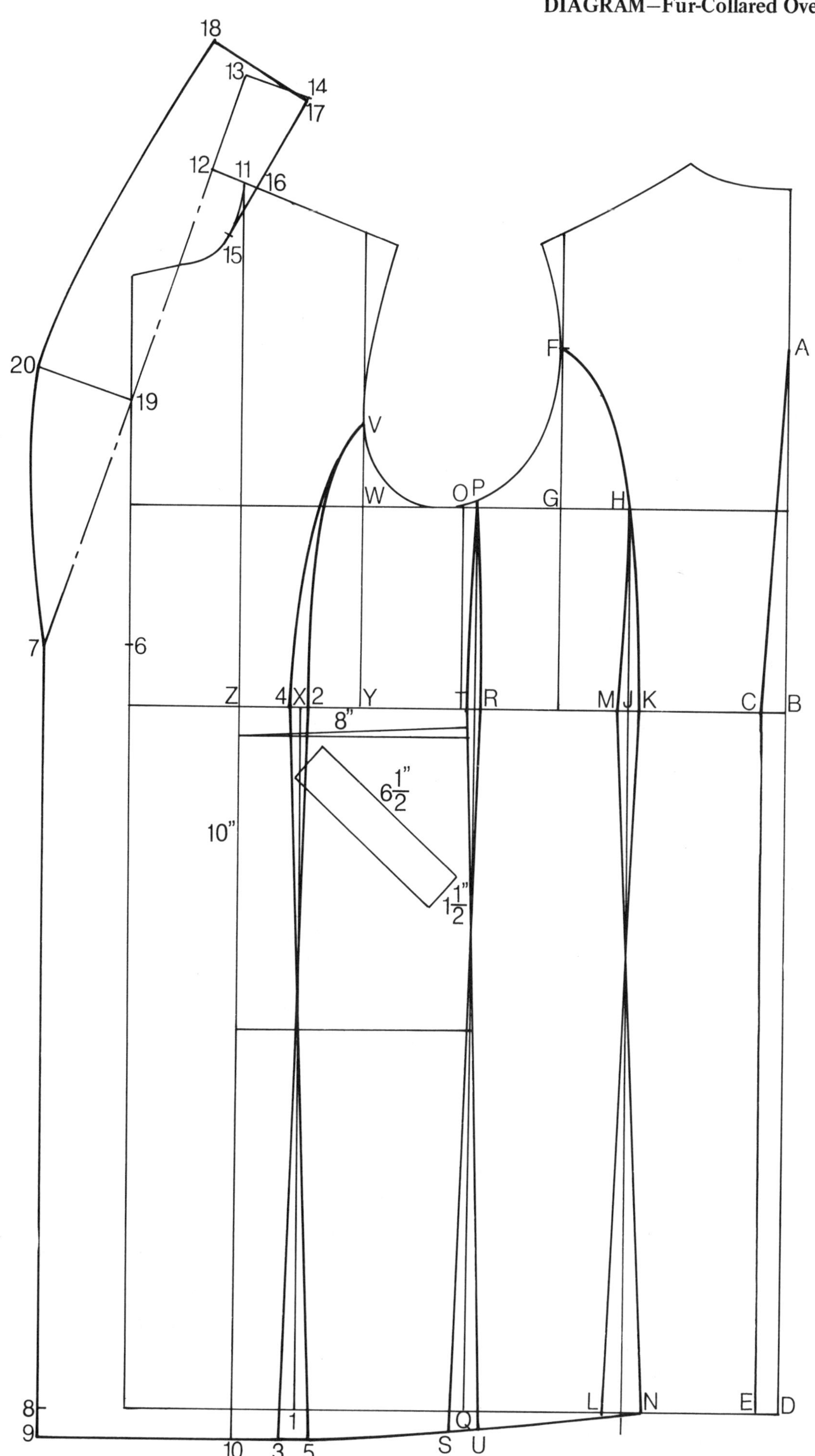

SHOULDER TORSO CUT COAT

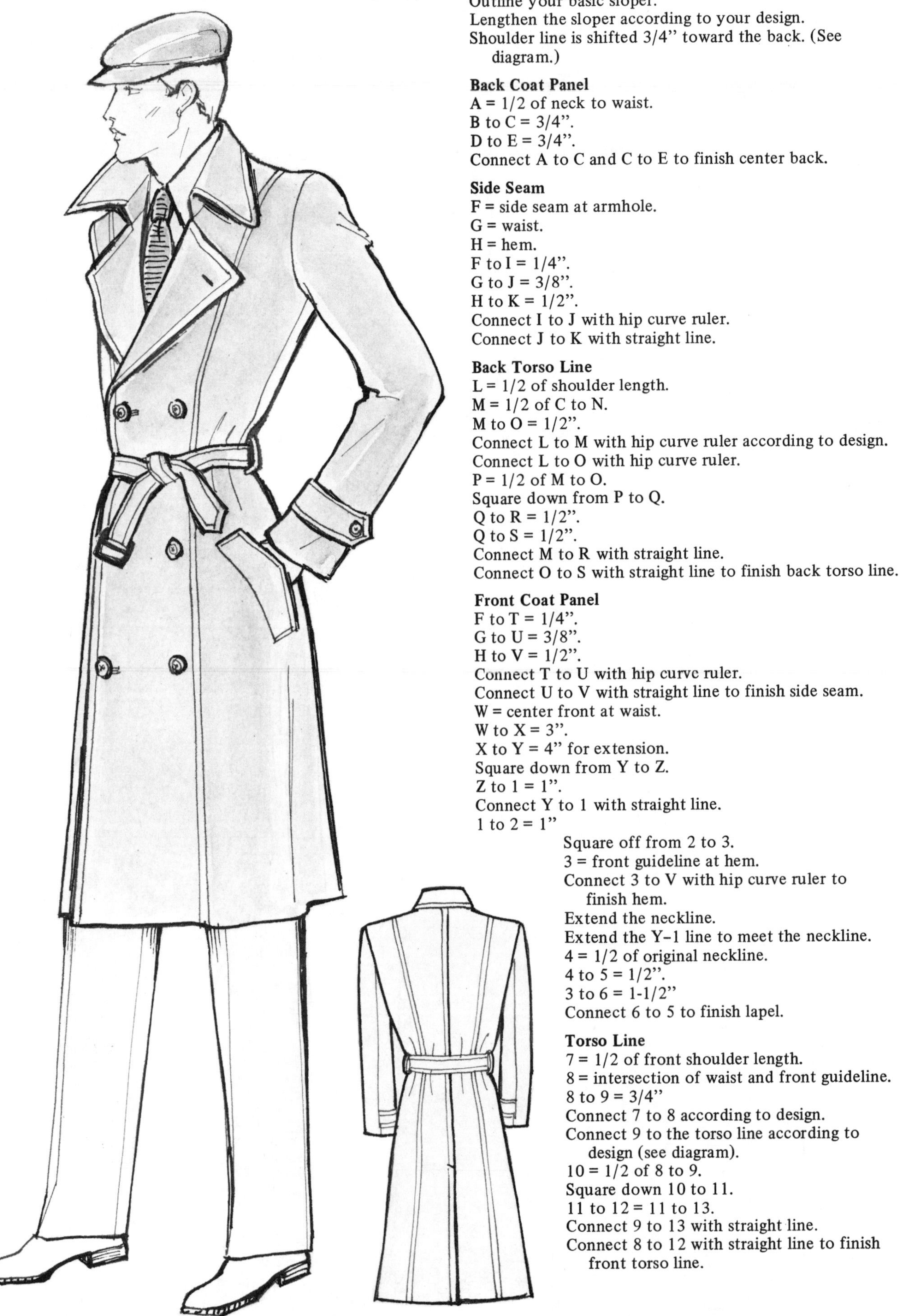

Outline your basic sloper.
Lengthen the sloper according to your design.
Shoulder line is shifted 3/4" toward the back. (See diagram.)

Back Coat Panel
A = 1/2 of neck to waist.
B to C = 3/4".
D to E = 3/4".
Connect A to C and C to E to finish center back.

Side Seam
F = side seam at armhole.
G = waist.
H = hem.
F to I = 1/4".
G to J = 3/8".
H to K = 1/2".
Connect I to J with hip curve ruler.
Connect J to K with straight line.

Back Torso Line
L = 1/2 of shoulder length.
M = 1/2 of C to N.
M to O = 1/2".
Connect L to M with hip curve ruler according to design.
Connect L to O with hip curve ruler.
P = 1/2 of M to O.
Square down from P to Q.
Q to R = 1/2".
Q to S = 1/2".
Connect M to R with straight line.
Connect O to S with straight line to finish back torso line.

Front Coat Panel
F to T = 1/4".
G to U = 3/8".
H to V = 1/2".
Connect T to U with hip curve ruler.
Connect U to V with straight line to finish side seam.
W = center front at waist.
W to X = 3".
X to Y = 4" for extension.
Square down from Y to Z.
Z to 1 = 1".
Connect Y to 1 with straight line.
1 to 2 = 1"
Square off from 2 to 3.
3 = front guideline at hem.
Connect 3 to V with hip curve ruler to finish hem.
Extend the neckline.
Extend the Y–1 line to meet the neckline.
4 = 1/2 of original neckline.
4 to 5 = 1/2".
3 to 6 = 1-1/2"
Connect 6 to 5 to finish lapel.

Torso Line
7 = 1/2 of front shoulder length.
8 = intersection of waist and front guideline.
8 to 9 = 3/4"
Connect 7 to 8 according to design.
Connect 9 to the torso line according to design (see diagram).
10 = 1/2 of 8 to 9.
Square down 10 to 11.
11 to 12 = 11 to 13.
Connect 9 to 13 with straight line.
Connect 8 to 12 with straight line to finish front torso line.

DIAGRAM–Shoulder Torso Cut Coat

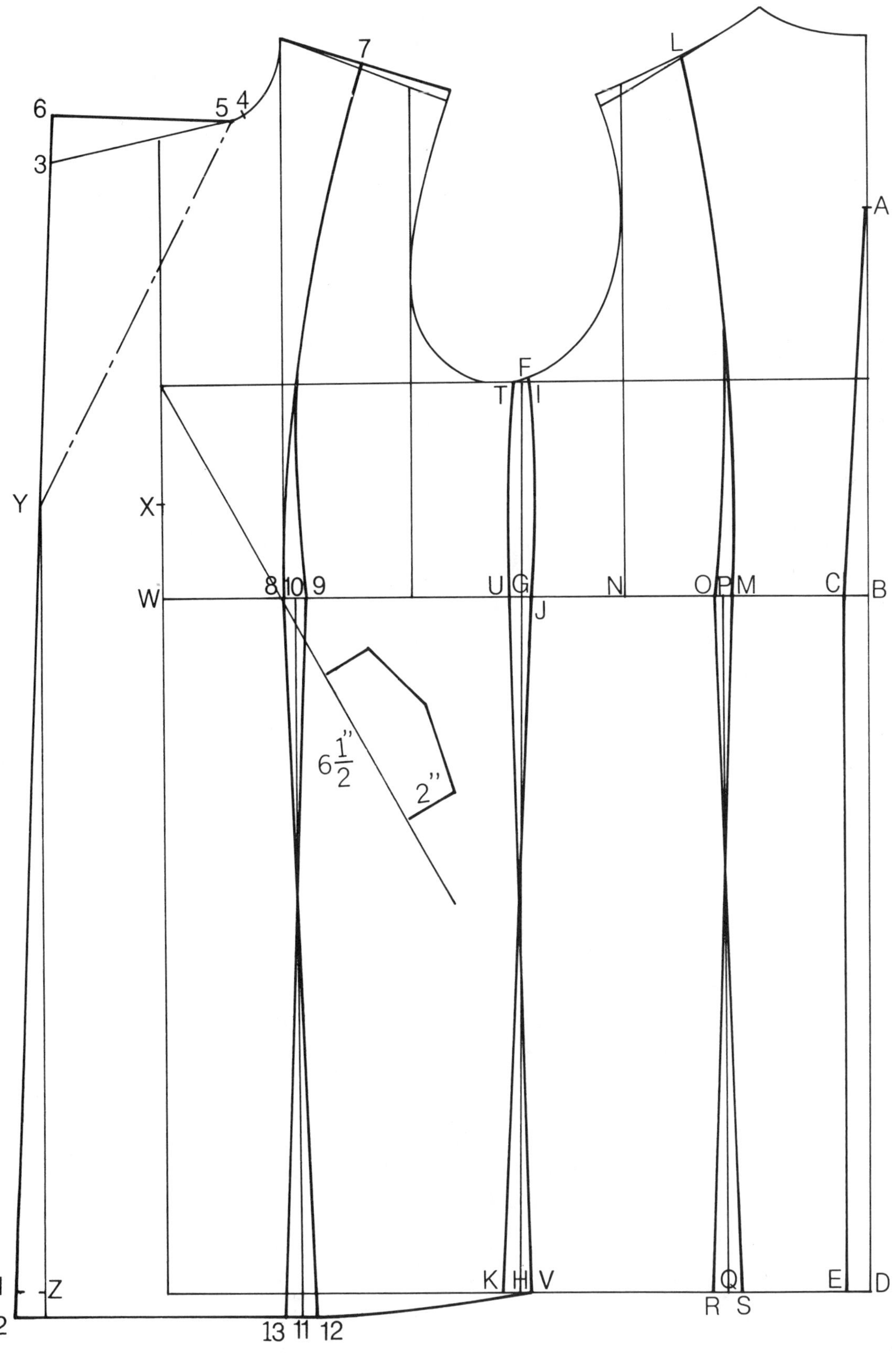

Collar. See page 194.
Sleeve. See page 110.

BONAPARTE COAT (ARMHOLE TORSO CUT)

Outline the basic sloper.
Lengthen the sloper to your overcoat design.

Back Coat Panel
A = 1/2 of neck to chest line.
B to C = 3/4".
D to E = 3/4".
Connect A to C to E to finish center back.
F to G = 4-1/4".
I = 1/2 of H to C.
I to J = 3/4".
K = 1/2 of I to J.
Square down from K to L.
L to M = 1-1/4".
Connect G to I with sleigh curve ruler.
Connect I to M with straight line to finish back coat panel.

Back Coat Side Panel
L to N = 1-1/4".
Connect G to J with sleigh curve ruler.
Connect J to N with straight line.
O = side seam at armhole.
O to P = 1".
Square up from P to Q and down from P to R.
S = waist.
S to T = 1/2".
R to U = 2-1/2".
Connect Q to T with hip curve ruler.
Connect T to U with straight line to finish back coat side panel.

Front Coat Side Panel
S to V = 1/2".
R to W = 2-1/2".
Connect Q to V with hip curve ruler.
Connect V to W with straight line to finish side seam.
X to Y = 4-1/2".
Z = front side guide line.
Z to 1 = 3-1/4".
1 to 2 = 1".
3 = 1/2 of 1 to 2.
Square down from 3 to 4.
Connect Y to 1 with sleigh curve ruler.
Connect Y to 2 with sleigh curve ruler.
4 to 5 = 1-1/4".
Connect 2 to 5 with straight line to finish front coat side panel.

Front Coat Panel
4 to 6 = 1-1/4".
Connect 1 to 6 with straight line to finish torso line.
7 = center front chest line.
7 to 8 = 3-1/2" for extension.
Square from 8 to 9.
9 to 10 = 1" drop.
Square off from 10 to 5.
Connect 5 to W with hip curve ruler to finish hem.

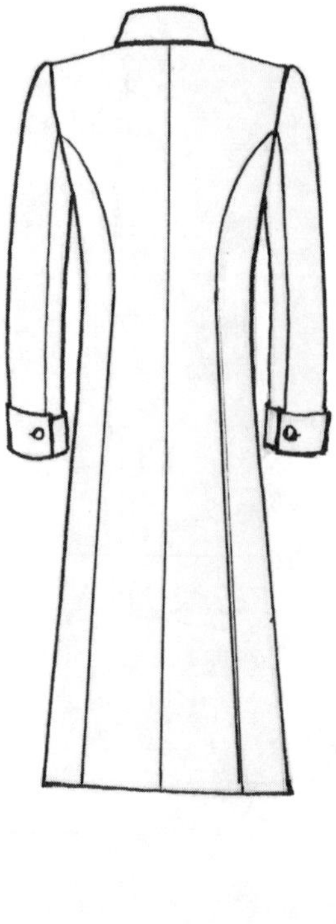

Lapel
11 = 1/2 of 12 to 13.
11 to 14 = 1/2".
Connect 8 to 14 for roll line.
Square off 15 to 16 for 5" for lapel width to finish front panel.

Collar
a to b = back neck measurement plus 13 to 11.
Square up a to c = 4-3/4".
Square up b to d = 4-3/4".
b to e = 2"
Square off e to f for roll line.
a to g = 1/2".
g to h = 11 to 13 front neck measurement.
f to i = 1/2".
Connect g to i to c to finish collar.

Note: Collar between c to d needs stretching by iron.

Pocket (see diagram)
Length = 6-3/4".
Width = 2-1/2".
Place 3" below waist line.

DIAGRAM–Bonaparte Coat (Armhole Torso Cut)

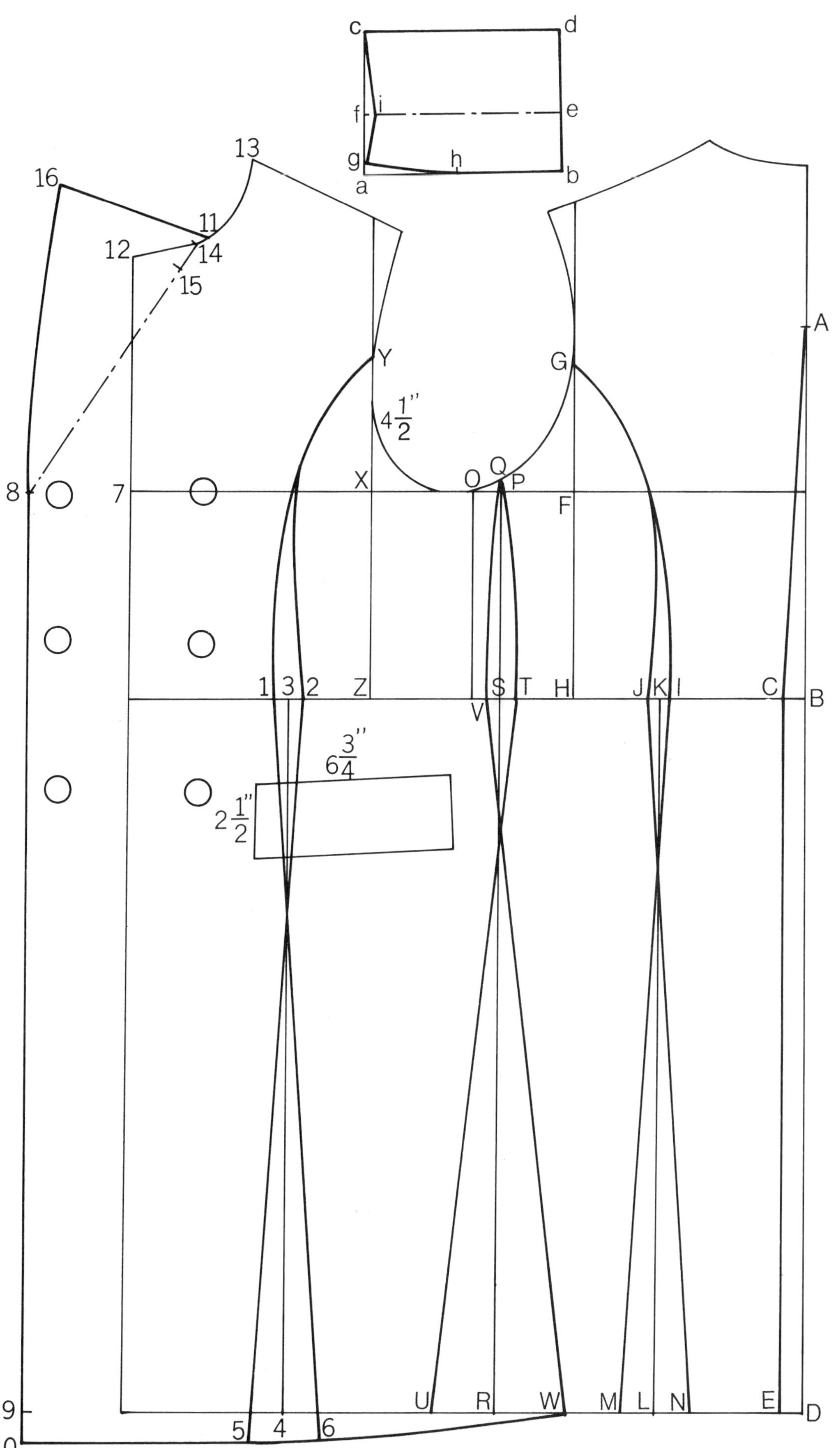

NECK TORSO CUT COAT

Outline your basic sloper and lengthen according to your design.

Back Coat Panel
A = 1/2 of neck to chest.
B to C = 1".
E to D = 1".
Connect A to C to E with straight line to finish center back.
F = 2-3/4" above chestline.
G = back side seam guideline at waist.
H = hem.
G to I = 3/8".
H to J = 1/4".
Connect F to I with hip curve ruler.
Connect I to J with straight line to finish back panel.

Back Side Panel
G to K = 3/8" at waist.
H to L = 1/4".
Connect F to K with hip curve ruler.
Connect K to L with straight line to finish back side seam.
M to O = 1/3 of N to O.
Square down from M to P.
Q = waist.
M to R = 1/4".
Q to S = 3/8".
P to T = 1/2".
Connect R to S with hip curve ruler.
Connect S to T with straight line to finish back side panel.

Front Side Panel
M to U = 1/4".
Q to V = 3/8".
P to W = 1/2".
Connect U to V with hip curve ruler.
Connect V to W with straight line to finish side seam.
X = 1/2 of Y to Z.
1 to 2 = 3/4" at chest.
Square down from 2 to 3.
4 = waist.
4 to 5 = 3/8".
3 to 6 = 1/4"
Connect X to 2 with hip curve ruler.
Connect 2 to 5 with straight line.
Connect 5 to 6 with straight line to finish front side panel.

Front Coat Panel
4 to 7 = 3/8".
3 to 8 = 1/4"
Connect 2 to 4 with straight line.
Connect 7 to 8 with straight line to finish torso cut line.
9 to X = 3/8".
Connect 9 to 2 with hip curve ruler.
10 = chest at center front.
10 to 11 = 2".
11 to 12 = 1-1/4" for extension.
Square down 12 to 13 at hem.
13 to 14 = 3/4".
Square off from 14 to 3.
Connect 3 to L with hip curve ruler to finish hemline.
Z = intersection of neck and shoulder points.
Z to 15 = 3/8".
Connect 15 to 12 with hip curve ruler to finish V neckline.
12 to 16 = 1/3 of 12 to 15.
16 = collar point.
17 = intersection of back neck and shoulder.
17 to 18 = 3/8".
Blend 18 into the original neckline.

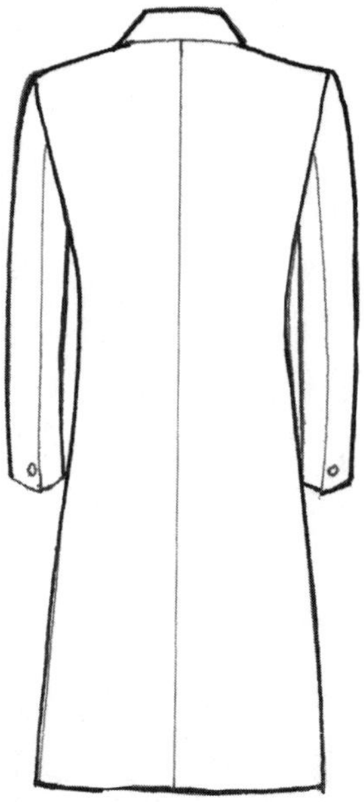

Pocket
For size, angle, and position of the pocket see diagram.

DIAGRAM—Neck Torso Cut Coat

Collar

a to b = 15 to 16 plus the back neck measurement minus 1/4".
b to c = 1/2".
Connect c to a with hip curve ruler (see diagram).
c to d = 3-1/2".
Square off from a to e and d to e.
e to f = 1/2" down.
f to g = 1".
Connect g to d with hip curve ruler (see diagram)
Connect g to a with straight line to finish collar.

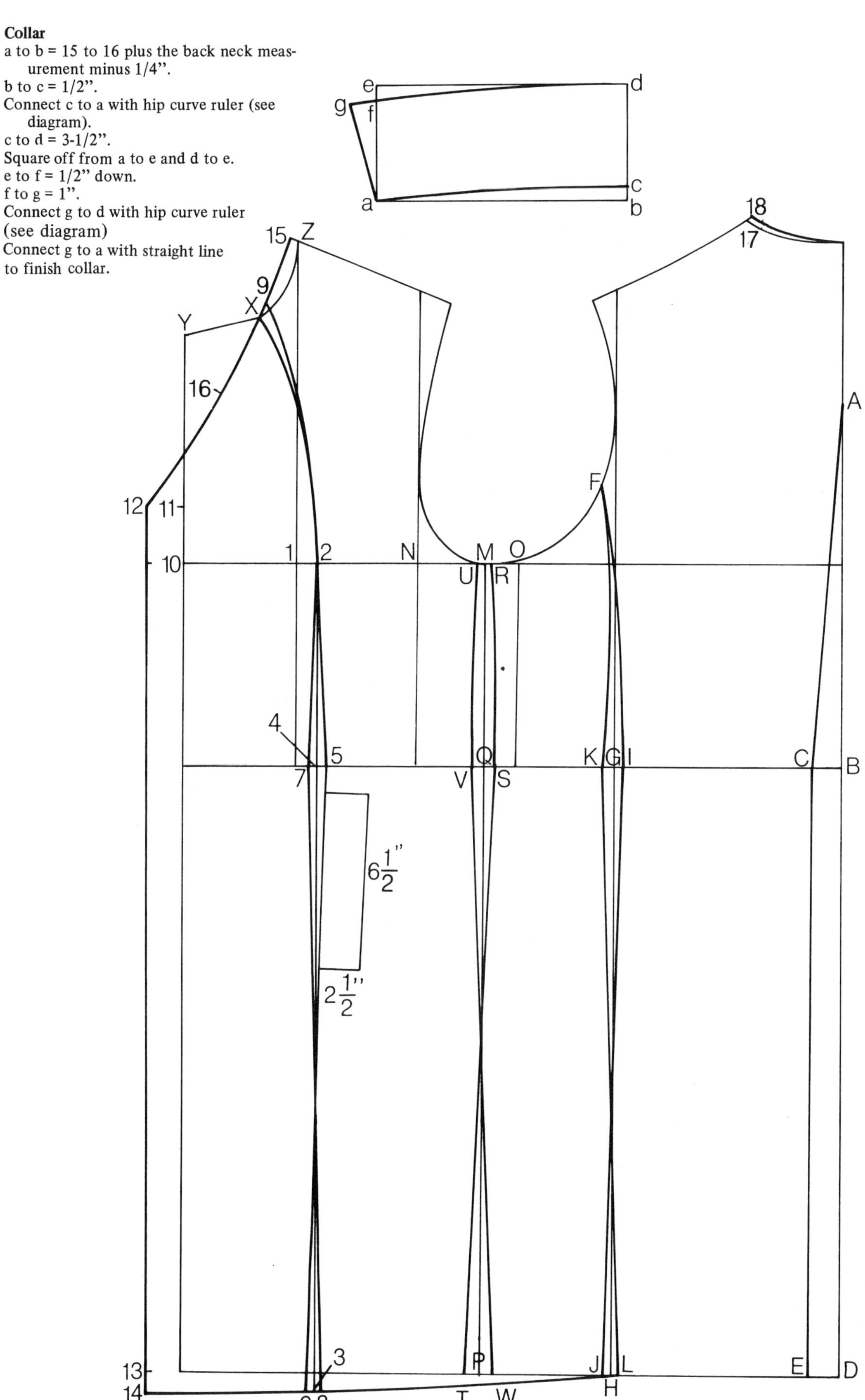

WELT-SEAM TORSO CUT COAT – CENTER FRONT

Outline the basic sloper.
Lengthen the sloper according to the design.
Shift shoulder line 3/8" toward back (see diagram).

Back Coat Panel
A = 1/2 of neck to waist.
B to C = 1".
D to E = 1".
Connect A to C to E to finish center back.
F = side seam at armhole.
F to G = 1".
Square down from G to H.
I to J = 1/2" at waist.
H to K = 1/2".
Connect G to J with hip curve ruler.
Connect J to K with straight line to finish back side seam.

Front Coat Panel
I to L = 1/2".
H to M = 1/2".
Connect G to L with hip curve ruler.
Connect L to M with straight line to finish side seam.
N = center front at chest.
N to O = 1".
O to P = 1-1/2" extension.
Square down P to Q.
Q to R = 1".
Square off R to S.
Connect S to M with hip curve ruler to finish hemline.
T = intersection of neck and shoulder points.
Extend T to U = 1-1/8".
Connect P to U with straight line to establish the roll line.
V = neck point.
Extend V to W = 2".
Connect W to P with hip curve ruler, the deepest part toward P.
W to X = 1-1/4".
Y to roll line = 1/2".
Connect X to Y to finish lapel.

Front Torso Cut
N to Z = 4"
1 = front torso guideline at chest.
Connect Z to 1 according to design.
2 to 3 = 3/8" at waist.
S to 4 = 1/4".
Connect 1 to 3 and 3 to 4 with straight line.
2 to 5 = 3/8" at waist.
S to 6 = 1/4".
Connect 1 to 5 and 5 to 6 with straight line to finish torso cut.

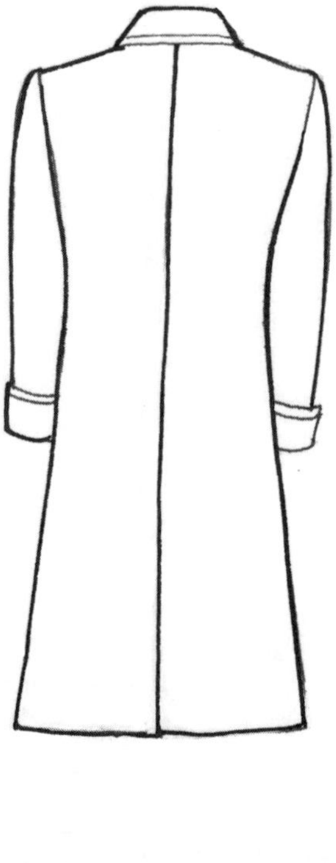

Collar. See page 188.
Sleeve. See page 110.

Pocket
See diagram.

DIAGRAM—Welt-Seam Torso Cut Coat – Center Front

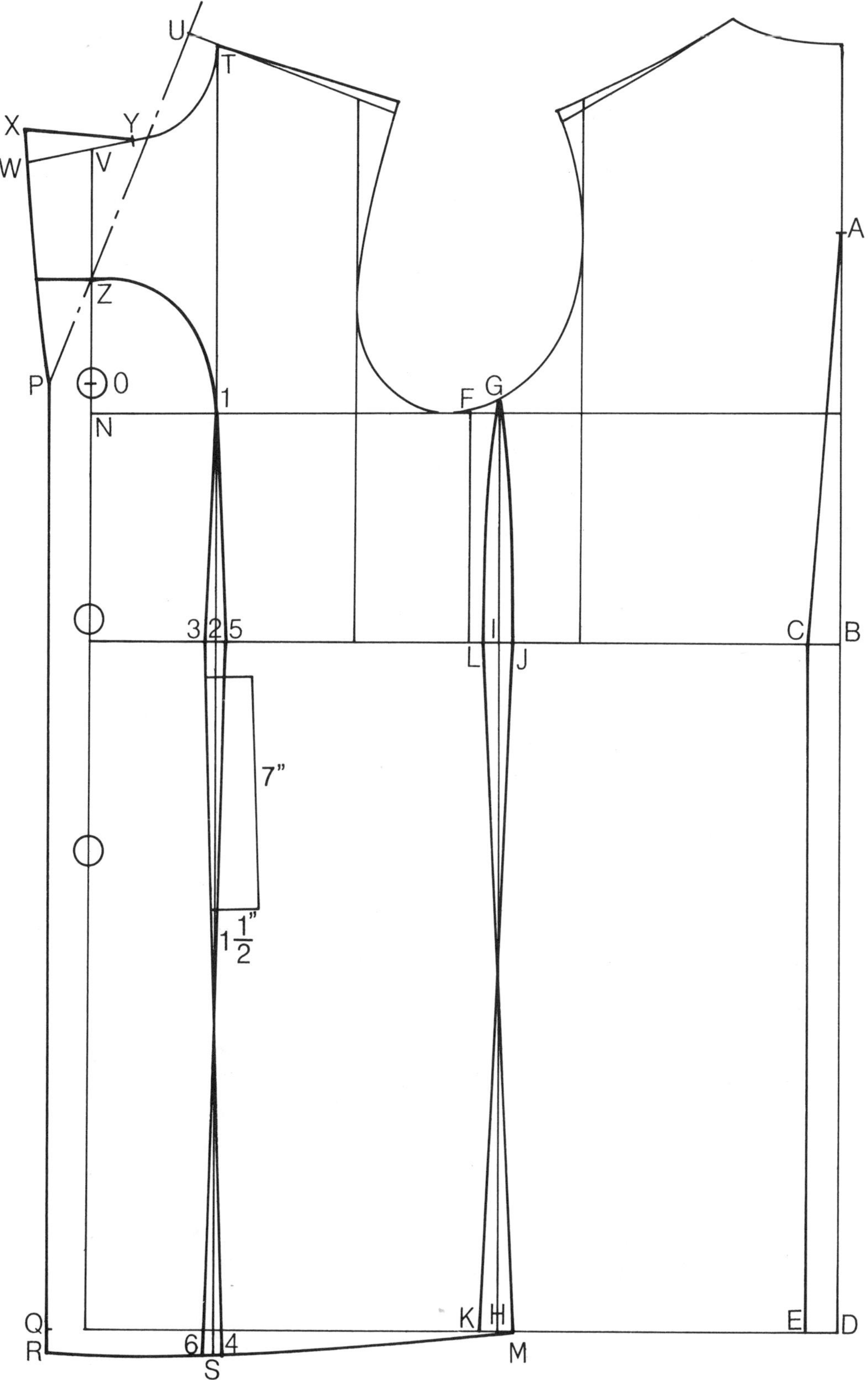

BRITISH RAINCOAT

Outline your basic sloper and lengthen according to the design.

Back Coat Panel
A = 1/2 of neck to chest measurement.
B to C = 1".
D to E = 1".
Connect A to C to E to establish center back.
F = 3-1/2" above chestline.
Square off F to G.
H to F = 3/4".
Connect G to H with hip curve ruler to establish the back yoke.
I = 1-1/2" squared up from chest line.
Square down to J.
K = waistline.
K to L = 1/2".
J to M = 3/4".
Connect I to L with hip curve ruler.
Connect L to M with straight line to finish back coat panel.

Side Coat Panel
K to N = 1/2".
J to O = 1".
Connect I to N with hip curve ruler.
Connect N to O with straight line to finish the side seam.

Side Dart
P = 1/3 of Q to R.
Square down from P to T.
S to T = 3-1/2".
P to U = 1/4".
P to V = 1/4".
S to W = 3/8".
S to X = 3/8".
Connect U to W to T with hip curve ruler.
Connect V to X to T with hip curve ruler to finish the side dart.

Y = intersection of neck and shoulder points.
Y to Z = 2".
1 to 2 = 1/2" at waist.
2 to 3 = 3/4".
4 to 5 = 1" at hem.
Connect Z to 2 with hip curve ruler.
Connect 2 to 4 with straight line.
Blend in from 3 to torso line with sleigh curve ruler.
Connect 3 to 4 with straight line to finish side coat panel.

Front Coat Panel
6 = center front at waist.
6 to 7 = 3".
7 to 8 = 3-1/2" for extension.
Square down 8 to 9.
9 to 10 = 1".
10 to 11 = 1/2".
Connect 8 to 11 with straight line.
Square off 11 to 12.
Connect 12 to O with hip curve ruler to finish hem.
Y to 13 = collar stand.
Connect 8 to 13 to establish roll line.
14 = neck point.
14 to 15 = 1/2".
17 = Square off from 16 through 15 for 5".
17 to 18 = 1-1/2".
Connect 18 to 8 with hip curve ruler.
Connect 18 to 15 with straight line to finish lapel.

Center Back Pleat (See diagram.)

Collar. See page 178.
Sleeve. See page 110.

Pocket
For size, angle, and position of pocket see diagram.

DIAGRAM—British Raincoat

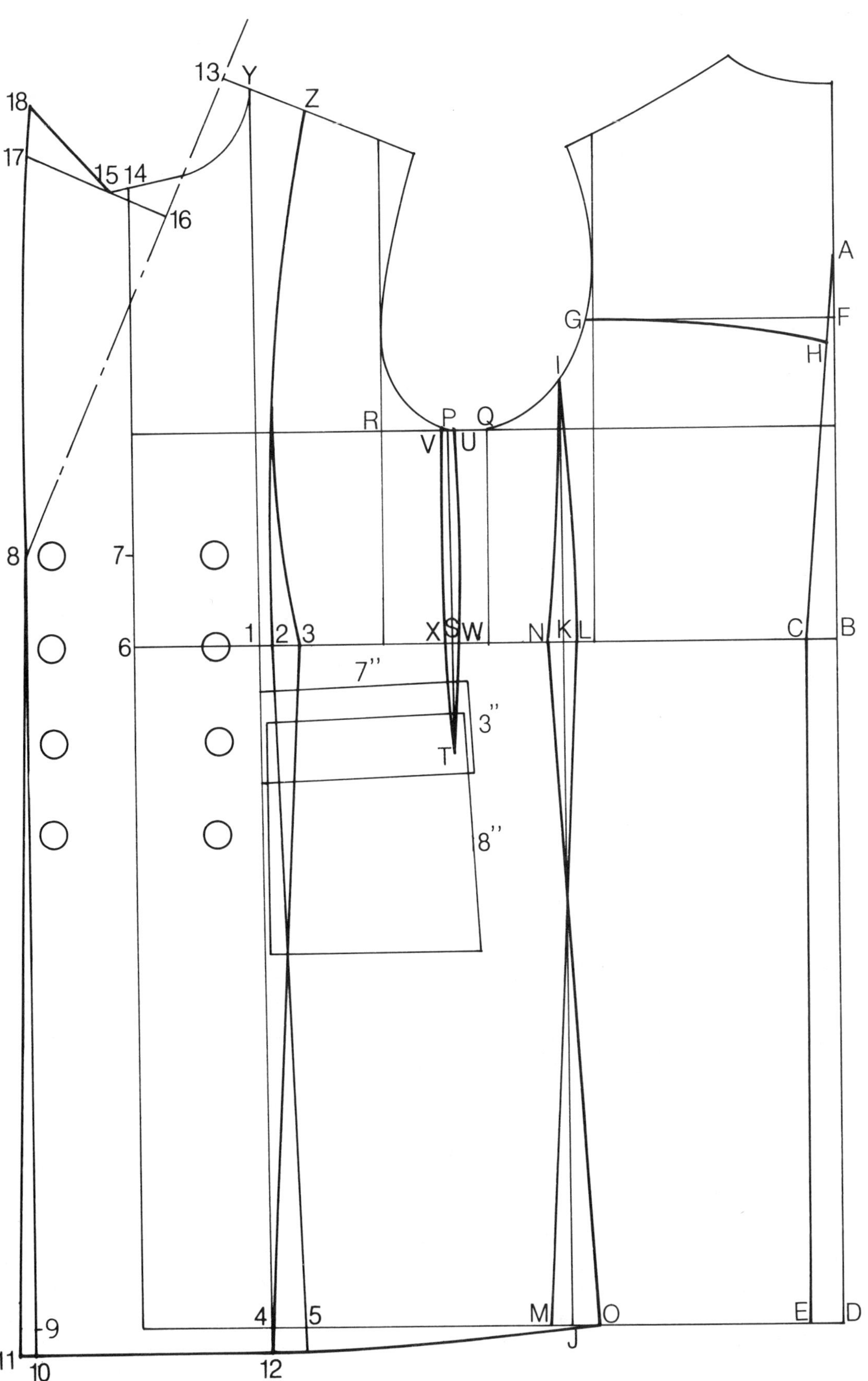

CARDIGAN COAT

Outline your basic sloper.
Lengthen sloper according to design.

Back Coat Panel
A = 1/2 of neck to chest.
B to C = 1".
D to E = 1".
Connect A to C to E to finish center back.
F = according to your design at armhole.
G to C = 4".
G to H = 1".
Connect F to G with sleigh curve ruler according to design.
Connect F to H with sleigh curve ruler according to design (see diagram).
I = 1/2 of G to H.
Square down from I to J.
J to K = 1-1/4".
J to L = 1-3/4".
Connect G to L with straight line.
Connect H to K with straight line.
Draw the tab line according to design (see diagram).

Front Coat Panel
Side Darts:
M = side seam at armhole.
M to N = 1".
O = 1/3 of P to Q.
Connect N to O and extend the line downward.
O to R = 5".
N to S = 1/4".
N to T = 1/4".
O to U = 3/8".
O to V = 3/8".
Connect S to U to R with hip curve ruler.
Connect T to V to R with hip curve ruler to finish side darts.
W = center front at chest.
W to X = 1" - half of tab width.
Square down X to Y.
Y to Z = 1".
Square off Z to 1.
Connect 1 to K with hip curve ruler to finish hemline.
2 = intersection of neck and shoulder points.
2 to 3 = 1".
2 to 4 = 1".
3 to 5 = 1/4".
Connect 5 to 4.
Connect 5 to X with hip curve ruler to finish tab.

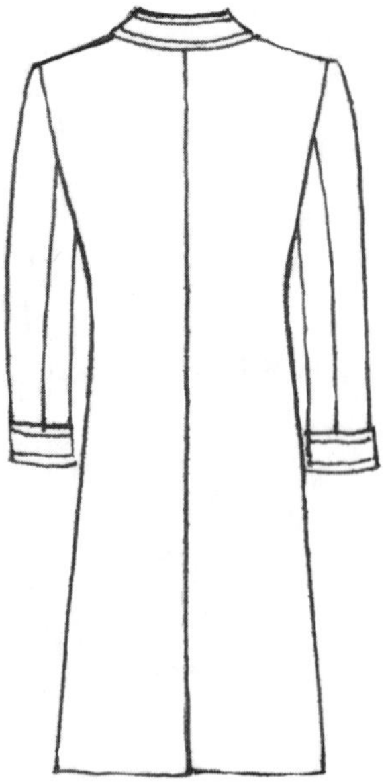

Back Neck Band
6 to 7 = original neckline.
6 to 8 = 3/4" down.
8 to 9 = 2".
7 to 10 = 1".
10 to 11 = 3/8" down.
8 to 11 = 8 to 10.
Square off from 11 to 12 = 2".
Connect 9 to 12 with sleigh curve ruler to finish neck band.

Front Dart
13 = front torso guideline at waist.
13 to 14 = 2".
14 to 15 = 3/4".
Square up and down from midpoint between 14 and 15.
16 at chest.
Midpoint to 17 = 3-1/2".
Connect 16 to 14 and 16 to 15.
Connect 17 to 14 and 17 to 15 to finish front dart.

Pocket (See diagram.)

DIAGRAM–Cardigan Coat

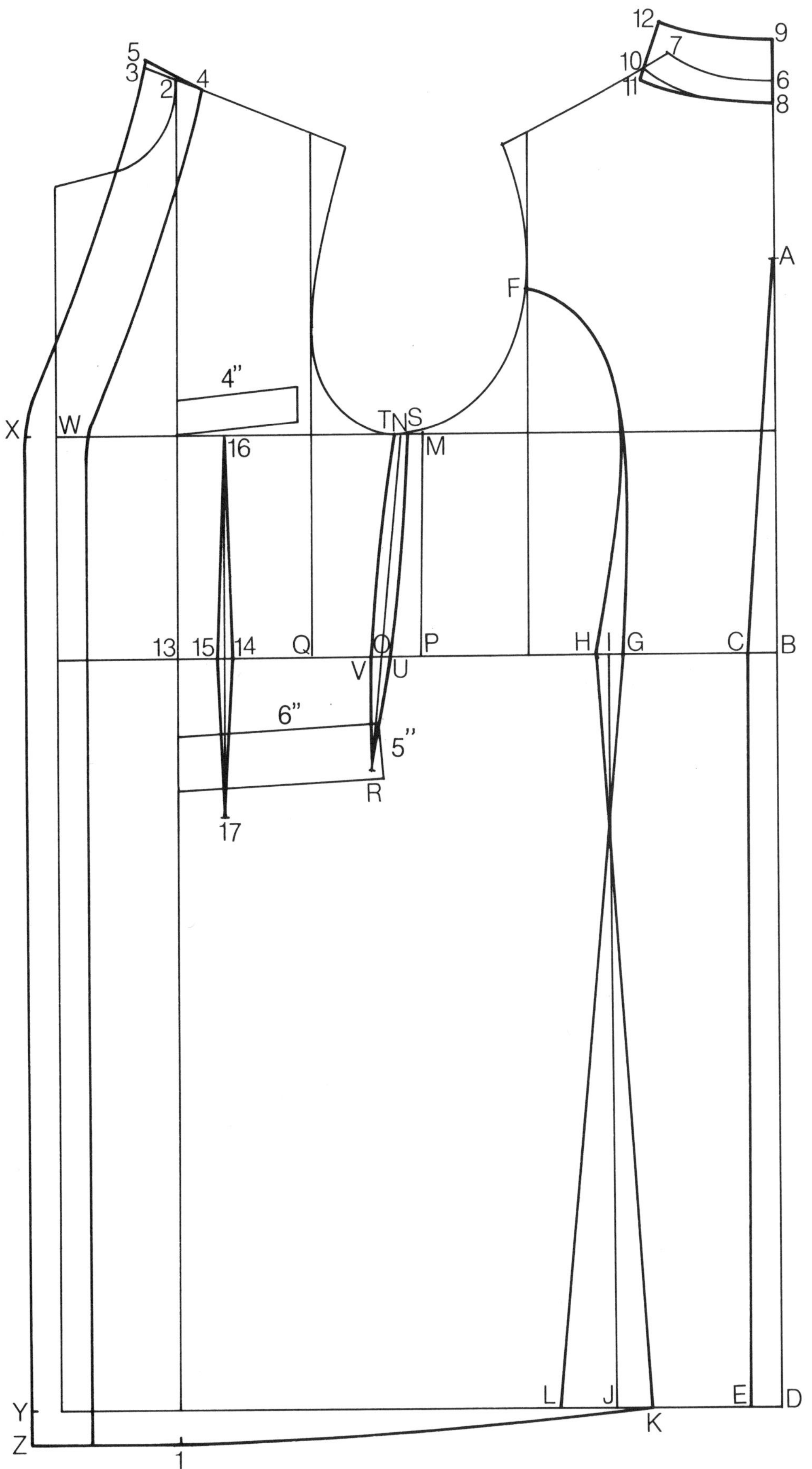

SECTION V

FUNDAMENTALS OF SLEEVE DESIGN

BASIC SLEEVE SLOPER

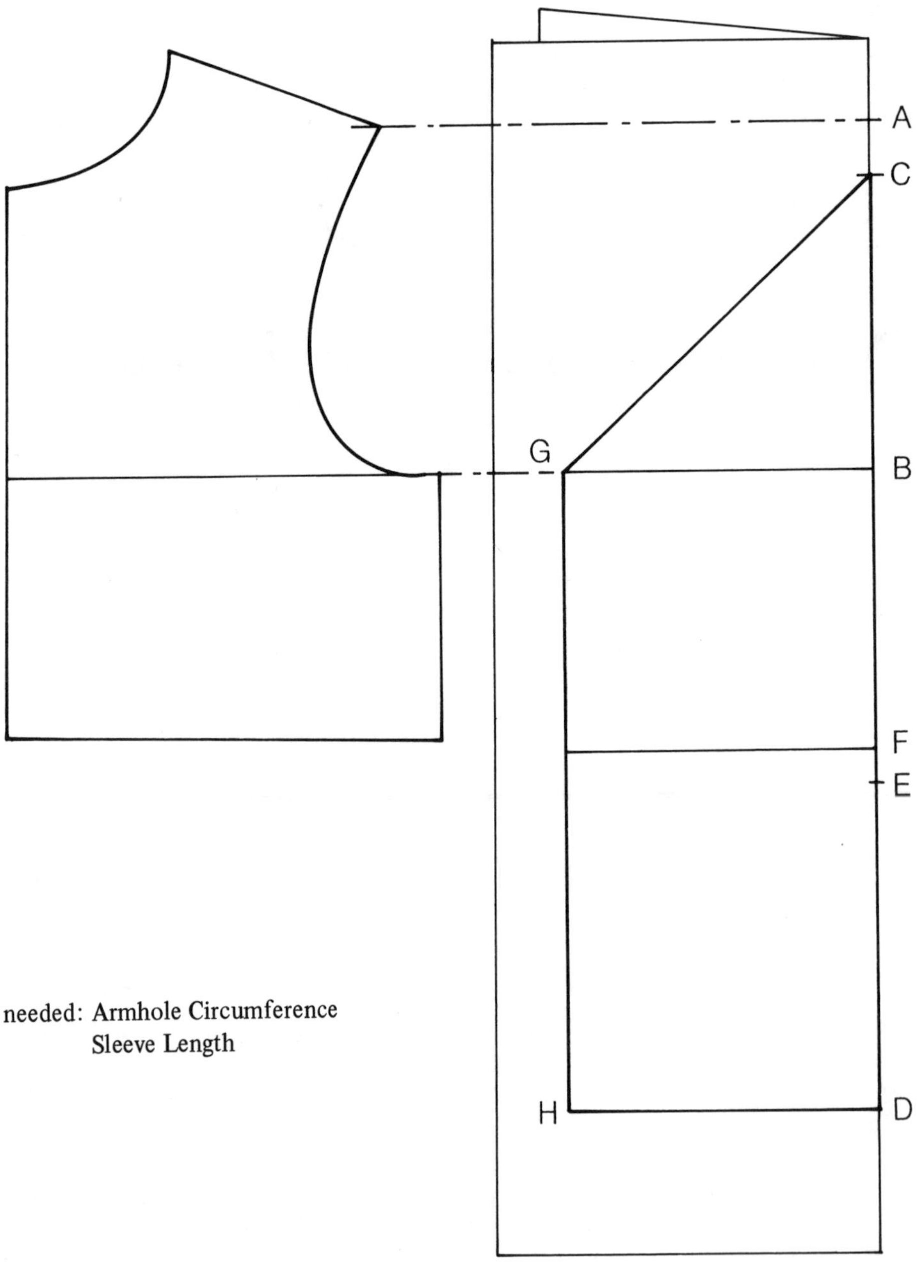

Measurements needed: Armhole Circumference
Sleeve Length

Diagram A

A to B = armhole height (see diagram).
A to C = 1-3/8".
C to D = sleeve length
E = 1/2 of B to D.
E to F = 1" up.
Square off from B, F, and D to the left.
C to G = 1/2 armhole circumference plus 3/8" for ease.
Square down from G to H.

BASIC SLEEVE SLOPER

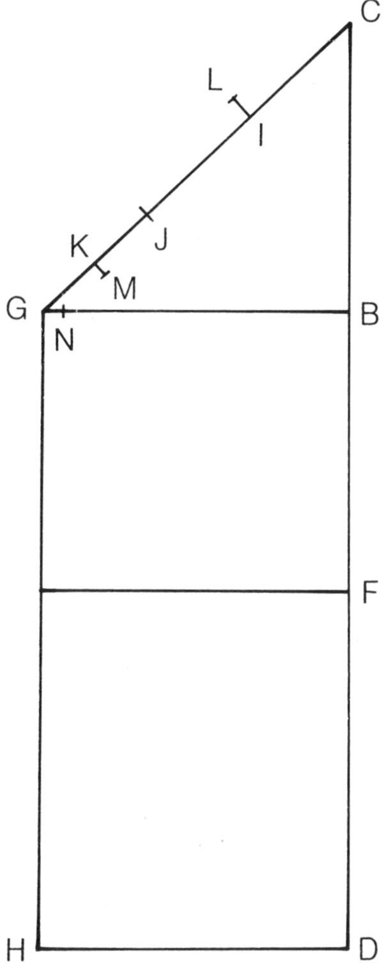

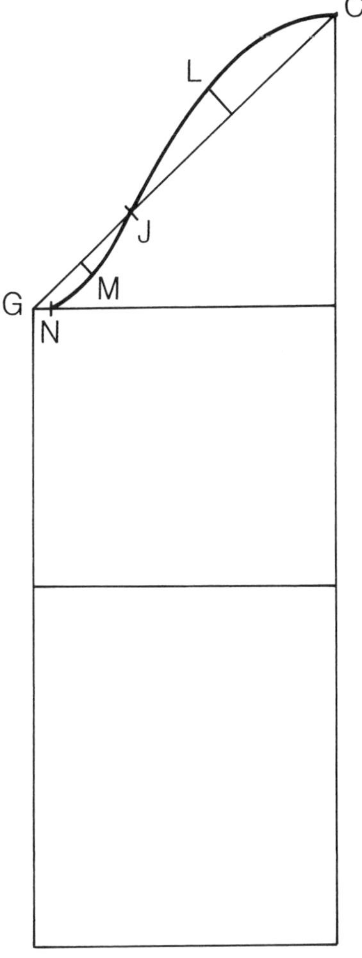

Diagram B

Divide C to G into three equal sections.
K = 1/2 of J to G.
I to L = 3/4".
K to M = 3/8".
G to N = 3/8".

Diagram C

Connect C to L to J with sleigh curve ruler.
Connect J to M to N with sleigh curve ruler to finish up back sleeve cap.
Blend in at point N.

BASIC SLEEVE SLOPER

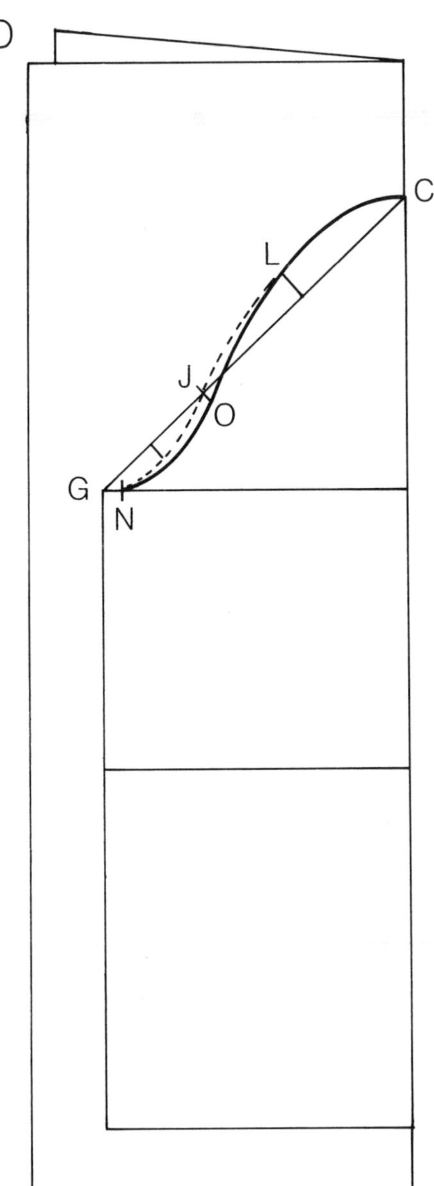

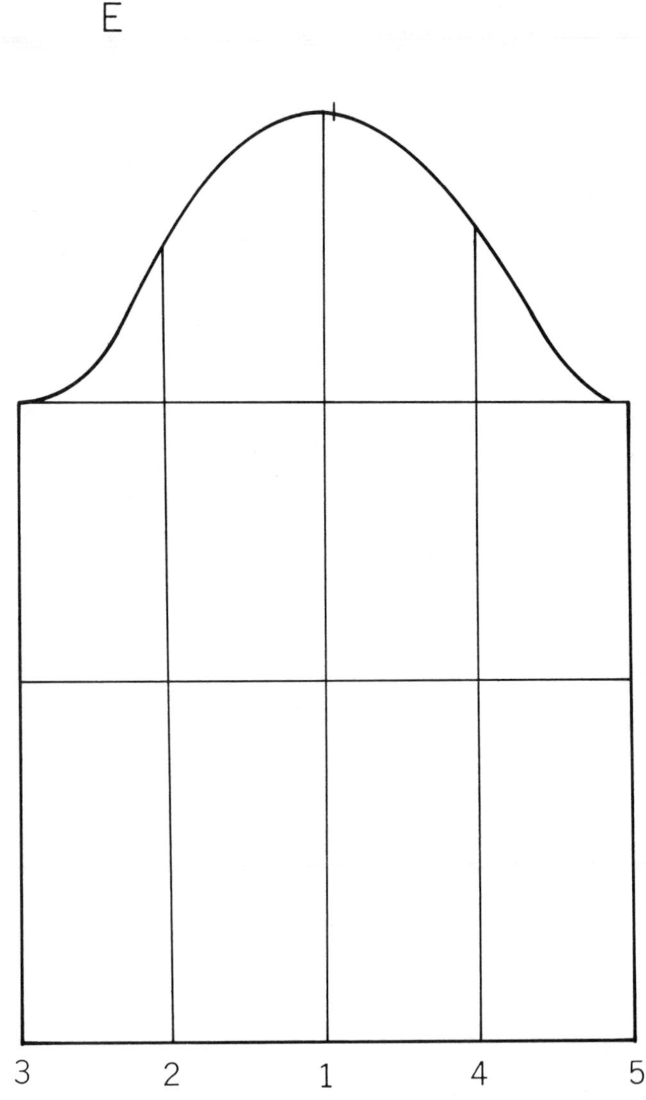

Diagram D

Front sleeve cap.
Square down from J for 3/8" to O.
Connect L to O with sleigh curve ruler.
Connect O to N with sleigh curve ruler to finish front sleeve cap.
Trace through back sleeve cap into the other side of paper.
Trace through the remainder of the sleeve including the elbow line.

Diagram E

1 = grainline.
2 = 1/2 of 1 to 3.
4 = 1/2 of 1 to 5.
Square up from 2 and 4 as guide lines.

BASIC SLEEVE SLOPER

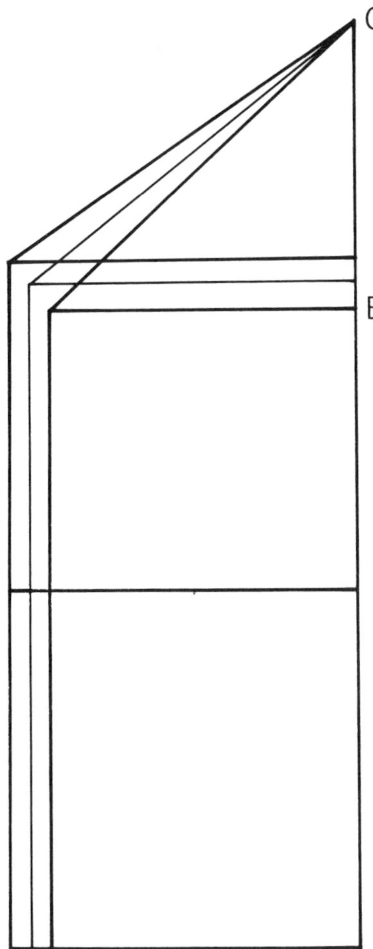

Diagram F

For additional underarm ease, shorten the cap height. For action clothes shorten cap height 1/2" to 1" (see diagram).

TWO-PIECE SLEEVE

DIAGRAM–Two-Piece Sleeve

Under Sleeve

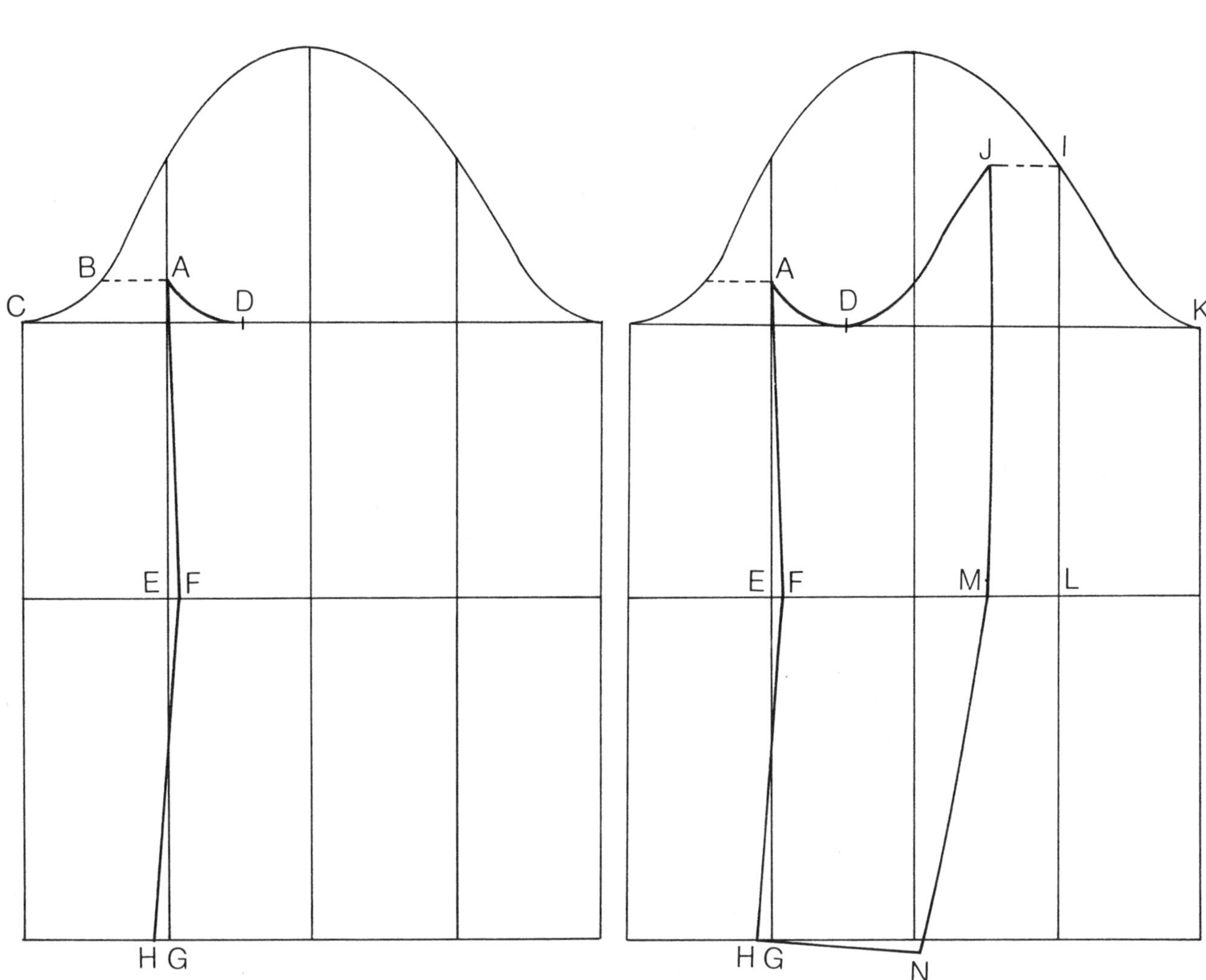

Outline sleeve sloper.

Two-piece sleeve consists of upper sleeve and under sleeve.

On front guideline, square off from A to B for 2".
Transfer curve between B and C to A and D.
E to F = 3/8".
H to G = 3/8".
Connect A to F and F to H to finish inseam.

Square off top of back guideline I to J for 2".
Transfer curve between I and K to J and D.
L to M = I to J.
Square off from H to N.
H to N = 1/2 cuff minus 1".
Connect J to M with shallowest part of hip curve ruler.
Connect M to N with shallowest part of hip curve ruler to finish under sleeve.

UPPER SLEEVE

Diagram C

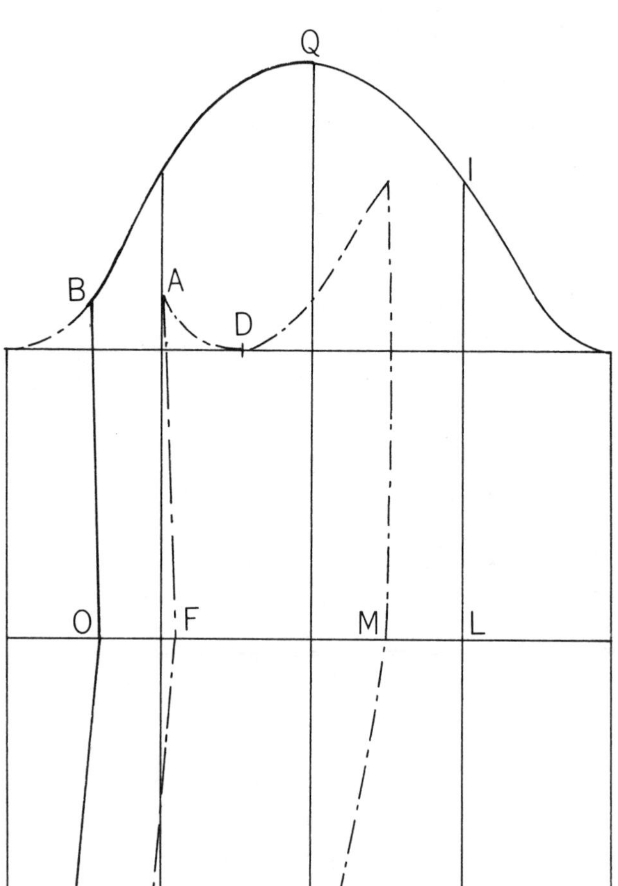

F to O = 2".
H to P = 2".
Connect B to O and O to P with straight line to finish inseam.
Connect P to H to N to finish cuff.
Cap of upper sleeve is curve between B and Q and I.

Diagram D

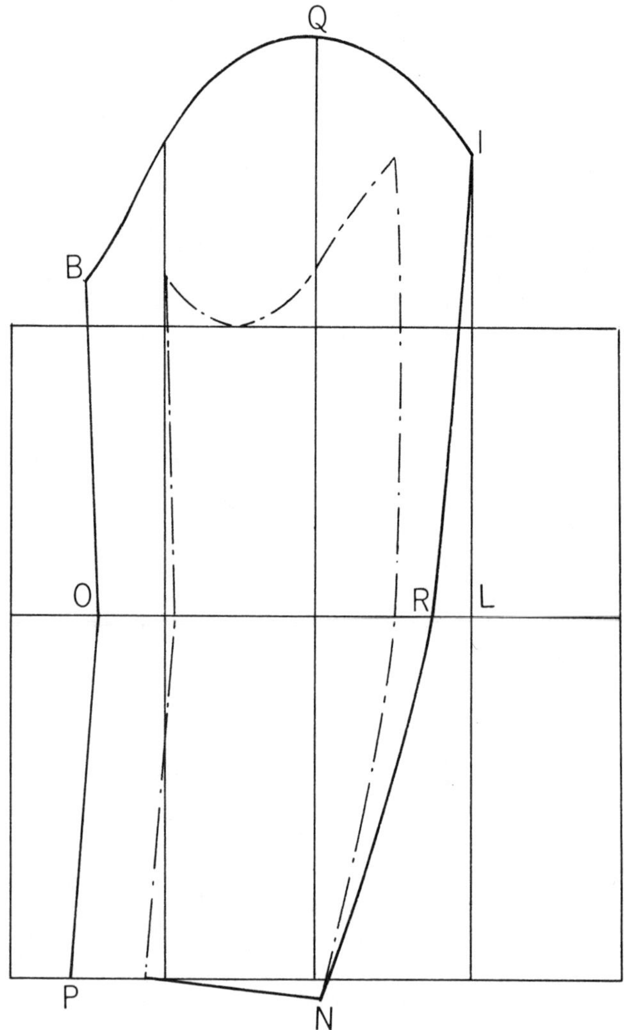

L to R = 1".
Connect I to R with hip curve ruler.
Connect R to N with hip curve ruler to finish upper sleeve.

TWO-PIECE SLEEVE CROSSMARK

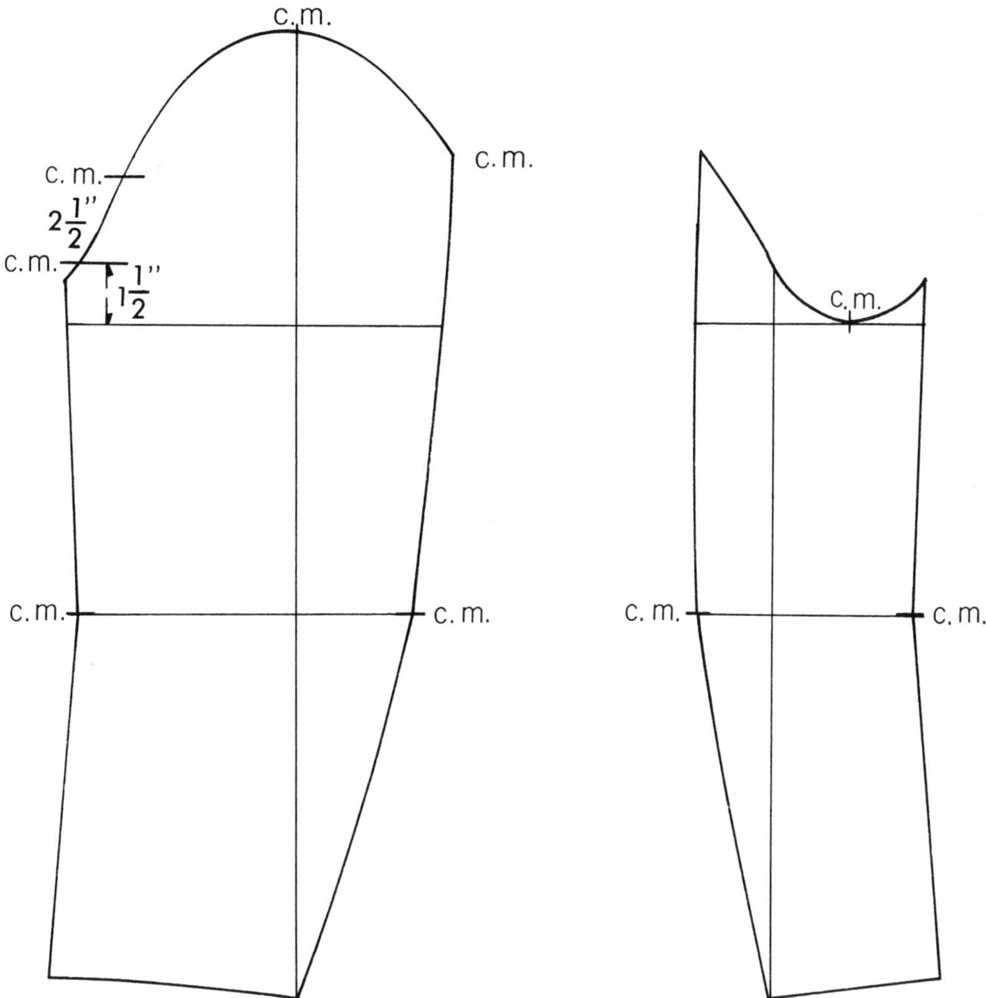

Upper Sleeve

Under Sleeve

CUFFED SLEEVE

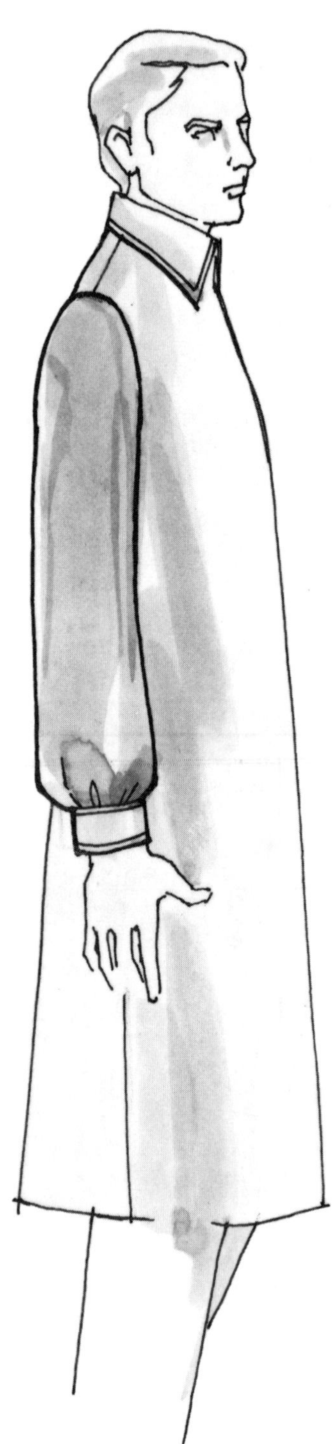

Cuff measurement – 11" to 13".
Outline the basic sleeve sloper.
Subtract the cuff width (2-1/2") from the bottom of the sleeve sloper.
A to B = cuff length plus 3" ease for tucks or shirring according to design.
C = 1/2 of A to B.
Connect A to D with straight line.
Connect B to E with straight line.
F = 1/2 of C to B.
F to G = 3/8".
Connect G to B with sleigh curve ruler and blend in G to A.
G to H = 3" (see diagram).

DIAGRAM—Cuffed Sleeve

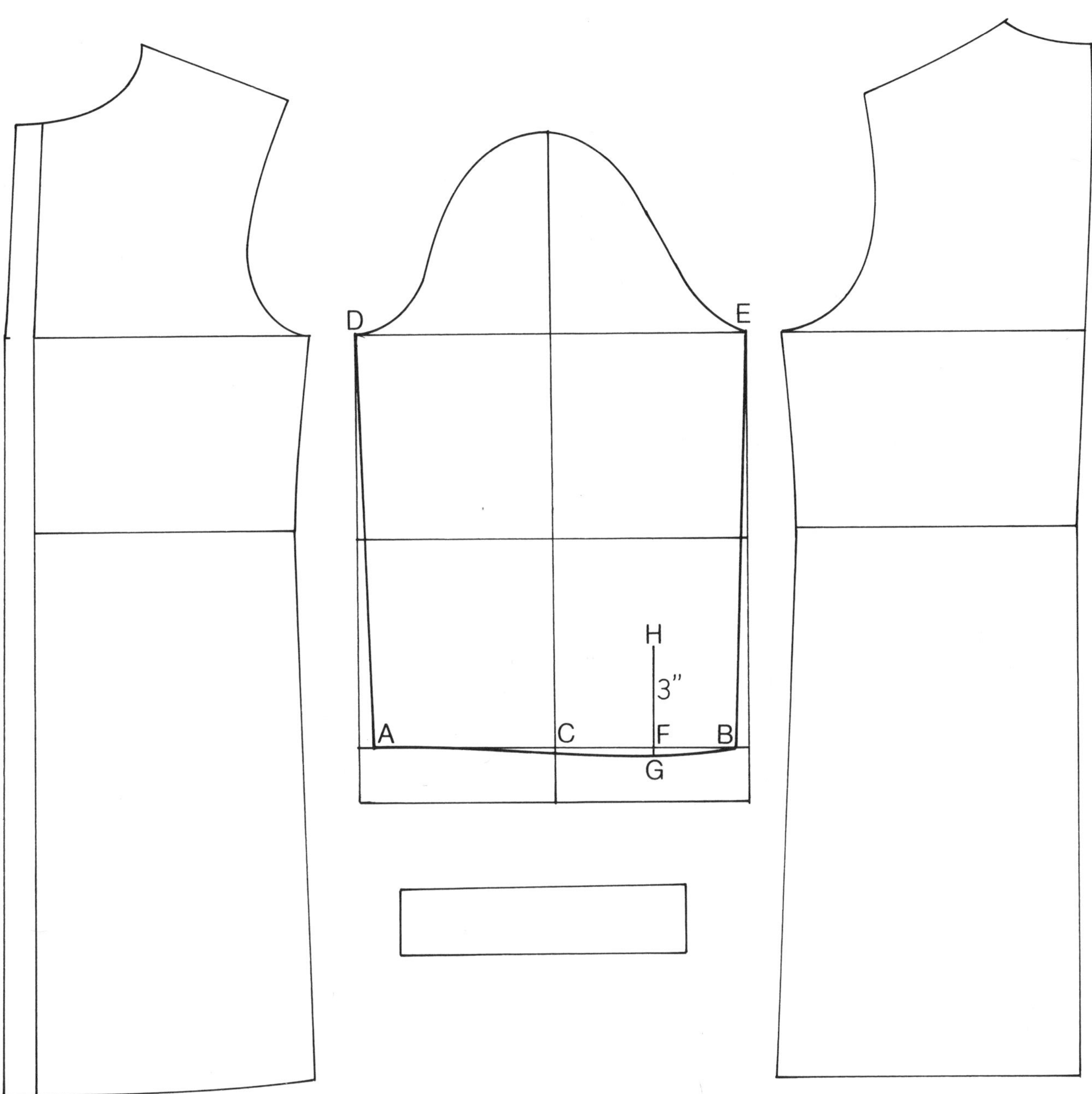

TWO-PIECE SLEEVE

DIAGRAM—Two-Piece Sleeve

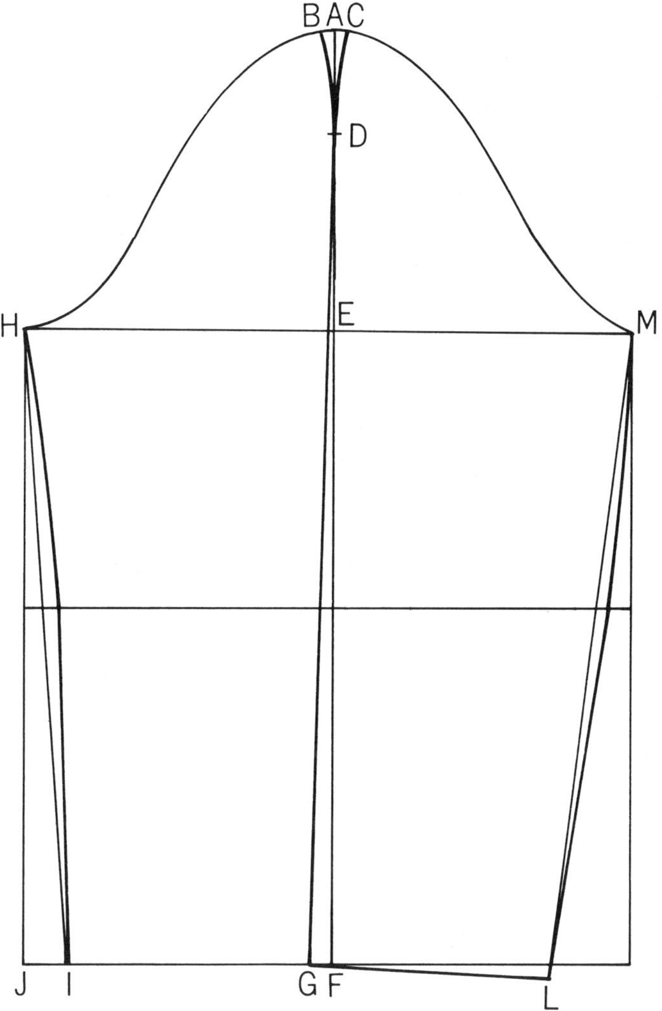

A = apex of sleeve cap.
A to B = 1/4".
A to C = 1/4".
A to D = 1/3 of A to E.
F to G = 1/2".
Connect B to D with sleigh curve ruler.
Connect D to G with straight line.
F to I = 6 1/2".
Connect H to I with hip curve ruler.
Connect C to D with sleigh curve ruler.
L to G = 6 1/2".
Connect L to M with hip curve ruler to finish two piece sleeve.

SEMI-RAGLAN SLEEVE

SEMI-RAGLAN SLEEVE

DIAGRAM A

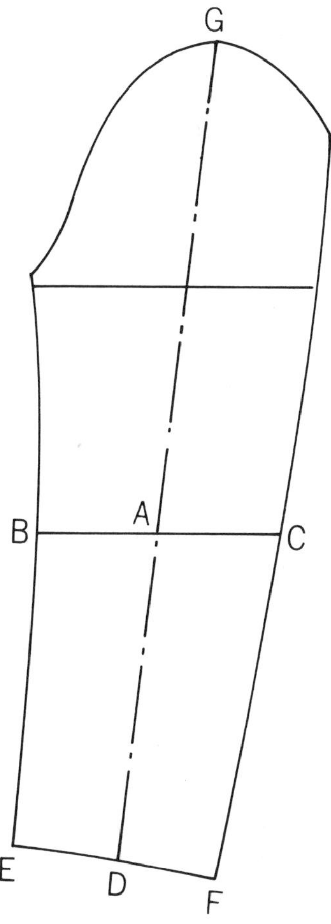

Outline upper sleeve.
Indicate elbow line.
A = 1/2 B to C.
D = 1/2 E to F.
G = center top of cap.
Connect G to A and A to D with straight line.

DIAGRAM B

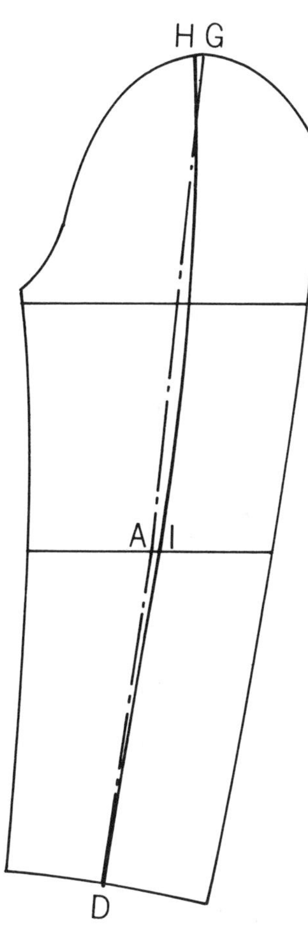

G to H = 1/4".
A to I = 1/8".
Connect H to I with hip curve ruler.
Connect I to D with straight line.

DIAGRAM C

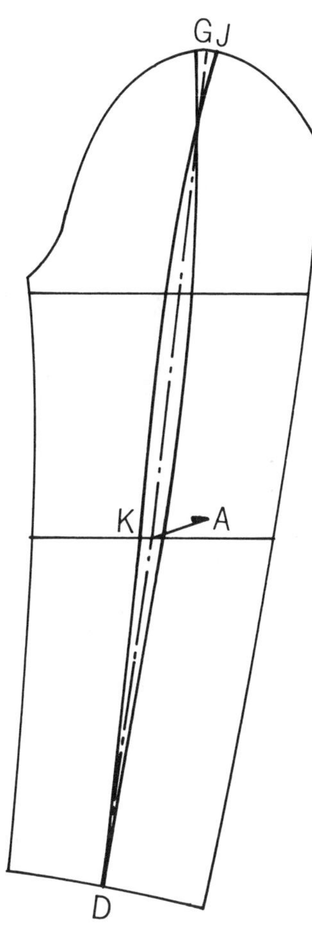

G to J = 1/4".
A to K = 1/8".
Connect J to K with hip curve ruler.
Connect K to D with straight line, to finish three-piece sleeve.

BASIC TWO-PIECE RAGLAN SLEEVE

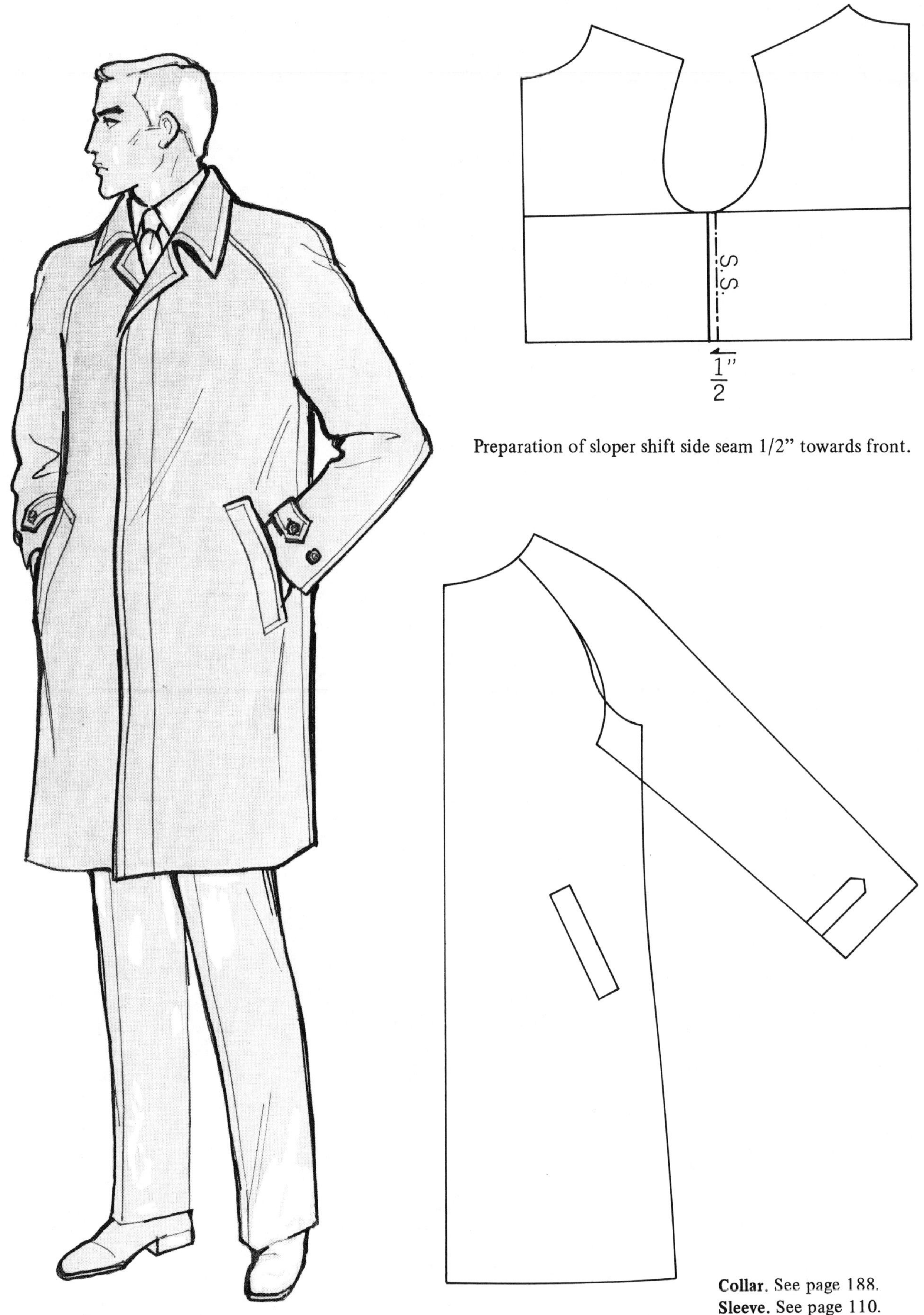

Preparation of sloper shift side seam 1/2" towards front.

Collar. See page 188.
Sleeve. See page 110.

DIAGRAM—Basic Two-Piece Raglan Sleeve

Outline your basic back coat sloper.
Lengthen according to your design.

BACK COAT PANEL

DIAGRAM A

A = 1/3 of B to C.
D = 1/3 of E to F.
Square off D to G.
H to I = 1" drop in armhole depth.
Blend in I to G with sleigh curve ruler to finish new dropped armhole curve.
J to K = 3/8" at waist side seam.
L to M = 1" at hem.
Connect I to K with hip curve ruler.
Connect K to M with straight line.

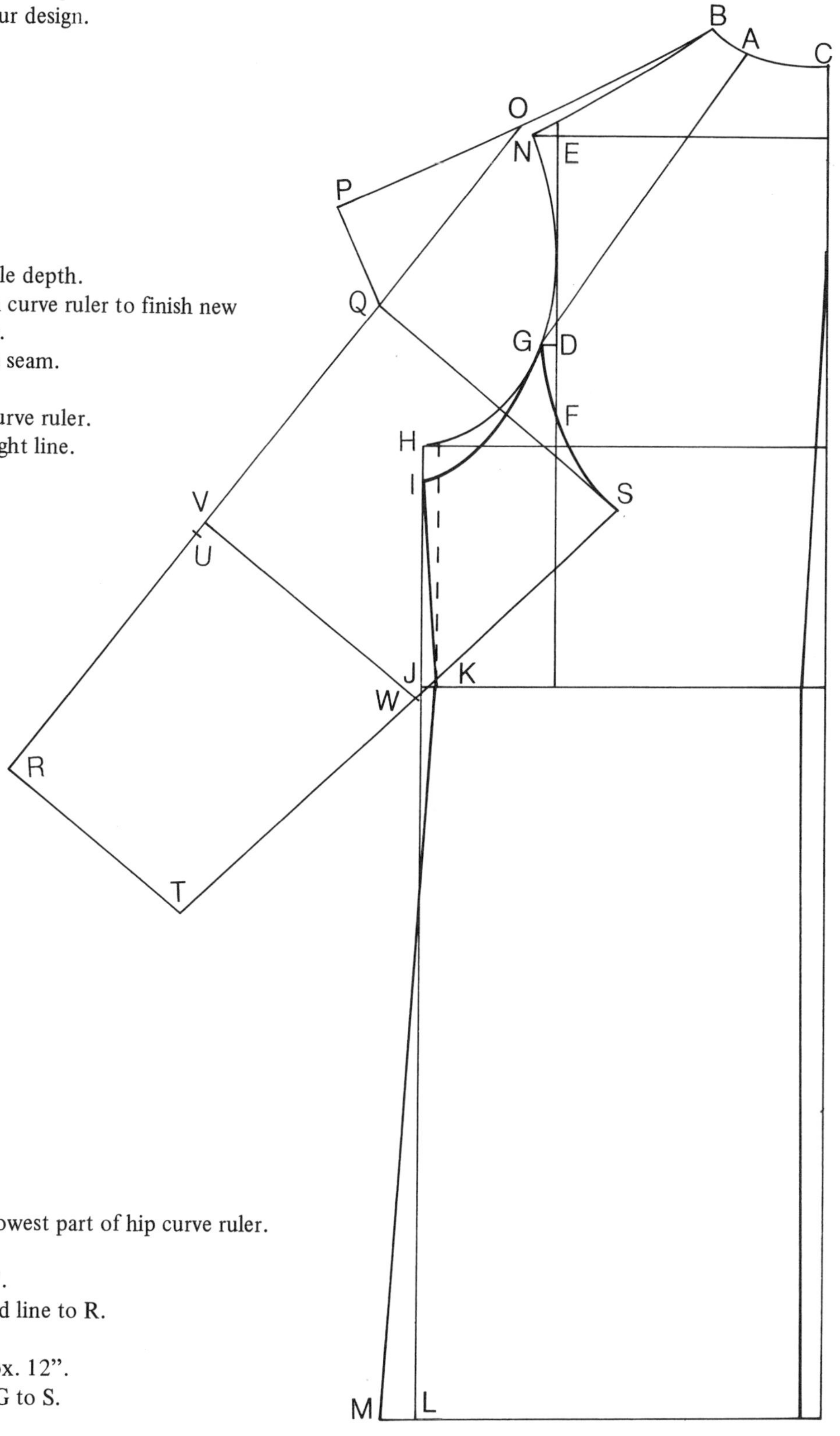

B
A
C
O
N
E
P
Q
G
D
F
H
I
S
V
U
J
K
W
R
T
M
L

N = shoulder at armhole.
N to O = 3/8" up.
Connect B to O with shallowest part of hip curve ruler.
Extend O to P = 6".
Square off P to Q = 3-3/4".
Connect O to Q and extend line to R.
O to R = sleeve length.
Square off from Q = approx. 12".
Pivot curved line G to I = G to S.
R to T = 6".
Connect S to T with straight line.
U = 1/2 of Q to R.
U to V = 5/8".
Square off from V to W.

DIAGRAM B

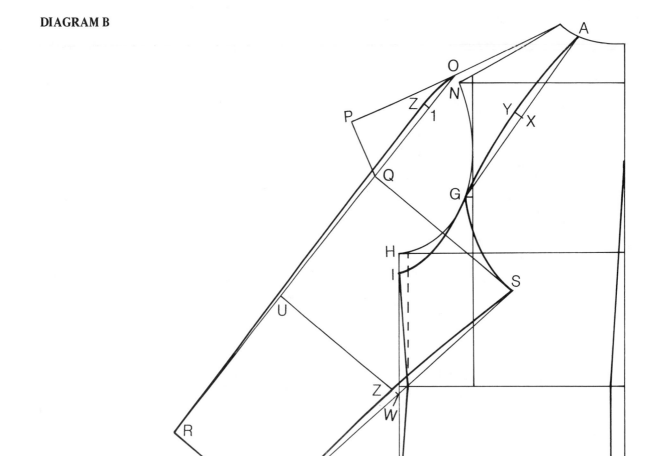

X = 1/2 of A to G.
X to Y = 1/2".
Connect A to Y to G with hip curve ruler.
W to Z = 3/8".
Connect S to Z with hip curve ruler.
Connect Z to T with straight line.
1 = 1/3 of O to Q.
1 to Z = 3/8".
Blend in Z to O with sleigh curve ruler.
Connect Z to R with straight line to finish back raglan sleeve.

Shape the center back seam the same as on the basic overcoat.

DIAGRAM–Basic Two-Piece Raglan Sleeve

DIAGRAM C

FRONT COAT PANEL

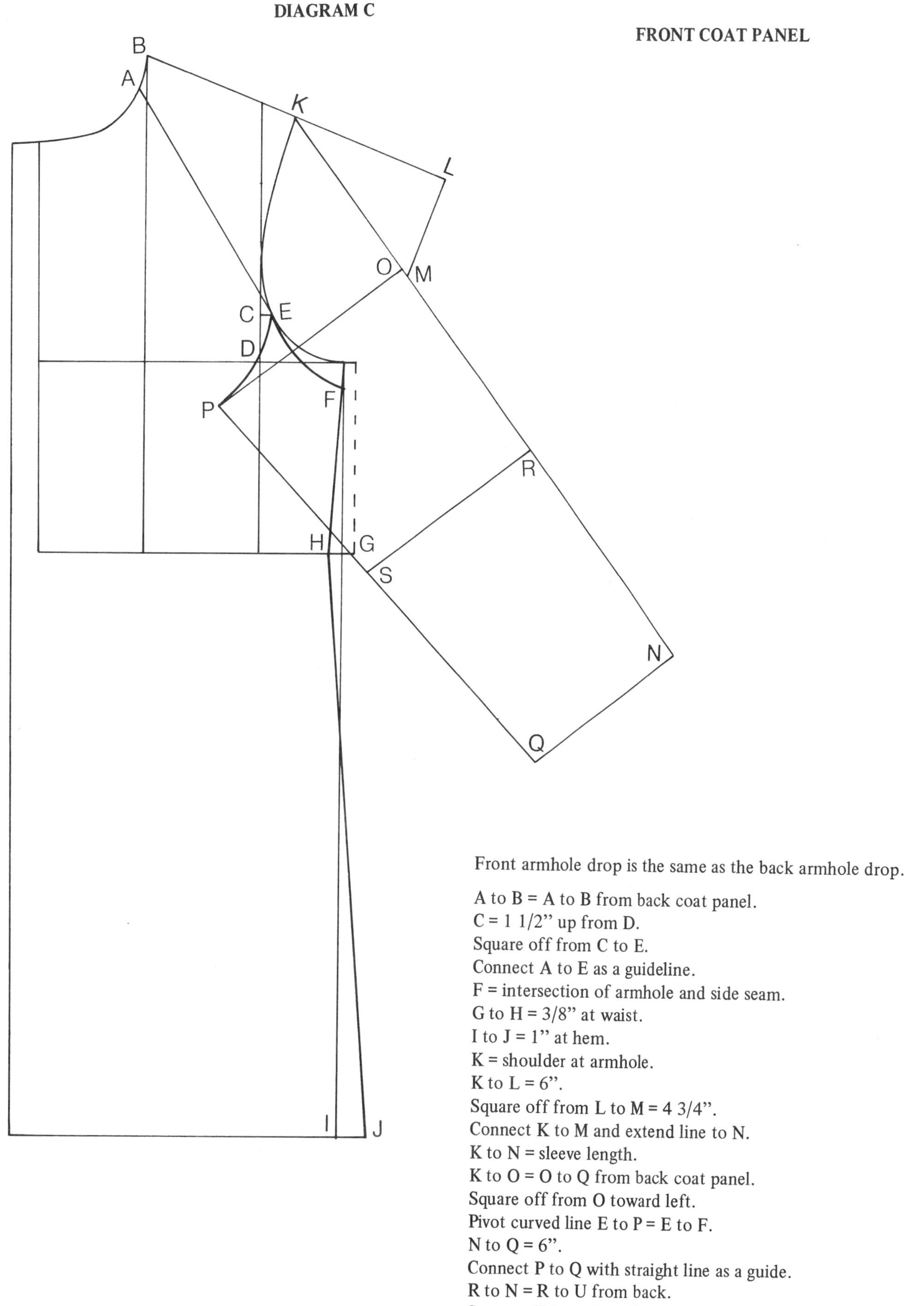

Front armhole drop is the same as the back armhole drop.

A to B = A to B from back coat panel.
C = 1 1/2" up from D.
Square off from C to E.
Connect A to E as a guideline.
F = intersection of armhole and side seam.
G to H = 3/8" at waist.
I to J = 1" at hem.
K = shoulder at armhole.
K to L = 6".
Square off from L to M = 4 3/4".
Connect K to M and extend line to N.
K to N = sleeve length.
K to O = O to Q from back coat panel.
Square off from O toward left.
Pivot curved line E to P = E to F.
N to Q = 6".
Connect P to Q with straight line as a guide.
R to N = R to U from back.
Square off from R to S.

DIAGRAM D

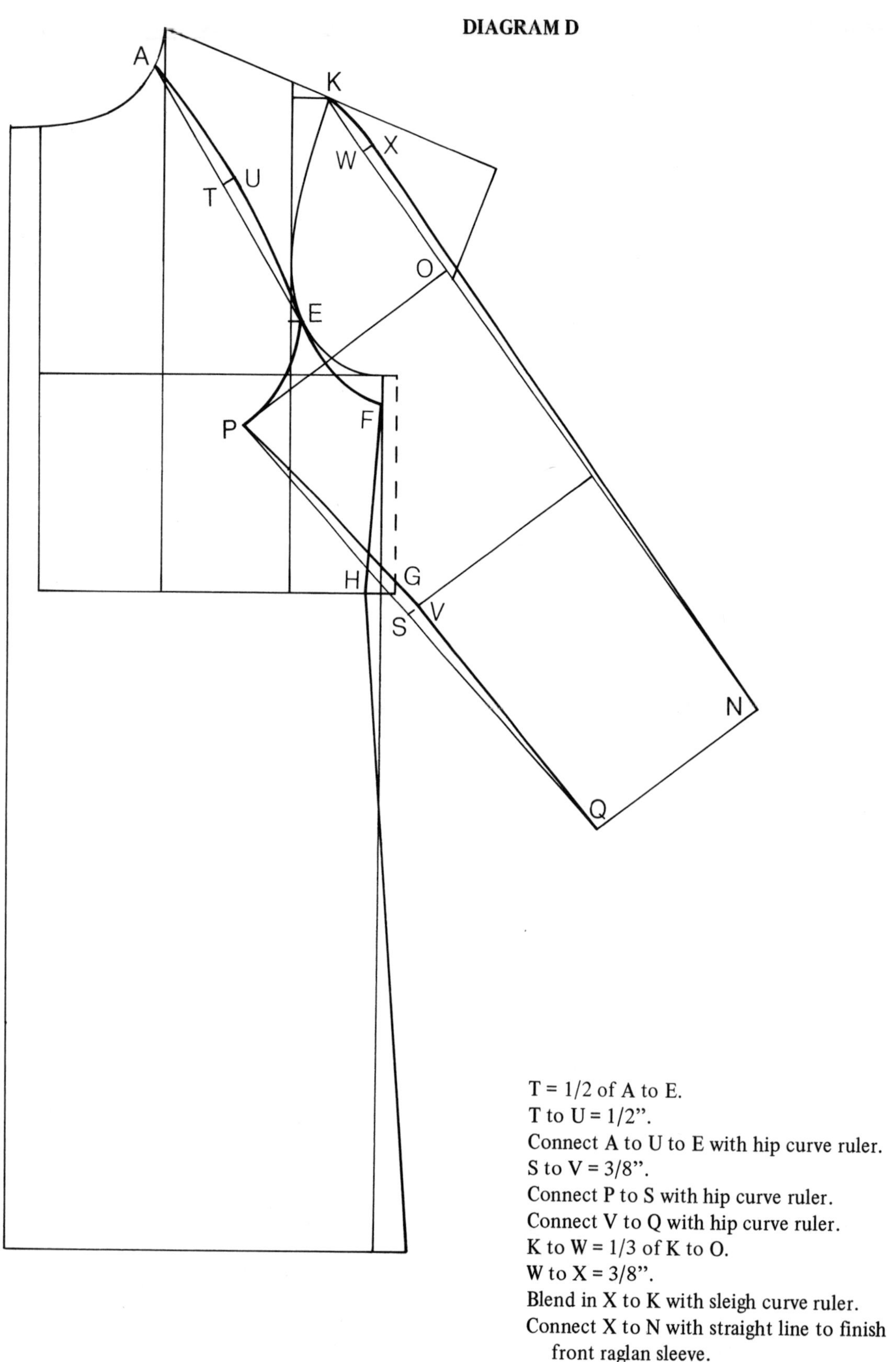

T = 1/2 of A to E.
T to U = 1/2".
Connect A to U to E with hip curve ruler.
S to V = 3/8".
Connect P to S with hip curve ruler.
Connect V to Q with hip curve ruler.
K to W = 1/3 of K to O.
W to X = 3/8".
Blend in X to K with sleigh curve ruler.
Connect X to N with straight line to finish front raglan sleeve.

NOTES

TRENCH COAT

Outline your basic sloper and lengthen according to design.

Drafting of Shoulder Parts (Front and Back) and Sleeve
Same as Basic Two-Piece Raglan Sleeve. (See Basic Raglan Sleeve, page 120.)

A = 5/8" from side seam toward front for crossmark to meet the raglan sleeve underseam.

Back Coat Panel
B = 1/2 of neck to chest.
C to D = 1".
E to F = 1".
Connect B to D and D to F with straight line to finish center back.
G = 1" from side seam toward the back.
Square down from G to H.
H to I = 2".
Connect G to I with straight line to finish back coat panel.

Front Coat Panel
H to J = 2".
Connect G to J with straight line.
K = center front at chest.
K to L = 3-1/2" for extension.
Square down from L to M and square up from L to U.
M to N = 3/4".
Square off from N to O.
Connect O to J with hip curve to finish hemline.

Lapel
P = 1/2" below L for breakpoint.
Q = intersection of shoulder and neck.
R = 1/2 Q to S.
Extend the neckline toward T.
T to U = 2-1/4".
Connect U to R.
V = 3/4" from R.
Connect P to V with straight line to finish lapel.

Pocket
W = chest line at front guideline.
Connect W to I with straight line as a guideline.
Size and position of pocket on the guide line, see diagram.

Sleeve drafting procedure is the same as the basic two piece raglan sleeve.

Coat Belt

Coat belt length – 70".
width – 2-1/4".

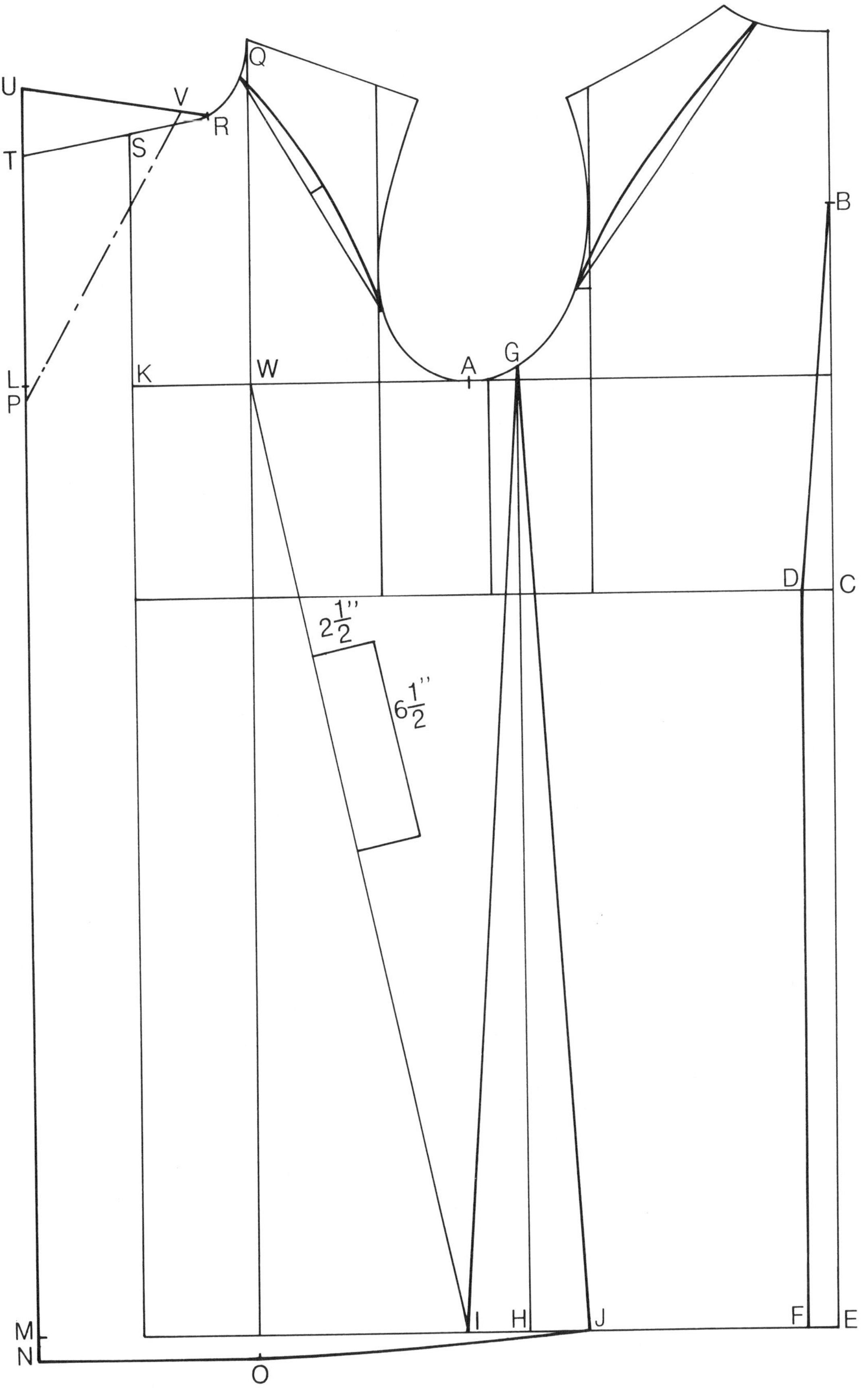
U
V
R
T
S
Q
B
L
P
K
W
A
G
D
C
$2\frac{1}{2}$''
$6\frac{1}{2}$''
M
N
I
H
J
F
E
O

DIAGRAM—Trench Coat

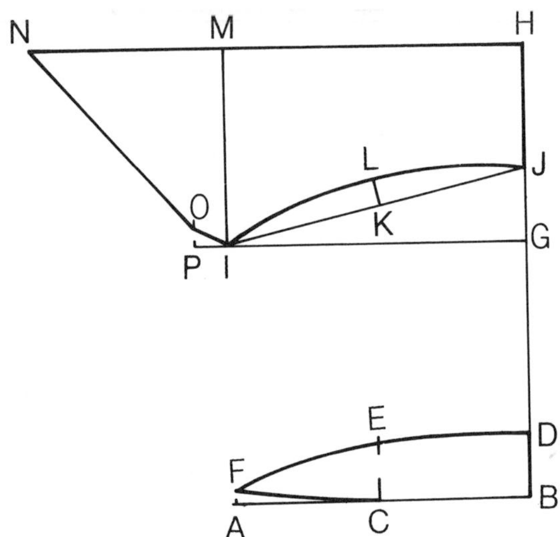

COLLAR

Stand

A to B = S to Q plus back neck measurement.
C to B = back neck measurement.
Square up B to D = 1-1/4" for stand.
Square up C to E = 1-1/4".
A to F = 1/4".
Connect F to C with sleigh curve.
Connect F to E with sleigh curve and blend in at E.

Square off G to H = 4".
G to I = D to F.
G to J = 1-1/2".
Connect J to I with straight line as a guide.
K = 1/2 of J to I.
Square up from K 1/2" to L.
Connect J to L to I with sleigh curve and square off at J.
Square off from H and I to M.
M to N = 4".
O = 3/4" from I and 3/8" from P.
Connect O to N to finish collar.

Designing Yoke
(See diagram.)

Designing Belted Cuff and Epaulet
(See diagram.)

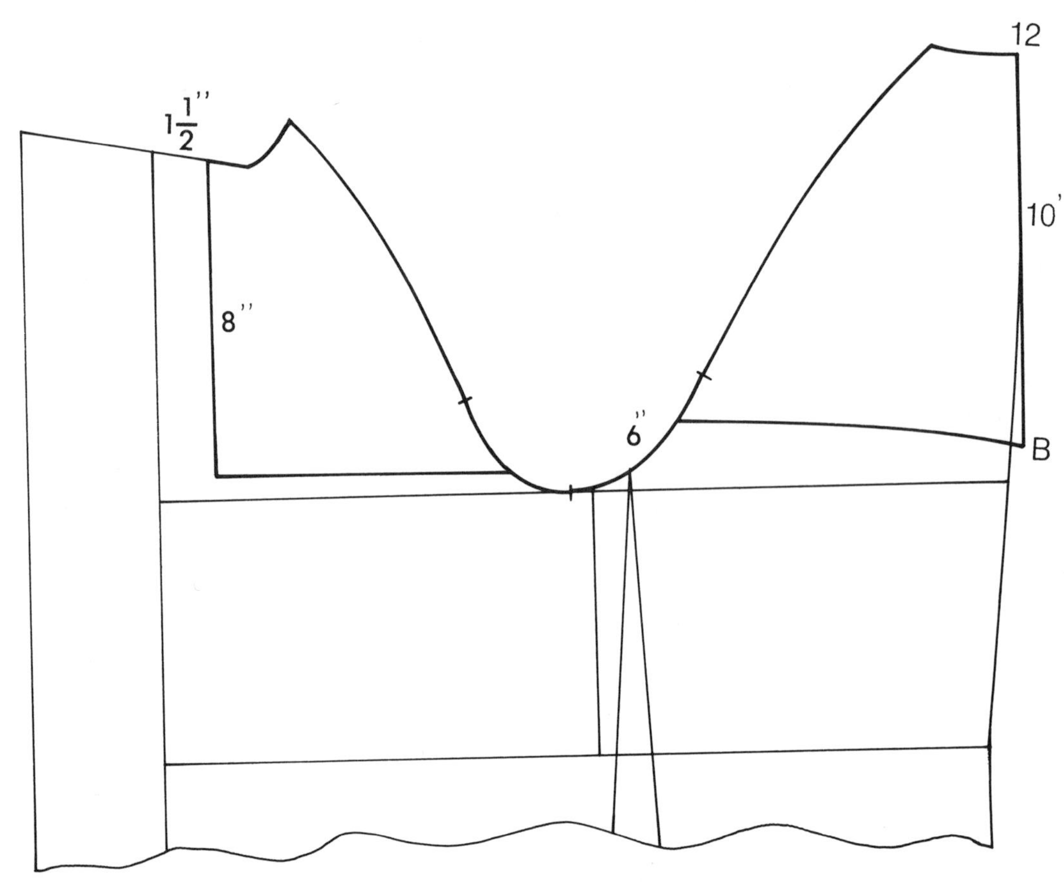

DIAGRAM–Trench Coat

Place front and back sleeve sections together.
See diagram, A and B.
Style the buckled wristband according to design.

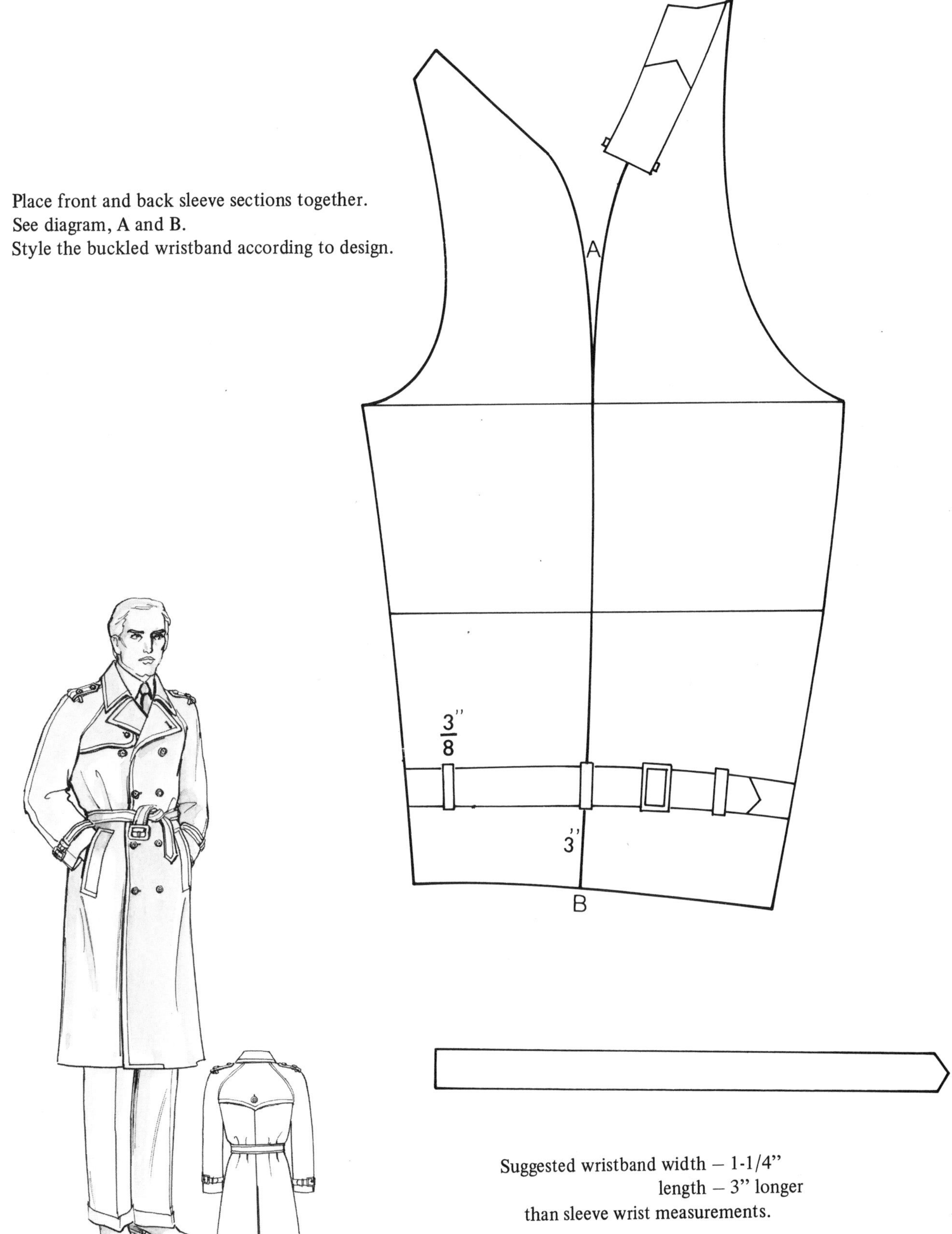

Suggested wristband width – 1-1/4"
length – 3" longer
than sleeve wrist measurements.

KIMONO RAGLAN CUT POLO COAT

Outline your basic sloper and lengthen according to your design.

Back Coat Panel
Armhole:
A = side seam at armhole.
A to B = 4".
C = 1/2 of D to E.
Connect C to B with straight line as a guide.
F = 1/2 of C to B.
F to G = 1/2".
Connect C to G and G to B with hip curve ruler.

H = side seam at waist.
H to I = 3/8".
J to K = 1-1/2".
Connect B to I with hip curve ruler.
Connect I to K with straight line to finish side seam.

Back Sleeve
Extend shoulder line L to M = sleeve length.
L to N = 5".
Square off from N to O.
G to P = G to B.
Square off M to Q = 6-1/2" (according to design).
Connect Q to P with straight line = Z to 1 from front sleeve.
R = 1/2 of Q to P.
R to S = 2-1/2".
S to T = 3/4".
Connect T to P with sleigh curve ruler.
Connect T to Q with straight line.
U = 1/2 of N to L.
U to V = 3/8".
L to W = 1/4".
Blend in W to D for shoulder line.
Connect W to V with hip curve ruler.
Connect V to M with straight line to finish sleeve.

Collar. See page 178.
Sleeve. See page 110.

DIAGRAM—Kimono Raglan Cut Polo Coat

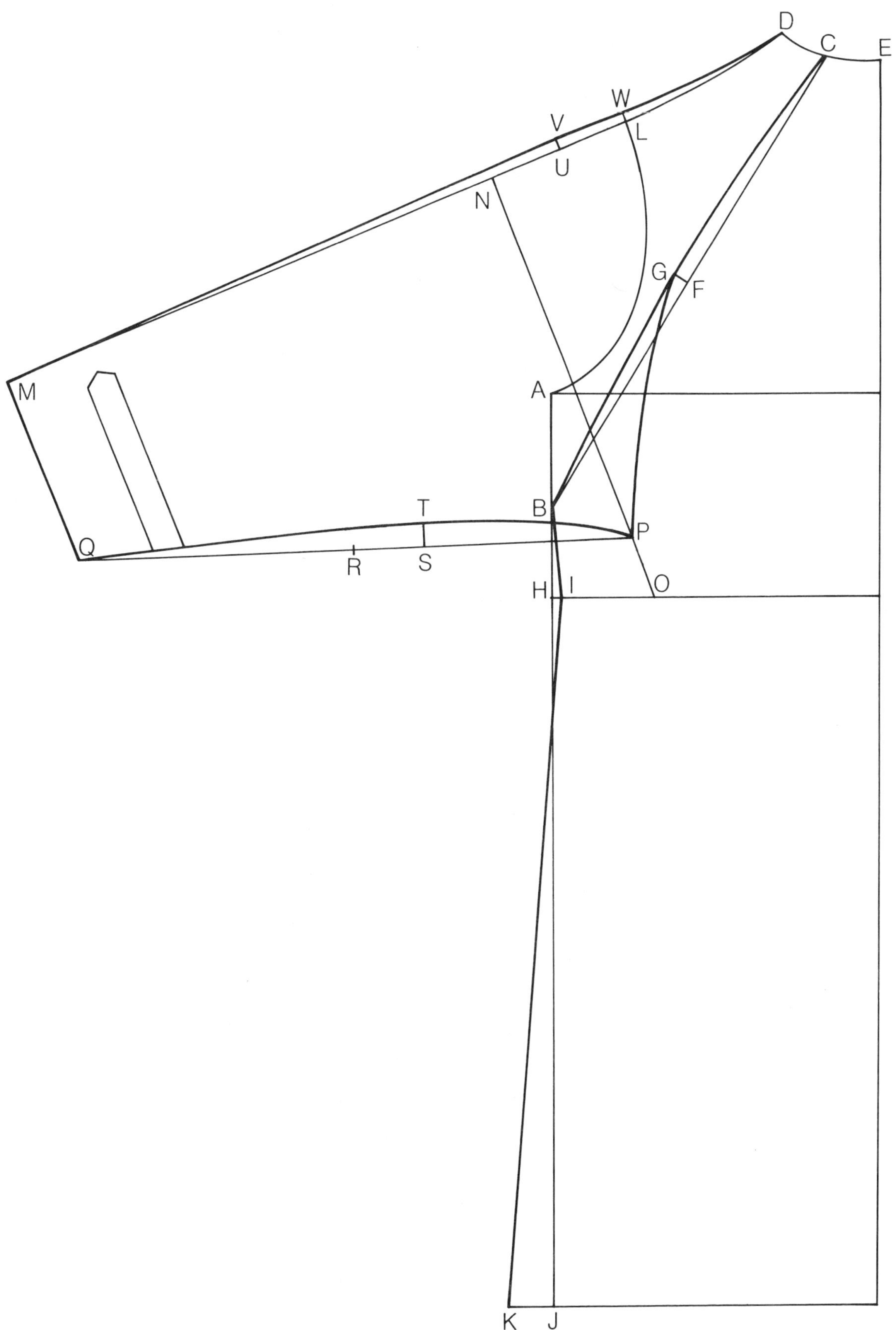

DIAGRAM—Kimono Raglan Cut Polo Coat

Front Coat Panel
A = side seam at armhole.
A to B = 4".
C to D = D to C from back neck.
Connect C to B with straight line.
E = 1/2 of C to B.
E to F = 3/8".
Connect C to F and F to B with hip curve ruler to finish armhole.
G = side seam at waist.
G to H = 3/8".
I to J = 1-1/2".
Connect B to H with hip curve ruler.
Connect H to J with straight line to finish side seam.
K = center front at waist.
K to L = 3".
L to M = 3" for extension.
Square down from M to N.
N to O = 3/4".
Square off O to P.
Connect P to J with hip curve ruler to finish hem.
D = intersection of shoulder and neck.
D to Q = 1" for stand.
Connect M to Q and extend the line upward.
Square off R to S = 5" for lapel width.
S to T = 1-1/2".
Connect T to U with straight line.
Connect T to M with hip curve ruler deeper curve toward M to finish lapel.

Pocket
For angle, size, and pocket position see diagram.

Kimono Sleeve
Same as Basic Two-Piece Raglan (page 120).

Collar
See Notch Collars (page 178).

Front Sleeve
Extend shoulder line V to W = sleeve length.
V to X = 5".
Square off X to Y at waistline.
F to Z = F to B.
Square off W to 1 = 6-1/2".
Connect Z to 1 with straight line.
2 = 1/2 of Z to 1.
2 to 3 = 2-1/2".
3 to 4 = 3/4".
Connect 4 to 1 with straight line.
Connect 4 to Z with sleigh curve ruler.
5 = 1/2 of V to X.
5 to 6 = 3/8".
V to 7 = 1/4".
Connect 6 to W with straight line.
Connect 6 to 7 with hip curve ruler.
Blend 7 into the shoulder to finish sleeve.

DIAGRAM—Kimono Raglan Cut Polo Coat

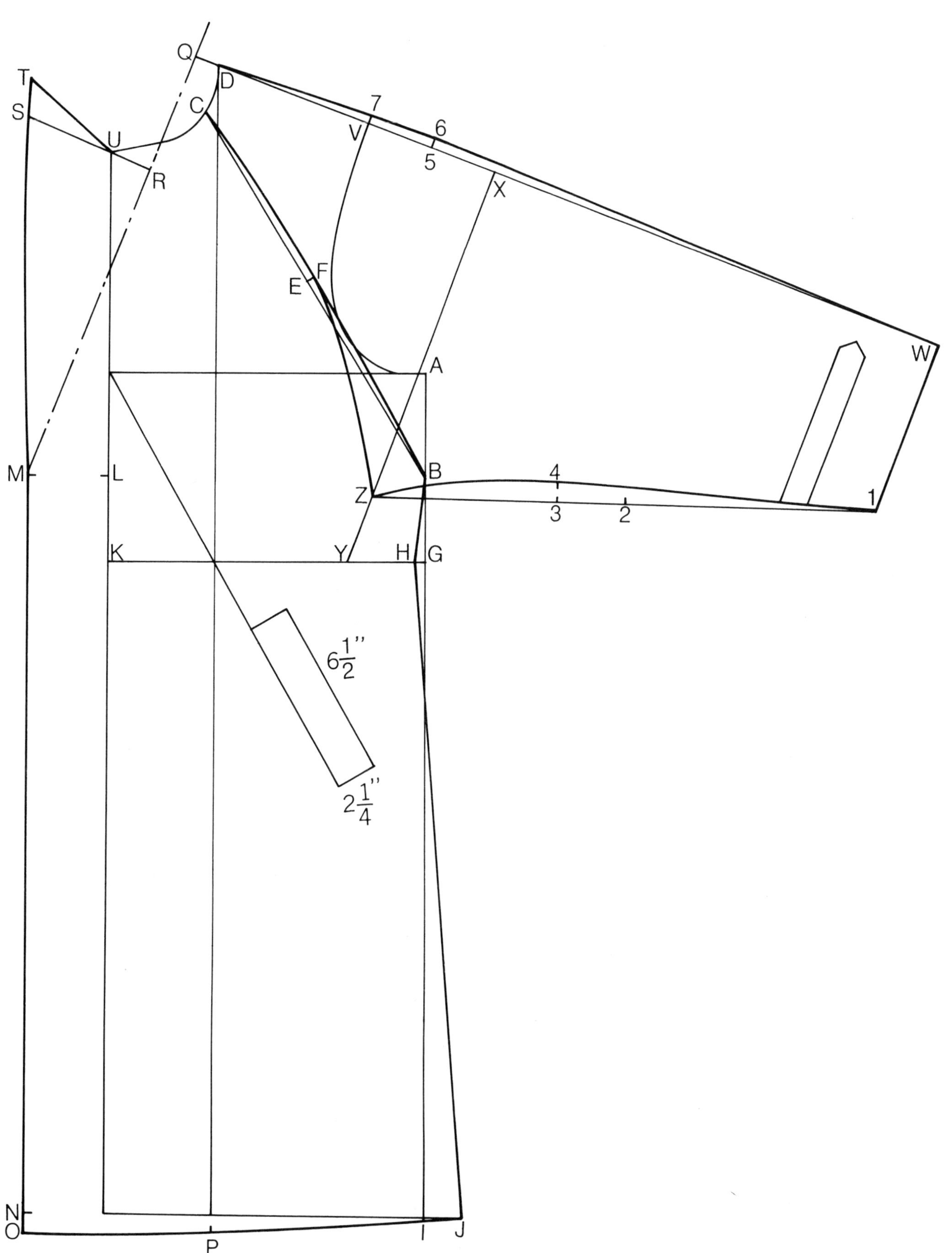

DIAGRAM–Kimono Raglan Cut Polo Coat

Back Shoulder. Close back shoulder dart by pivoting from A, putting B–C together.

To design one-piece kimono raglan seeve, place front and back sections together.
See diagram, A to B.

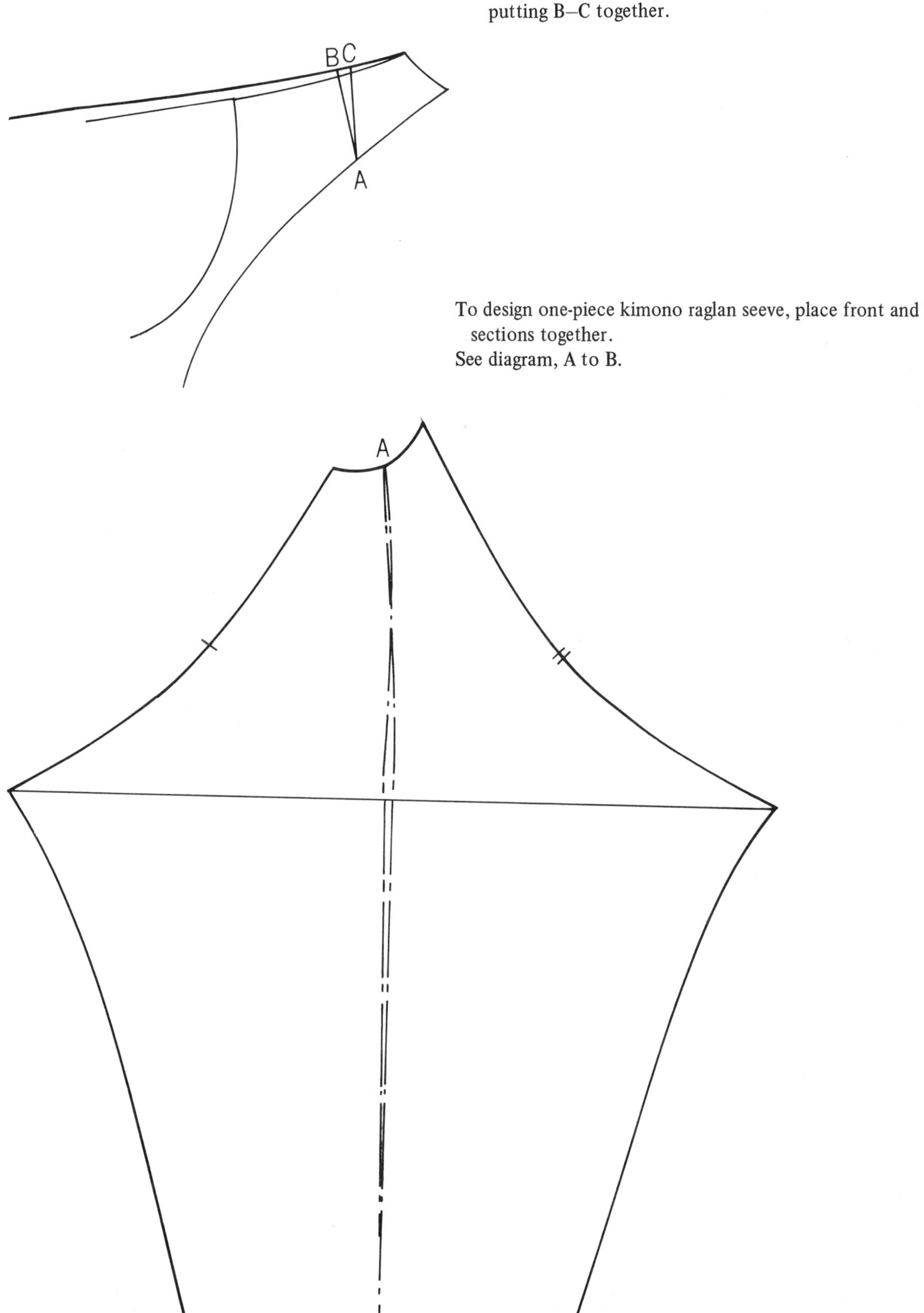

NOTES

ONE-PIECE RAGLAN SLEEVE

The draft of the One-Piece Raglan Sleeve is the same as the draft of the Basic Two-Piece Raglan Sleeve, only eliminate the over arm seam A to B. (See diagram.)

DIAGRAM—One-Piece Raglan Sleeve

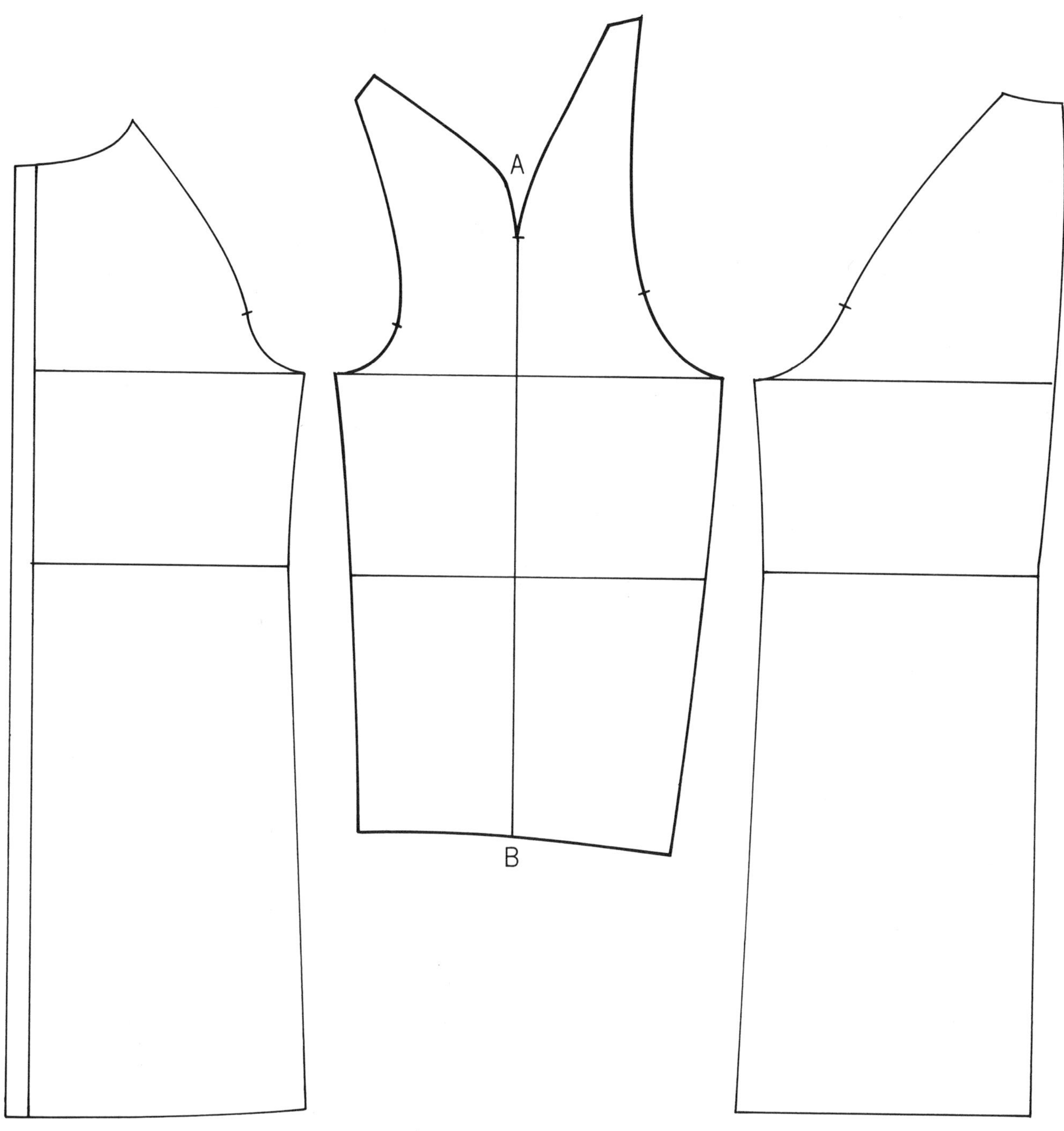

SPLIT RAGLAN SLEEVE

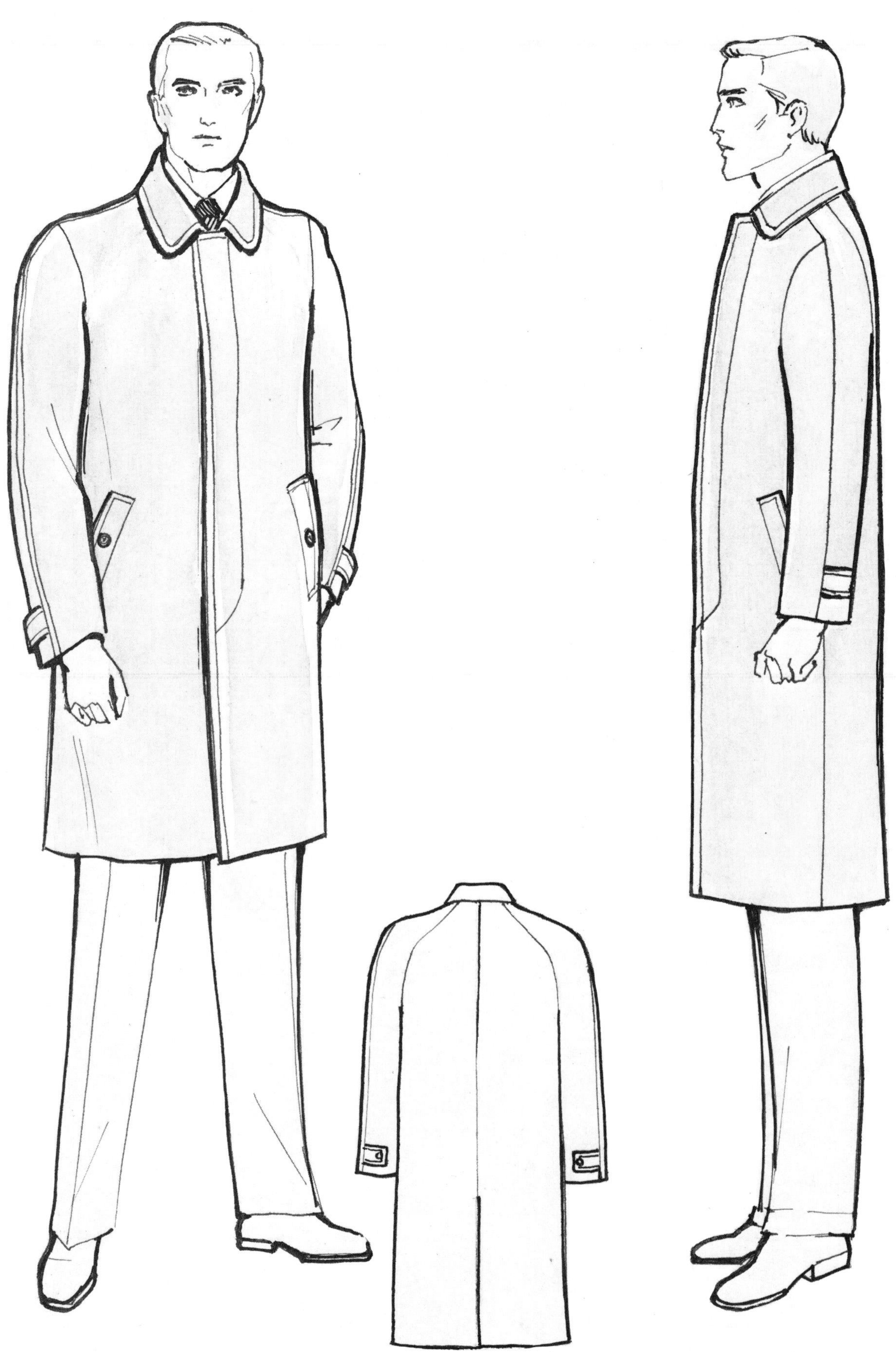

DIAGRAM–Split Raglan Sleeve

The draft of the Split Raglan Sleeve is the same as the draft of the Basic Two-Piece Raglan Sleeve, only the original sleeve cap on the front or back is the same. (See diagram.)

SHOULDER YOKED CAR COAT

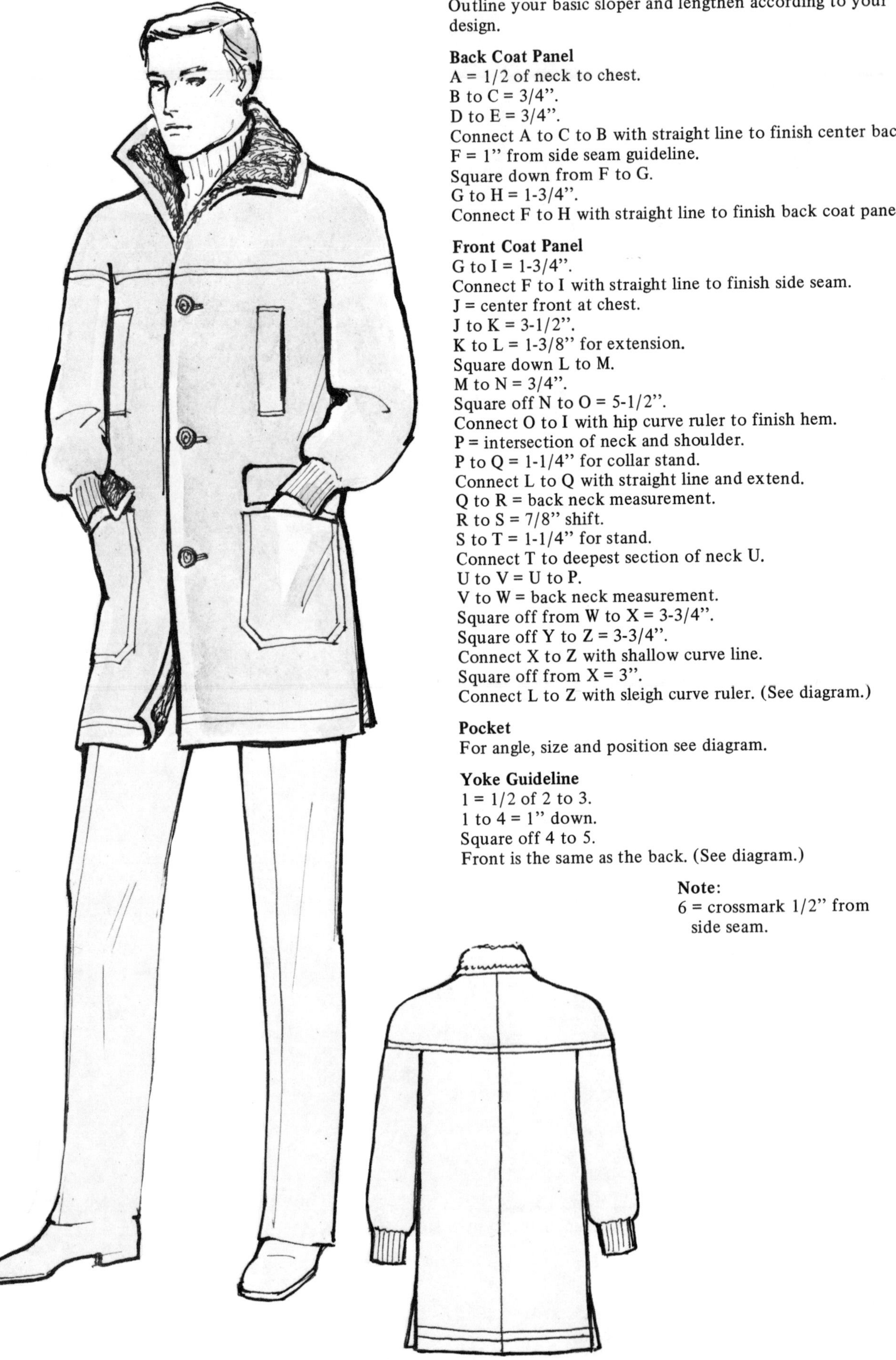

Outline your basic sloper and lengthen according to your design.

Back Coat Panel
A = 1/2 of neck to chest.
B to C = 3/4".
D to E = 3/4".
Connect A to C to B with straight line to finish center back.
F = 1" from side seam guideline.
Square down from F to G.
G to H = 1-3/4".
Connect F to H with straight line to finish back coat panel.

Front Coat Panel
G to I = 1-3/4".
Connect F to I with straight line to finish side seam.
J = center front at chest.
J to K = 3-1/2".
K to L = 1-3/8" for extension.
Square down L to M.
M to N = 3/4".
Square off N to O = 5-1/2".
Connect O to I with hip curve ruler to finish hem.
P = intersection of neck and shoulder.
P to Q = 1-1/4" for collar stand.
Connect L to Q with straight line and extend.
Q to R = back neck measurement.
R to S = 7/8" shift.
S to T = 1-1/4" for stand.
Connect T to deepest section of neck U.
U to V = U to P.
V to W = back neck measurement.
Square off from W to X = 3-3/4".
Square off Y to Z = 3-3/4".
Connect X to Z with shallow curve line.
Square off from X = 3".
Connect L to Z with sleigh curve ruler. (See diagram.)

Pocket
For angle, size and position see diagram.

Yoke Guideline
1 = 1/2 of 2 to 3.
1 to 4 = 1" down.
Square off 4 to 5.
Front is the same as the back. (See diagram.)

Note:
6 = crossmark 1/2" from side seam.

DIAGRAM–Shoulder Yoked Car Coat

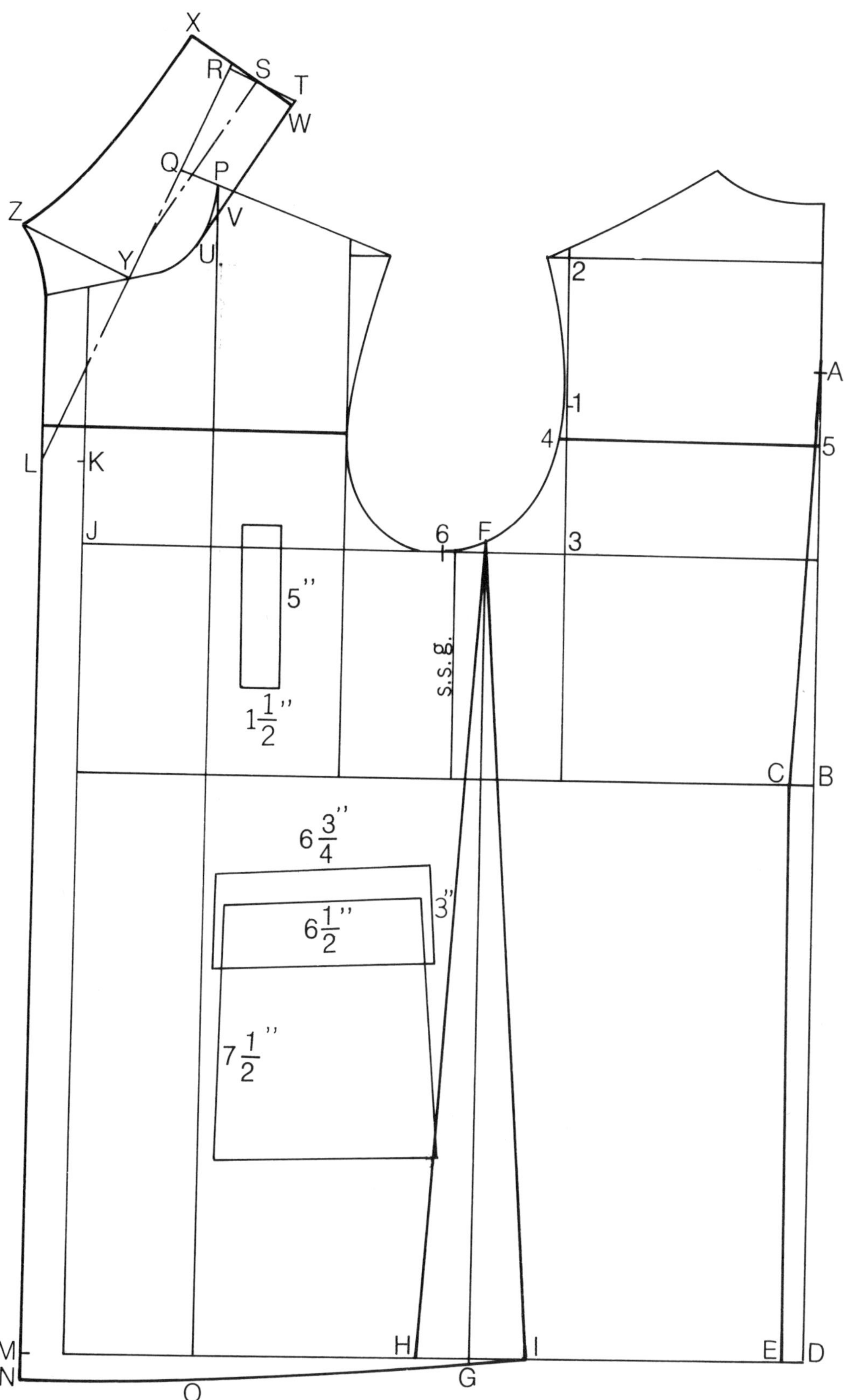

DIAGRAM—Shoulder Yoked Car Coat

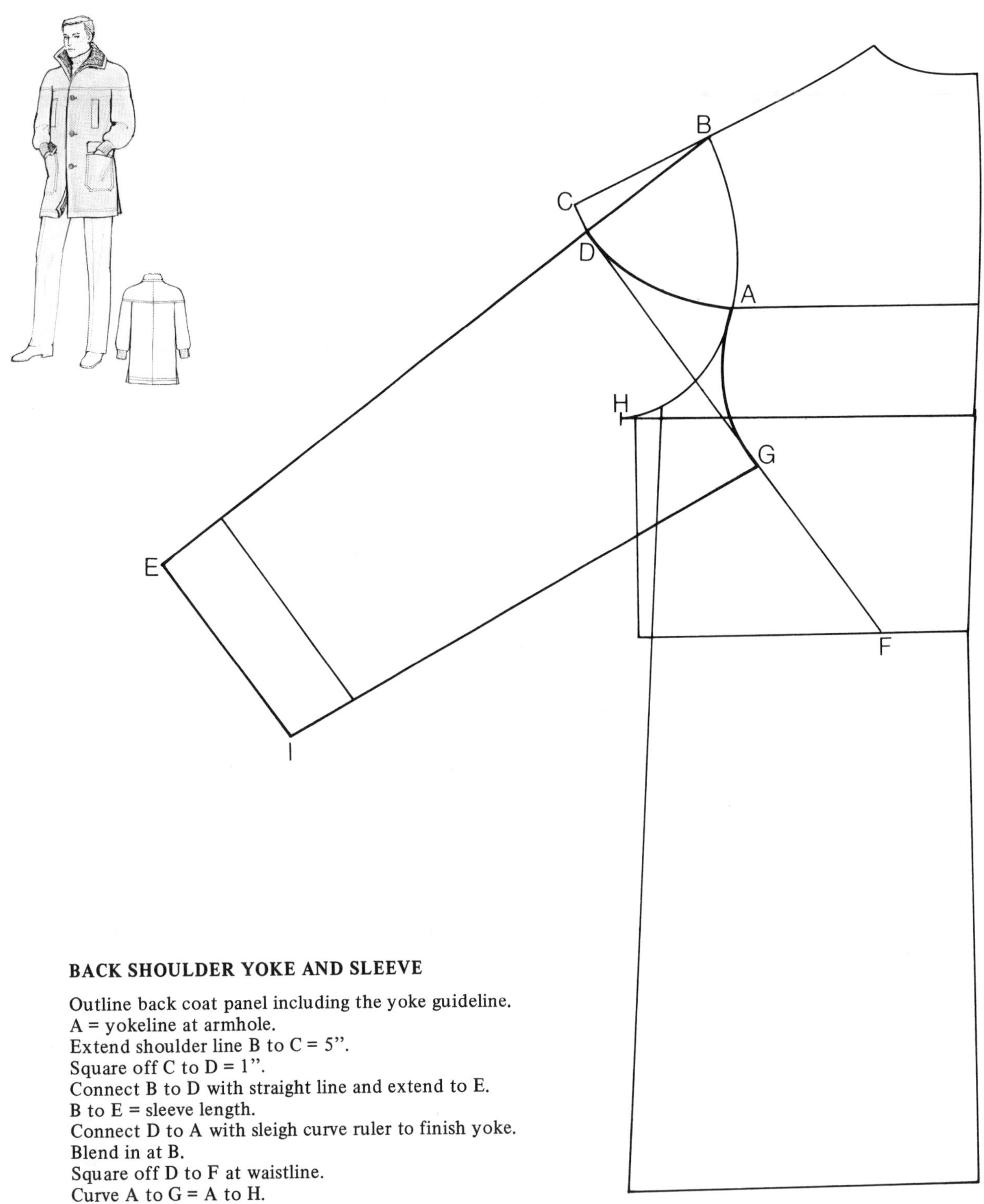

BACK SHOULDER YOKE AND SLEEVE

Outline back coat panel including the yoke guideline.
A = yokeline at armhole.
Extend shoulder line B to C = 5".
Square off C to D = 1".
Connect B to D with straight line and extend to E.
B to E = sleeve length.
Connect D to A with sleigh curve ruler to finish yoke.
Blend in at B.
Square off D to F at waistline.
Curve A to G = A to H.
Square off E to I = 7".
Connect I to G to finish sleeve.
Remove 2-1/2" at sleeve hem for knitted cuff.

DIAGRAM–Shoulder Yoked Car Coat

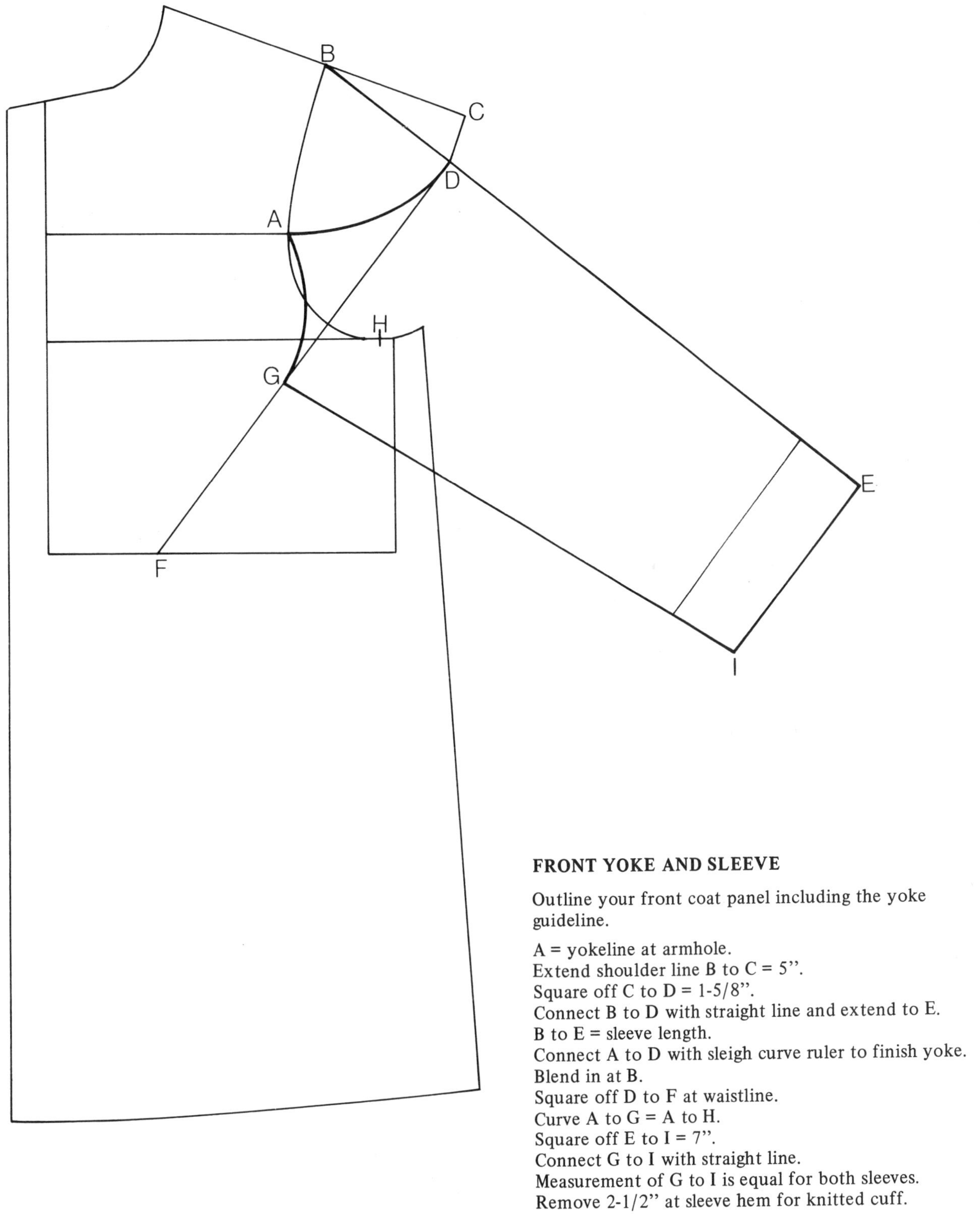

FRONT YOKE AND SLEEVE

Outline your front coat panel including the yoke guideline.

A = yokeline at armhole.
Extend shoulder line B to C = 5".
Square off C to D = 1-5/8".
Connect B to D with straight line and extend to E.
B to E = sleeve length.
Connect A to D with sleigh curve ruler to finish yoke.
Blend in at B.
Square off D to F at waistline.
Curve A to G = A to H.
Square off E to I = 7".
Connect G to I with straight line.
Measurement of G to I is equal for both sleeves.
Remove 2-1/2" at sleeve hem for knitted cuff.

DIAGRAM—Shoulder Yoked Car Coat

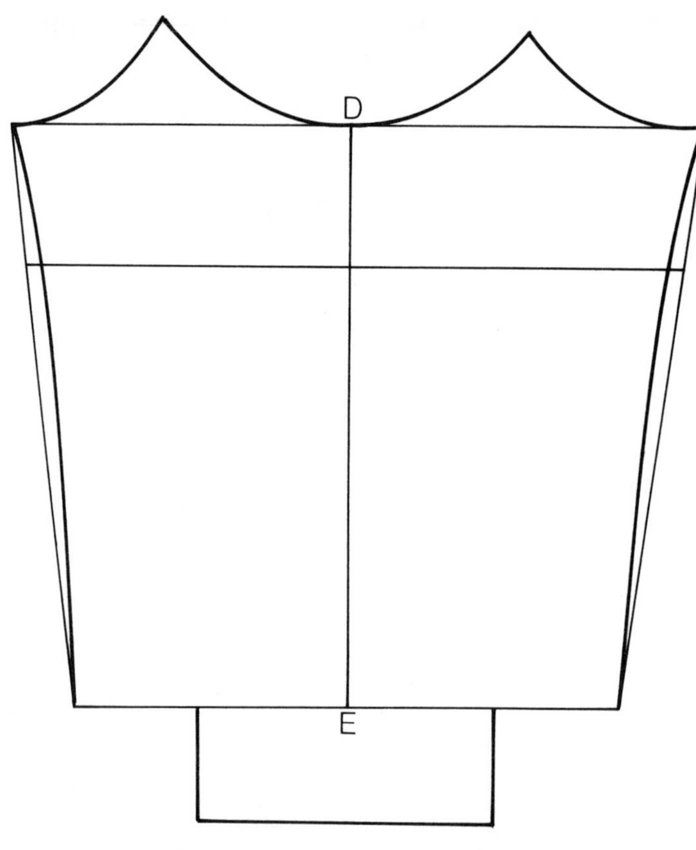

For one-piece sleeve match the front and back sleeves at the shoulder. (See diagram.)

NOTES

SADDLE-SLEEVE RAINCOAT

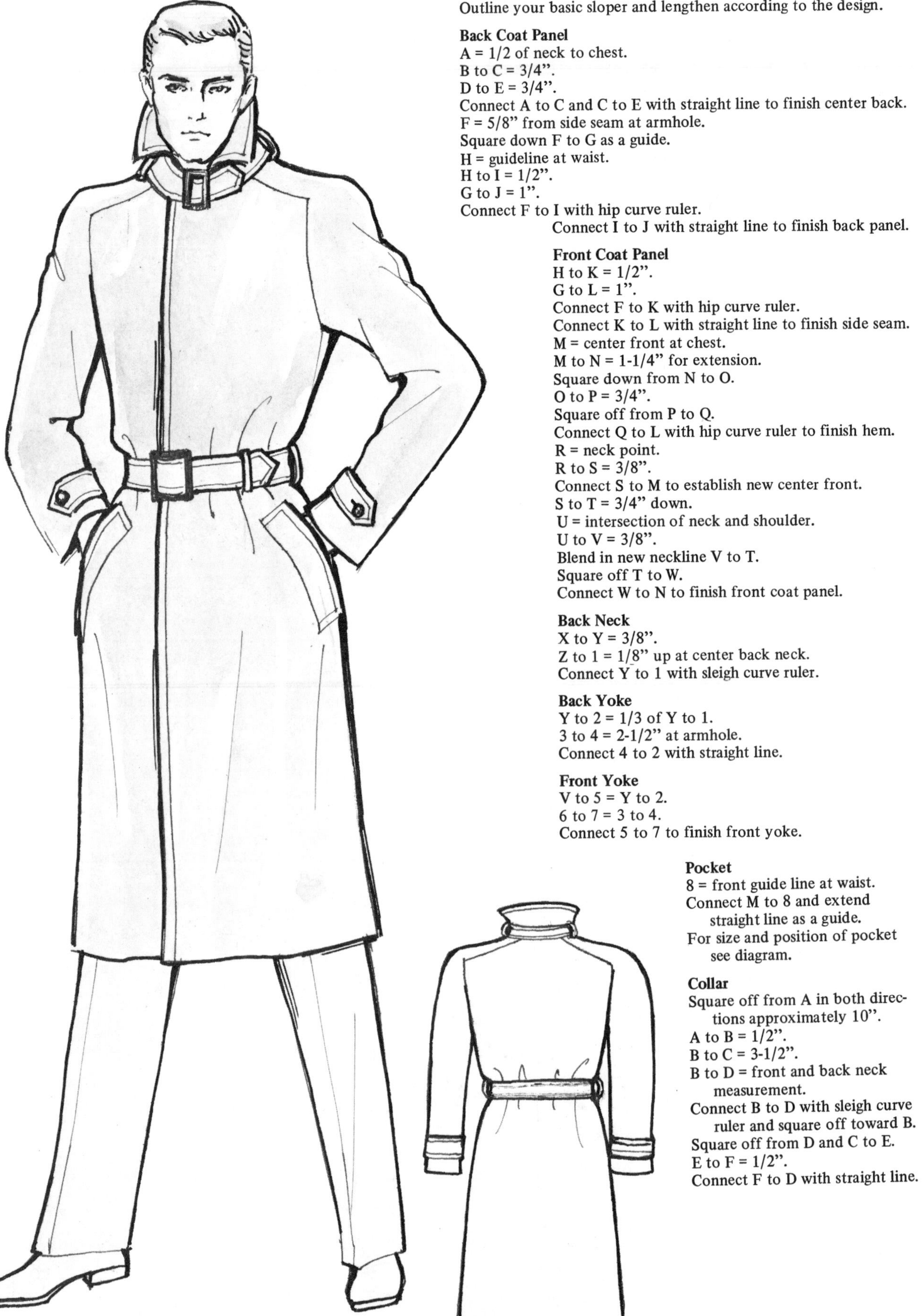

Outline your basic sloper and lengthen according to the design.

Back Coat Panel
A = 1/2 of neck to chest.
B to C = 3/4".
D to E = 3/4".
Connect A to C and C to E with straight line to finish center back.
F = 5/8" from side seam at armhole.
Square down F to G as a guide.
H = guideline at waist.
H to I = 1/2".
G to J = 1".
Connect F to I with hip curve ruler.
Connect I to J with straight line to finish back panel.

Front Coat Panel
H to K = 1/2".
G to L = 1".
Connect F to K with hip curve ruler.
Connect K to L with straight line to finish side seam.
M = center front at chest.
M to N = 1-1/4" for extension.
Square down from N to O.
O to P = 3/4".
Square off from P to Q.
Connect Q to L with hip curve ruler to finish hem.
R = neck point.
R to S = 3/8".
Connect S to M to establish new center front.
S to T = 3/4" down.
U = intersection of neck and shoulder.
U to V = 3/8".
Blend in new neckline V to T.
Square off T to W.
Connect W to N to finish front coat panel.

Back Neck
X to Y = 3/8".
Z to 1 = 1/8" up at center back neck.
Connect Y to 1 with sleigh curve ruler.

Back Yoke
Y to 2 = 1/3 of Y to 1.
3 to 4 = 2-1/2" at armhole.
Connect 4 to 2 with straight line.

Front Yoke
V to 5 = Y to 2.
6 to 7 = 3 to 4.
Connect 5 to 7 to finish front yoke.

Pocket
8 = front guide line at waist.
Connect M to 8 and extend straight line as a guide.
For size and position of pocket see diagram.

Collar
Square off from A in both directions approximately 10".
A to B = 1/2".
B to C = 3-1/2".
B to D = front and back neck measurement.
Connect B to D with sleigh curve ruler and square off toward B.
Square off from D and C to E.
E to F = 1/2".
Connect F to D with straight line.

DIAGRAM–Saddle-Sleeve Raincoat

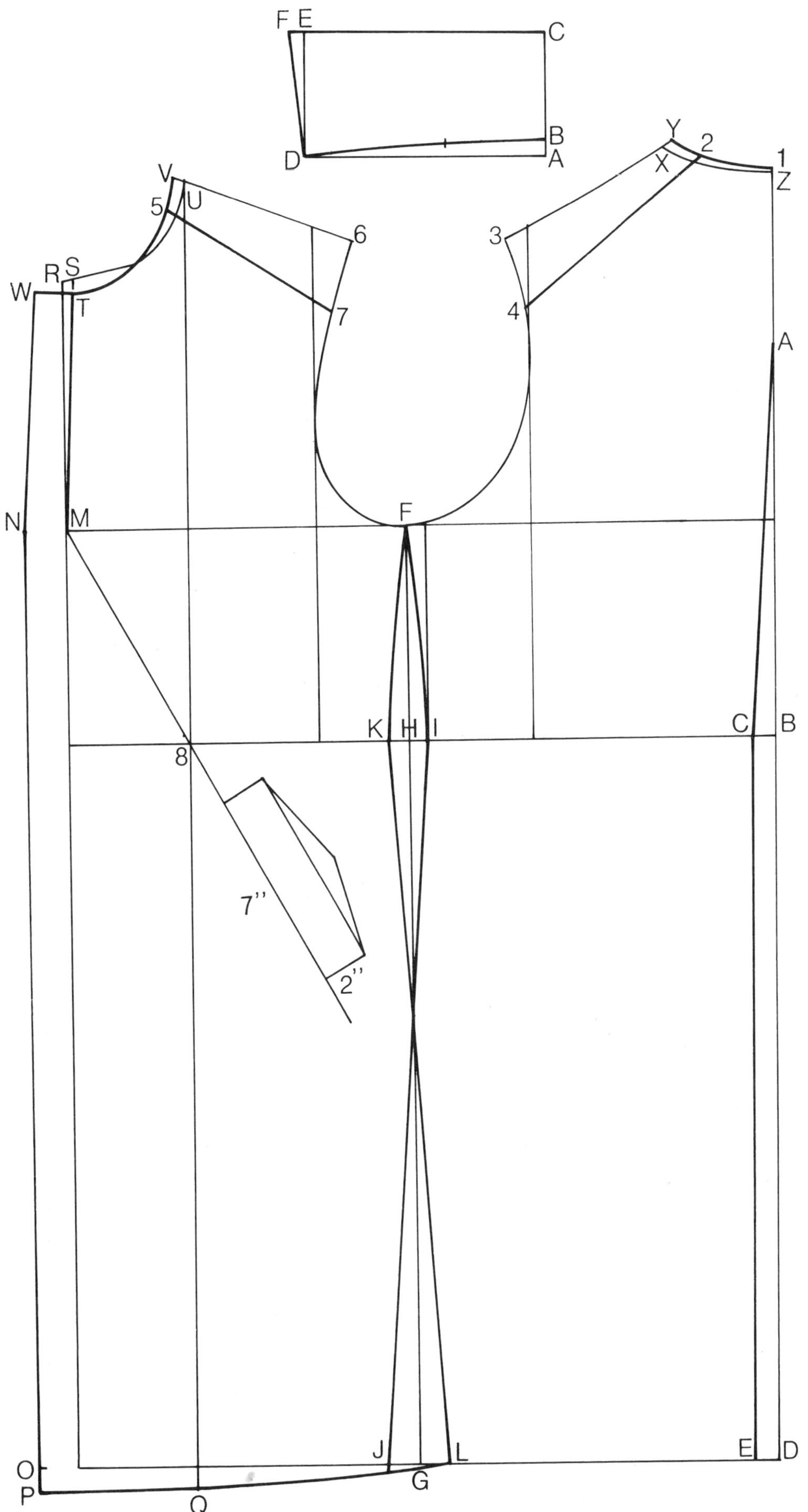

SADDLE SLEEVE

Outline the basic sleeve sloper.

For cap A to B = F to 7 from coat armhole plus 1/4" for ease.
C to D = F to 4 from coat armhole plus 1/4" for ease.
Join 7 on front shoulder piece to B on front sleeve cap and close the armhole (see diagram).
Join 4 on back shoulder piece to D on back sleeve cap and close the armhole (see diagram).
E = 1/3 of F to G.
H to I = 1/8".
J to K = 1/8".
Connect E to K with sleigh curve ruler and blend into shoulder to finish back sleeve.
Connect E to F with sleigh curve ruler and blend into shoulder to finish front sleeve.
L to M = 3/4".
M to N = 6".
Connect A to N with straight line as a guide.

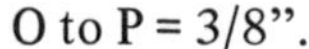

O to P = 3/8".
Connect A to P to N with hip curve ruler.
M to Q = 6".
Connect C to Q with straight line as a guide.
R to S = 3/8".
Connect C to S to Q with hip curve ruler.
Connect M to Q with sleigh curve to finish sleeve.

Cuff Belt
See diagram.

Neck Belt
Square off from A in both directions.
A to B = 2-3/4".
B to C = neck measurement (see neckline diagram).
Connect B to C with sleigh curve ruler.
C to D = 1-1/4".
Square up B to E = 1-1/4".
Connect E to D with sleigh curve ruler.
F = 1/4 of A to C.
Square off F to G and G to D.
Extend belt 4" toward H to finish band.

Neck Belt Loop
3/8" wider than belt width.

DIAGRAM–Saddle Sleeve

DIAMOND-SHAPED ARMHOLE RAINCOAT

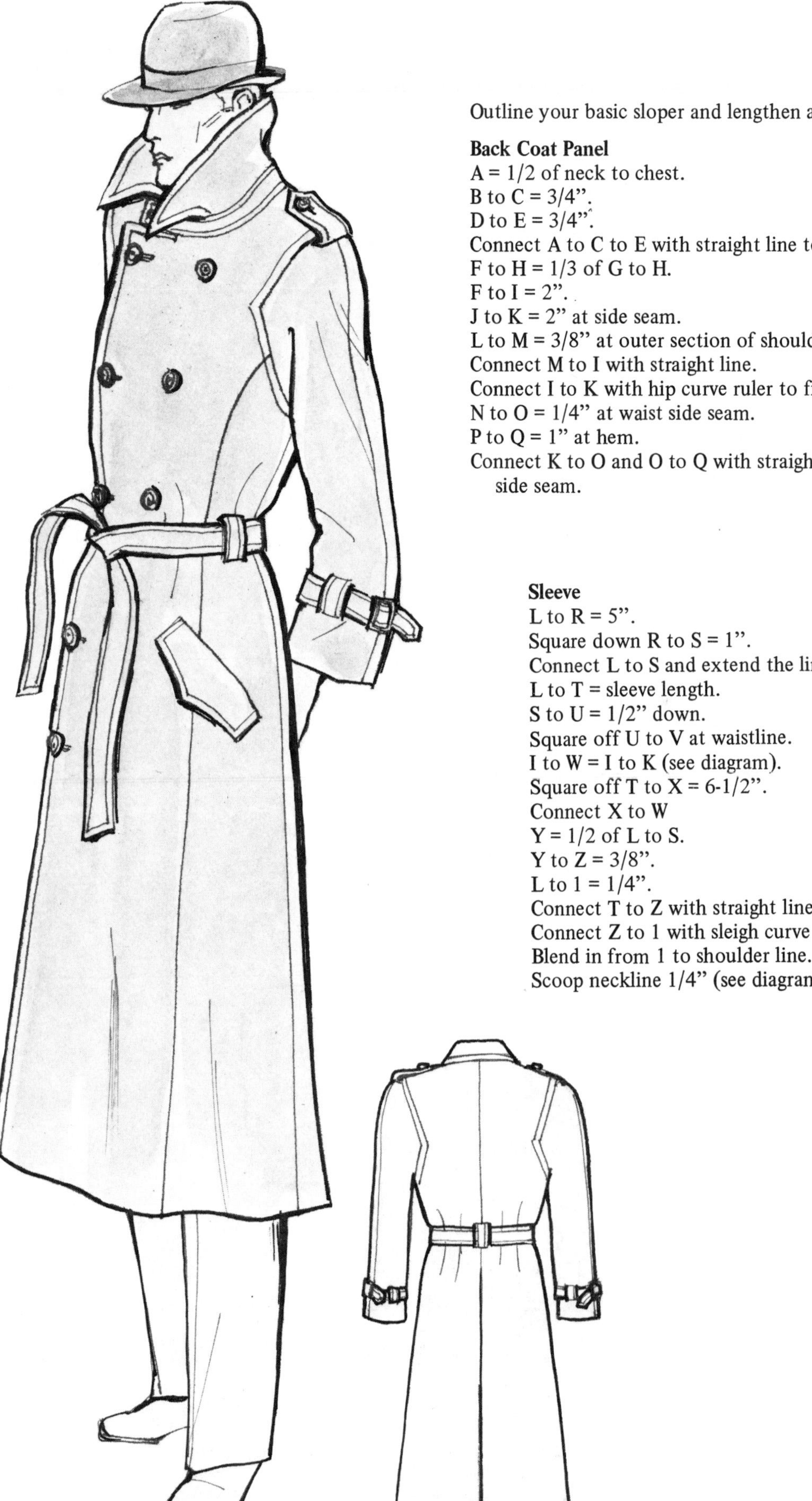

Outline your basic sloper and lengthen according to your design.

Back Coat Panel
A = 1/2 of neck to chest.
B to C = 3/4".
D to E = 3/4".
Connect A to C to E with straight line to finish center back.
F to H = 1/3 of G to H.
F to I = 2".
J to K = 2" at side seam.
L to M = 3/8" at outer section of shoulder.
Connect M to I with straight line.
Connect I to K with hip curve ruler to finish armhole.
N to O = 1/4" at waist side seam.
P to Q = 1" at hem.
Connect K to O and O to Q with straight line to finish side seam.

Sleeve
L to R = 5".
Square down R to S = 1".
Connect L to S and extend the line to T.
L to T = sleeve length.
S to U = 1/2" down.
Square off U to V at waistline.
I to W = I to K (see diagram).
Square off T to X = 6-1/2".
Connect X to W
Y = 1/2 of L to S.
Y to Z = 3/8".
L to 1 = 1/4".
Connect T to Z with straight line.
Connect Z to 1 with sleigh curve ruler.
Blend in from 1 to shoulder line.
Scoop neckline 1/4" (see diagram).

DIAGRAM—Diamond-Shaped Armhole Raincoat

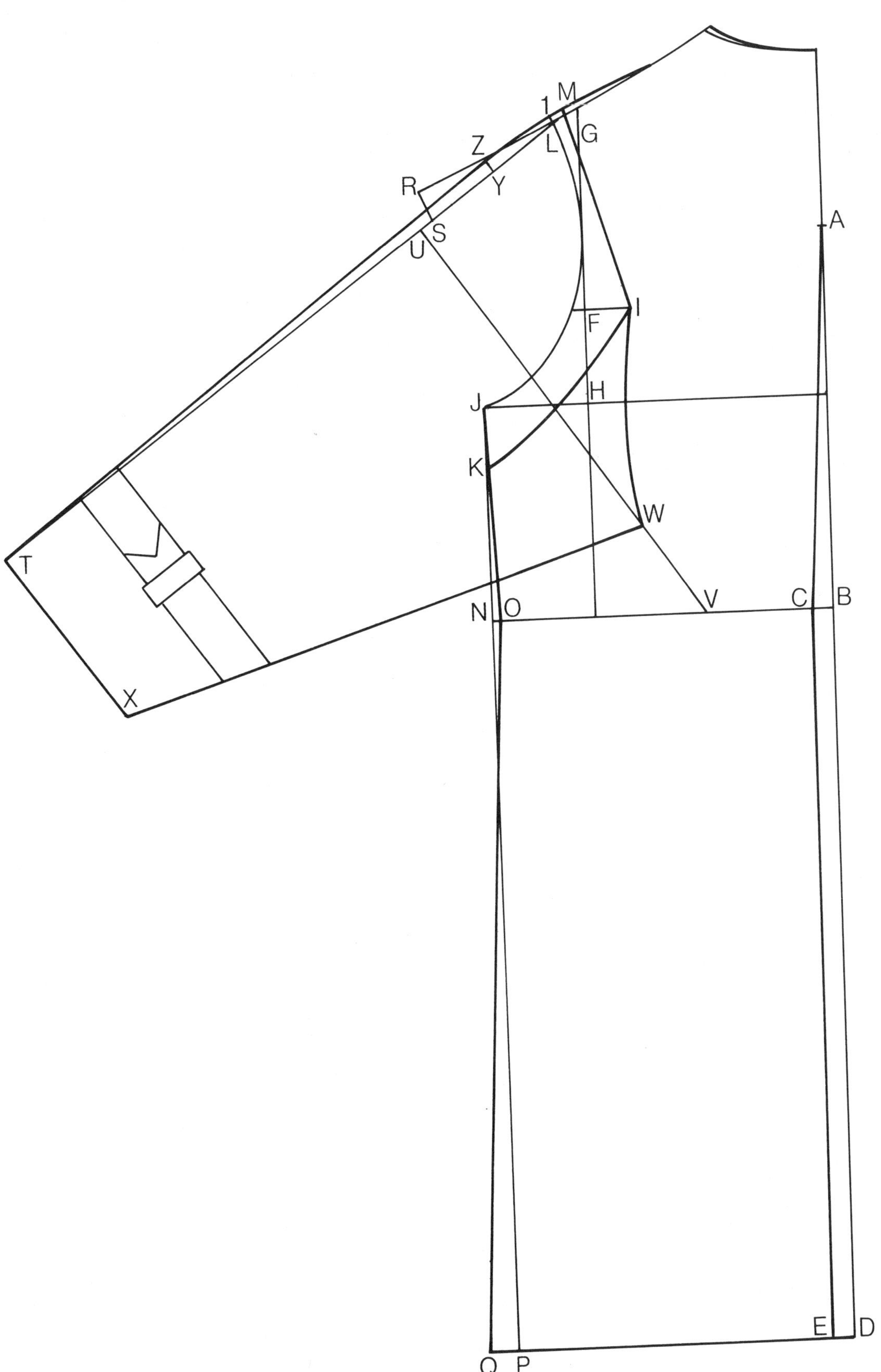

DIAGRAM–Diamond-Shaped Armhole Raincoat

Collar
Draft for new neckline.

Band
A to B = extension minus 1".
B to C = 1-1/4".
A to D = 1-1/4".
E = intersection of neck and shoulder.
E to F = 5/8" = 1/2 of stand width.
Blend F into the deepest section of the neckline G with sleigh curve ruler.
F to H = back neck measurement.
Square off H to I = 1/2".
Connect I to F with straight line.
Square off I to J = 1-1/4".
F to K = 1-1/4".
G to L = 1-1/4".
Connect J to K and K to L to D with sleigh curve ruler.

Collar
1 to 2 = J to C minus 1/2".
2 to 3 = 1-3/4".
1 to 4 = 1-3/4".
Square off 3 to 4.
5 to 1 = 1/3 of 2 to 1.
6 to 3 = 1/3 of 4 to 3.
Connect 6 to 1 with straight line.
7 = 1/2 of 1 to 6.
7 to 8 = 3/8".

Connect 6 to 8 to 1 with sleigh curve ruler.
3 to 9 = 3-1/4".
Square off 9 to 10.
10 to 11 = 4-1/4".
Square down 11 to 12 = 1-1/4".
Square down 10 to 13 = 1/2".
Connect 12 to 13 with sleigh curve ruler.
Connect 13 to collar edge toward 9.
Connect 12 to 1 with sleigh curve ruler to finish collar

Belt
Width = 2-1/4".
Length = 70" to 80".

DIAGRAM—Diamond-Shaped Armhole Raincoat

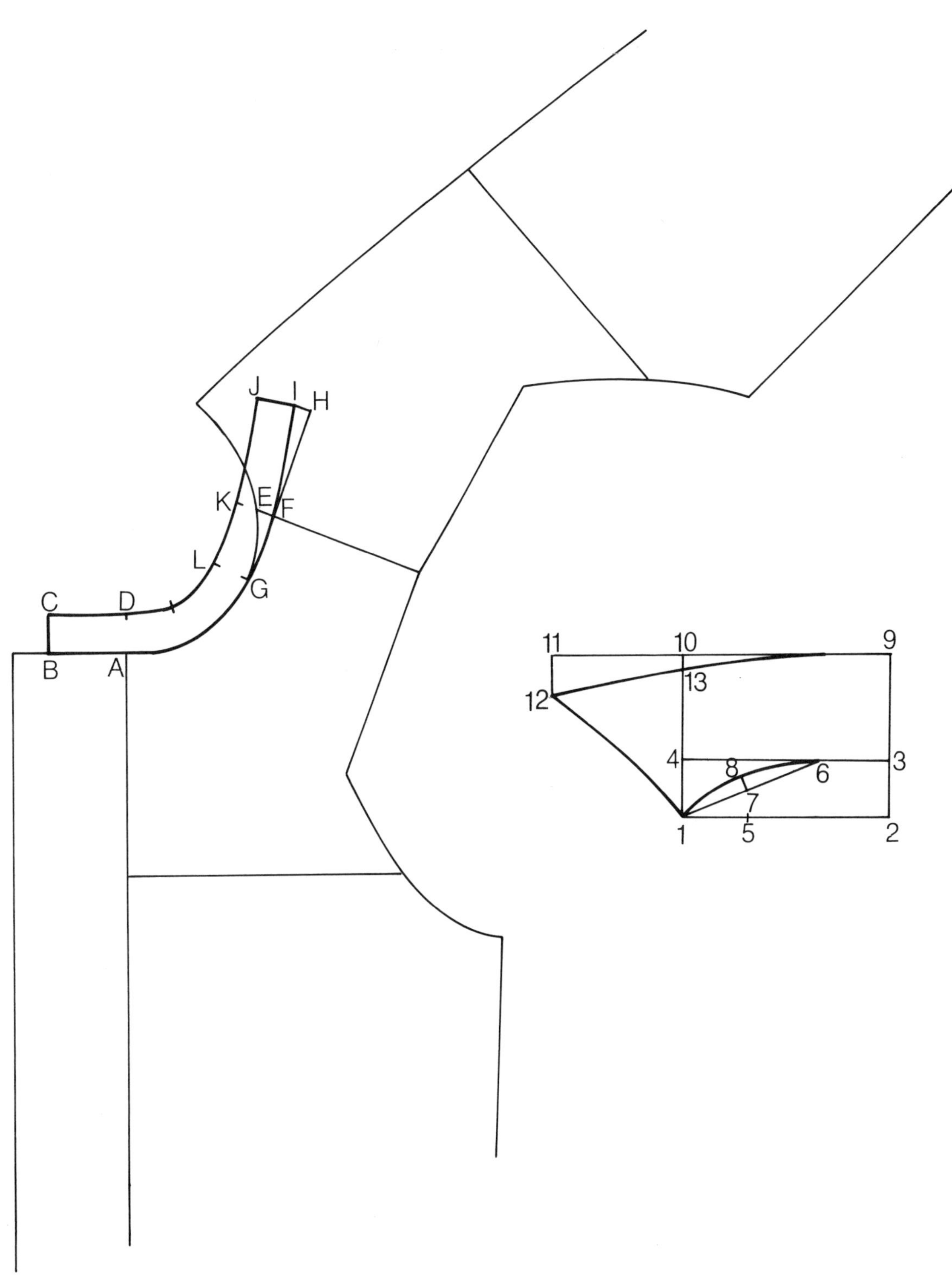

DIAGRAM—Diamond-Shaped Armhole Raincoat

Front Coat Panel
A to B = 2" at side seam.
C to D = 1/3 of D to E.
C to F = 1-1/2".
G to H = 3/8" at shoulder.
Connect H to F with straight line.
Connect F to B with sleigh curve ruler to finish armhole.
I to J = 1/4" at waist line.
K to L = 1".
Connect B to J to L with straight line to finish side seam.
M to C = 1-3/4".
N = 1/2 of O to P.
Square down from N to Q.
N to R = 3/8".
Q to S = 1".
Connect M to R with sleigh curve ruler.
Connect R to S with straight line to finish side panel.
N to T = 3/8".
Q to U = 1".
Connect M to T with sleigh curve ruler.
Connect T to U with straight line to finish torso cut seam.
Remove 1-1/4" at center front neck and 1/4" at neck and shoulder intersection.
Draw a new neckline and extend 3-1/2" = V to W for extension.
Square down W to X.

Sleeve
Extend shoulder line G to Y = 5".
Y to Z = 1-3/8".
Connect G to Z and extend the line to 1.
Z to 2 = 1/2".
Square off from 2 to 3 at waistline.
F to 4 = F to B.
Square off 1 to 5 = 6-1/2".
Connect 4 to 5 with straight line.
6 = 1/2 of G to 2.
6 to 7 = 3/8".
G to 8 = 1/4".
Connect 7 to 1 with straight line.
Connect 7 to 8 with sleigh curve ruler.
Blend in 8 to shoulder to finish sleeve.

DIAGRAM—Diamond-Shaped Armhole Raincoat

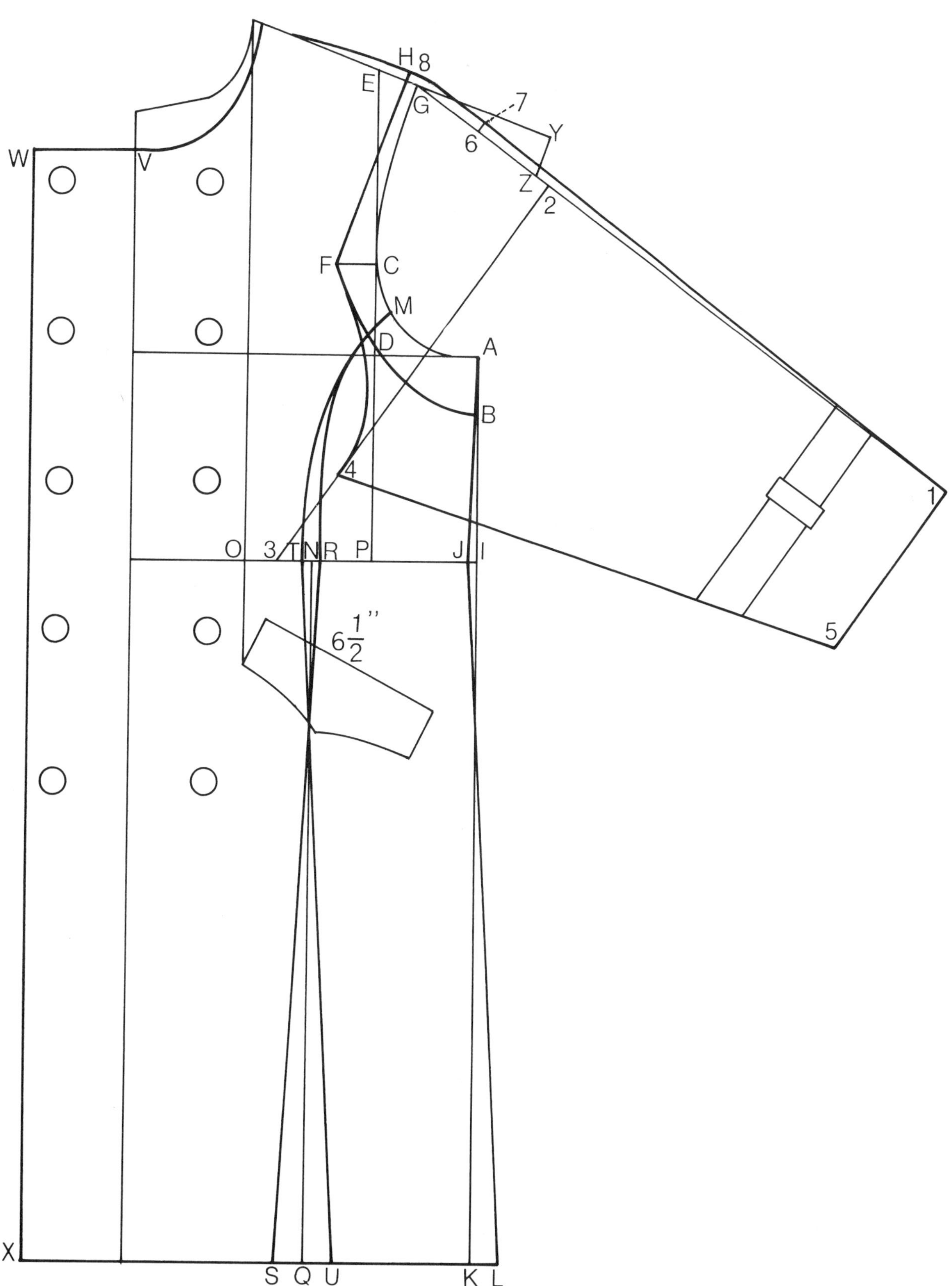

SQUARE ARMHOLE POLO COAT

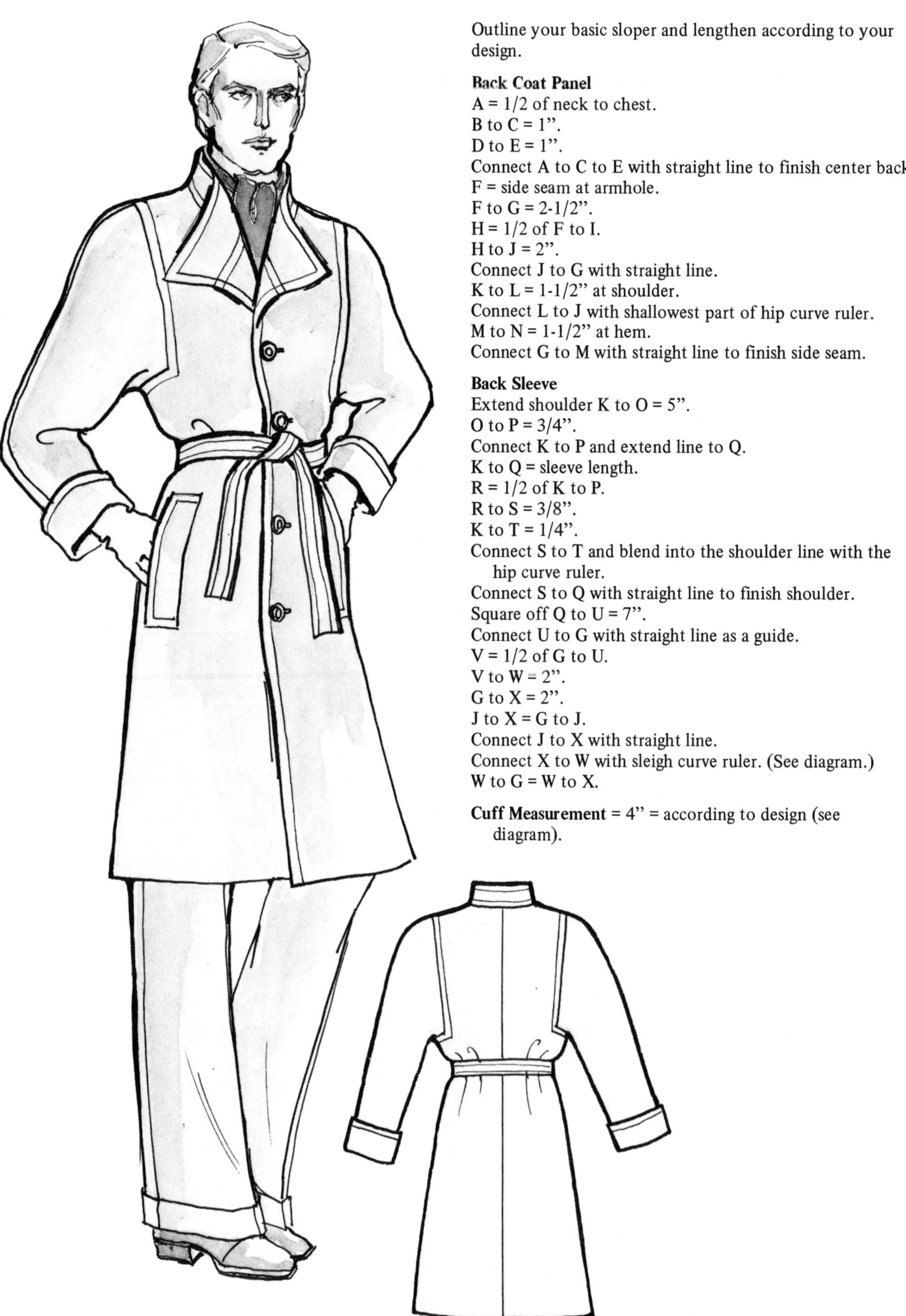

Outline your basic sloper and lengthen according to your design.

Back Coat Panel
A = 1/2 of neck to chest.
B to C = 1".
D to E = 1".
Connect A to C to E with straight line to finish center back.
F = side seam at armhole.
F to G = 2-1/2".
H = 1/2 of F to I.
H to J = 2".
Connect J to G with straight line.
K to L = 1-1/2" at shoulder.
Connect L to J with shallowest part of hip curve ruler.
M to N = 1-1/2" at hem.
Connect G to M with straight line to finish side seam.

Back Sleeve
Extend shoulder K to O = 5".
O to P = 3/4".
Connect K to P and extend line to Q.
K to Q = sleeve length.
R = 1/2 of K to P.
R to S = 3/8".
K to T = 1/4".
Connect S to T and blend into the shoulder line with the hip curve ruler.
Connect S to Q with straight line to finish shoulder.
Square off Q to U = 7".
Connect U to G with straight line as a guide.
V = 1/2 of G to U.
V to W = 2".
G to X = 2".
J to X = G to J.
Connect J to X with straight line.
Connect X to W with sleigh curve ruler. (See diagram.)
W to G = W to X.

Cuff Measurement = 4" = according to design (see diagram).

DIAGRAM—Square Armhole Polo Coat

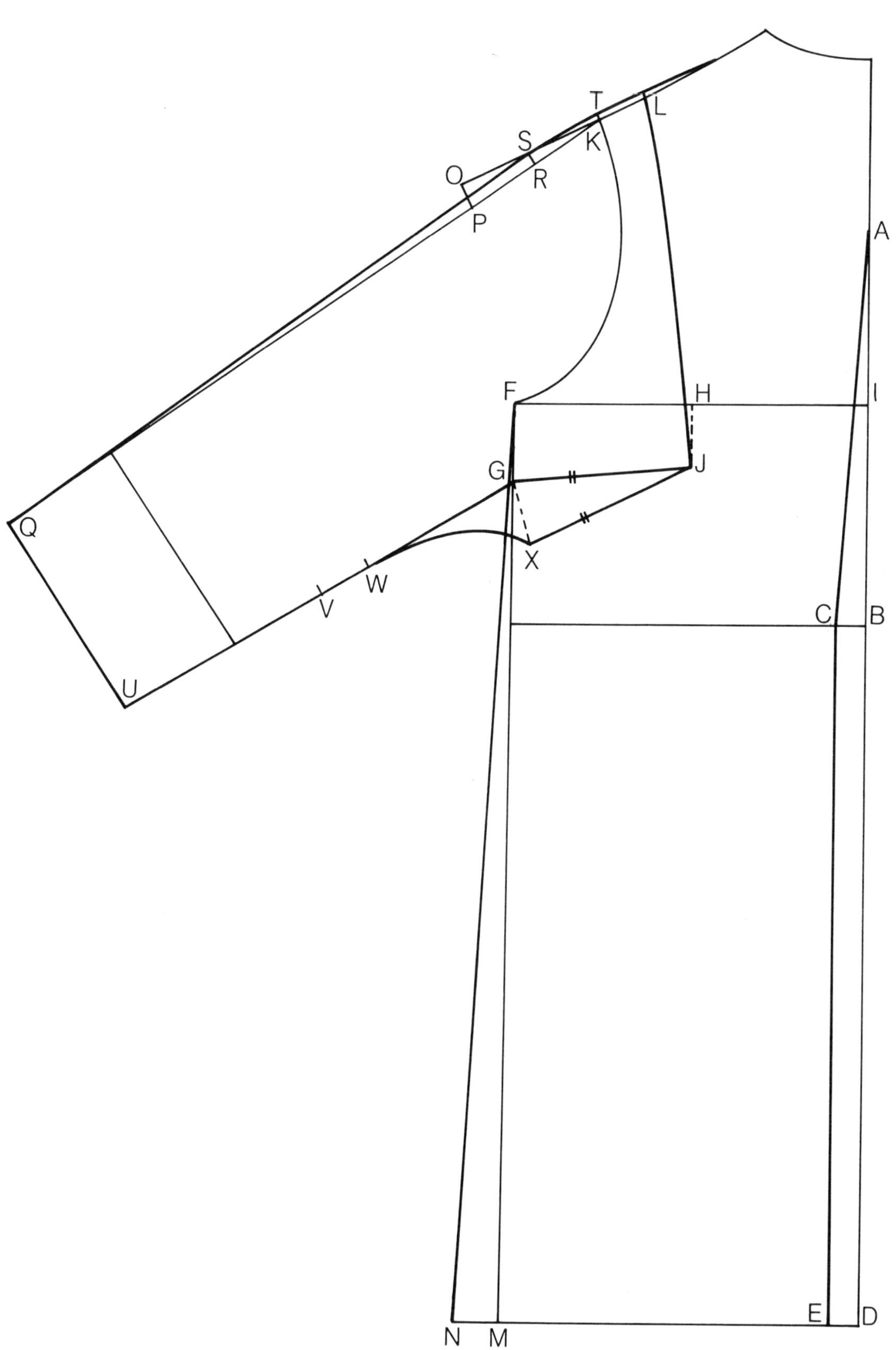

DIAGRAM—Square Armhole Polo Coat

Front Coat Panel
A = side seam at armhole.
A to B = 2-1/2".
C = 1/2 of A to D.
C to E = 1-3/4".
F to G = 1-1/2" at shoulder.
Connect G to E with shallowest part of hip curve ruler.
Connect E to B with straight line to finish armhole.
H to I = 1-1/2" at hem.
Connect B to I with straight line to finish side seam.
D = center front at chest.
D to J = 1-3/8".
J to K = 1-3/8" for extension.
Square down K to L.
L to M = 3/4".
Square off M to N.
Connect N to I with hip curve ruler to finish hem.
O = intersection of neck and shoulder.
O to P = 1-1/8" for collar stand as a guide.
Connect K to P with straight line as a guide.
Q = neck point.
Q to R = 1".
Blend in R to O for new neckline.
Q to S = 2".
R to S = Band width = 3".
Square off S to T = 3".
Connect T to K with straight line.
Square off R to U to finish neckline.

Collar
V = 1/3 of O to G.
Connect V to deepest section of neck = W.
W to X = W to O.
X to Y = back neck measurement.
X to Z = 1/8".
Connect Y to Z to W with hip curve ruler to finish collar neckline.
Y to 1 = 1-3/4" for center back collar width.
Square off 1 to 2.
Q to S = 2".
Square off S to T = 3".
Blend in 1 to 2 to S to T with sleigh curve ruler.
Extend the line K to U to T to finish lapel and collar.

Front Sleeve
F to 3 = 5".
Square off 3 to 4 = 1-3/8".
Connect F to 4 and extend the line to 5.
F to 5 = sleeve length.
6 = 1/2 of F to 4.
Square up 6 to 7 = 3/8".
F to 8 = 1/4".
Blend in 8 to shoulder with sleigh curve ruler.
Connect 7 to 5 with straight line.
Connect 7 to 8 with sleigh curve ruler to finish shoulder.
Square off 5 to 9 = 7".
B to 9 = G to U from back sleeve.
B to 10 = 1-3/8".
E to 10 = E to B.
11 = 1/2 of B to 9.
11 to 12 = 2".
Connect 10 to 12 with sleigh curve ruler.

Pocket
For angle, size, and pocket position see diagram.

Belt
See diagram.

Buttonhole
See page 164.

DIAGRAM—Square Armhole Polo Coat

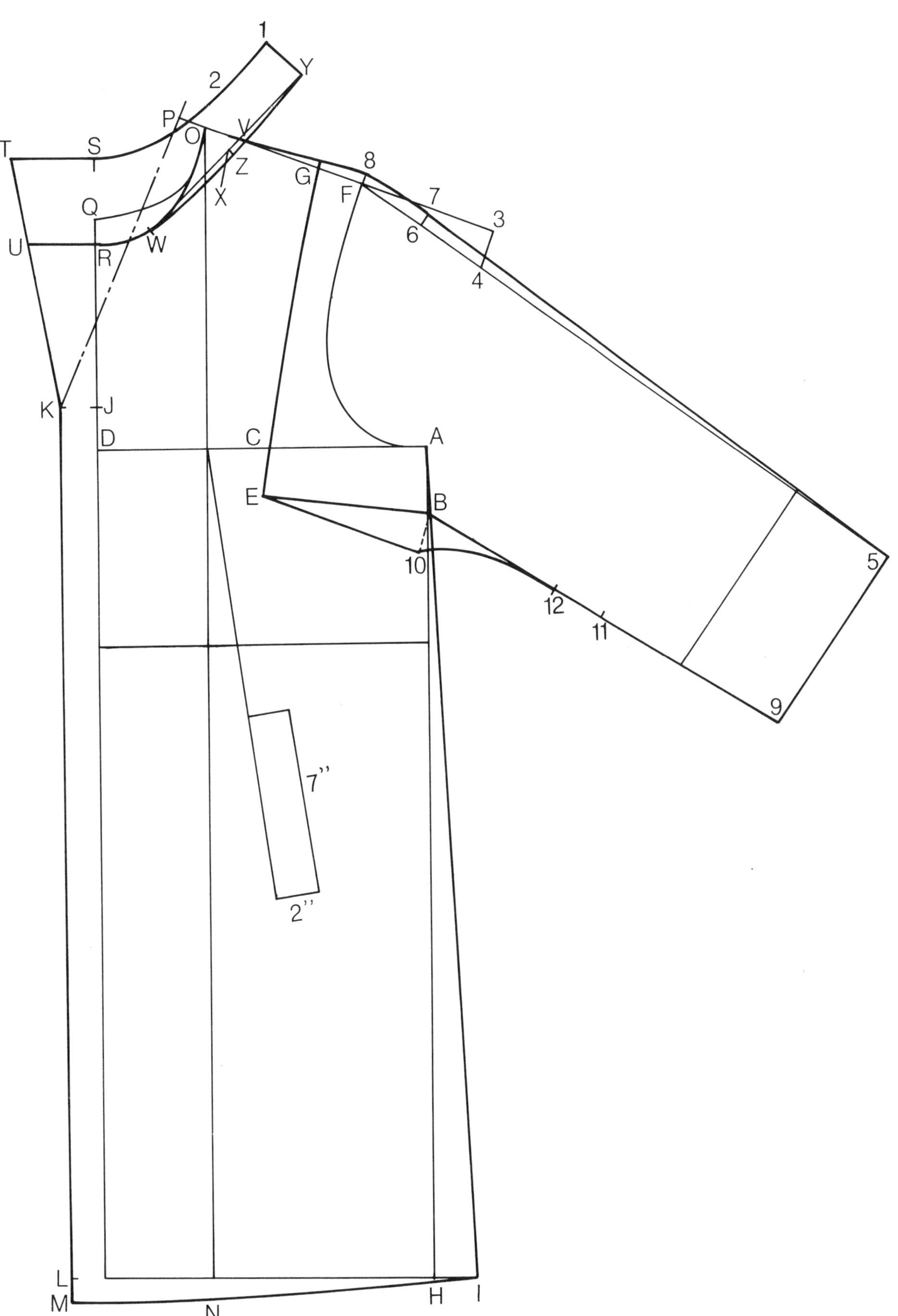

SECTION VI

DETAILS OF OUTERWEAR

(CUFF, BUTTONHOLES, NOTCH COLLAR)

CUFF DESIGNS

A

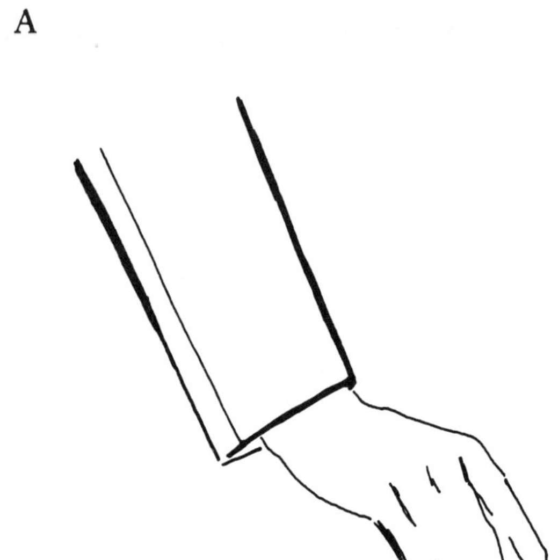

Basic Cuff

B

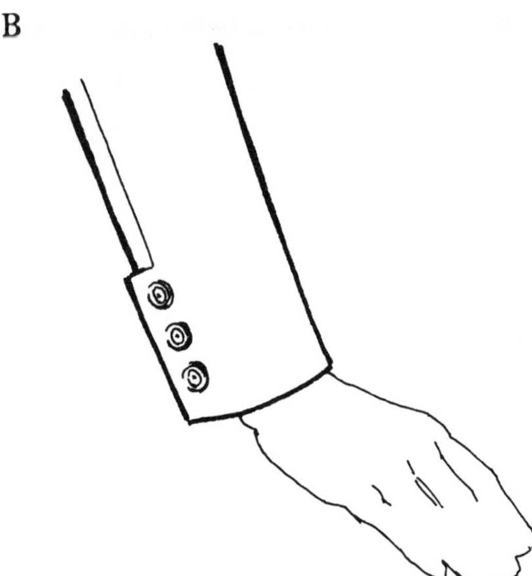

Vented Cuff

C

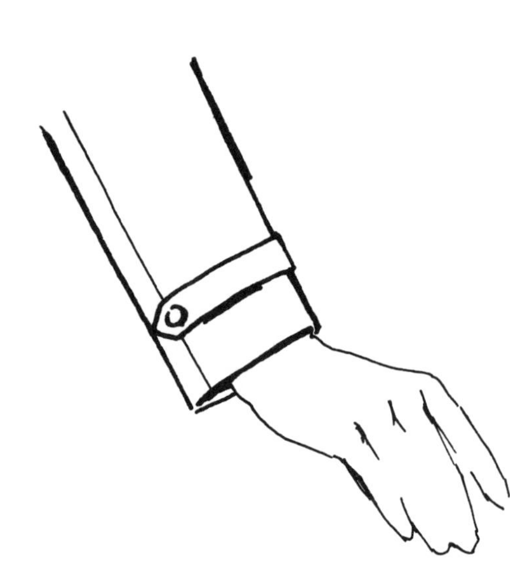

Button Strap Cuff

D

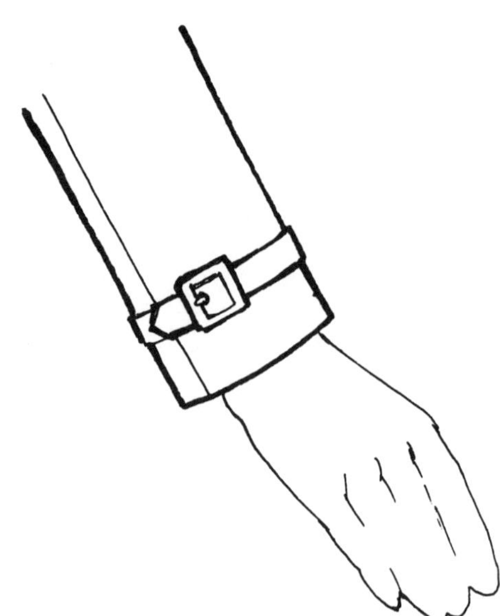

Buckle Strap Cuff

CUFF DESIGNS

E

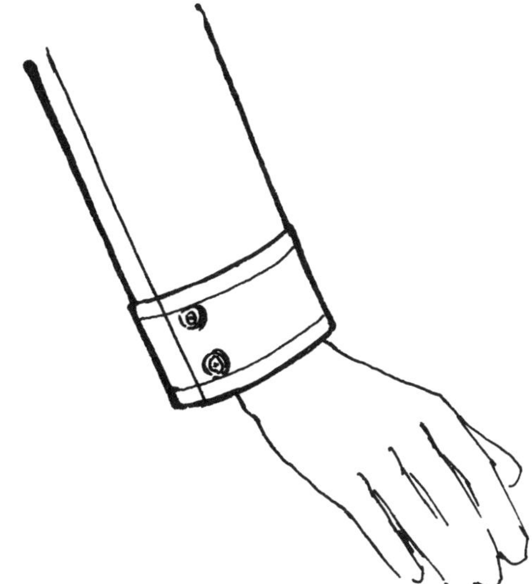

Barrel Cuff

F

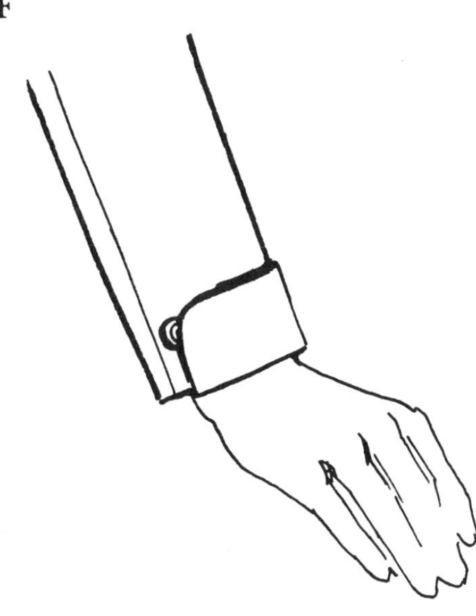

Semi-French Cuff

G

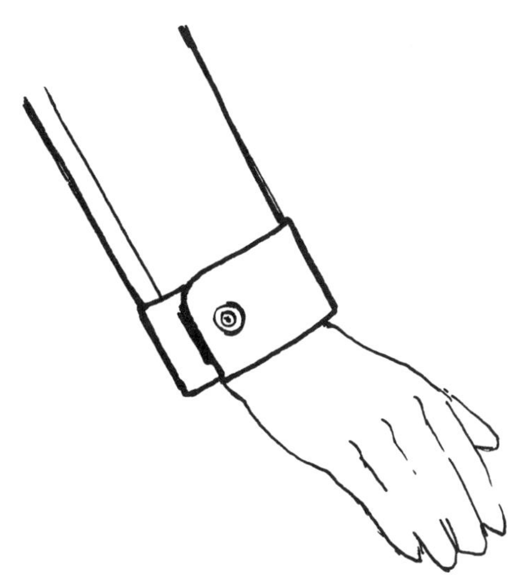

French Variation Cuff

H

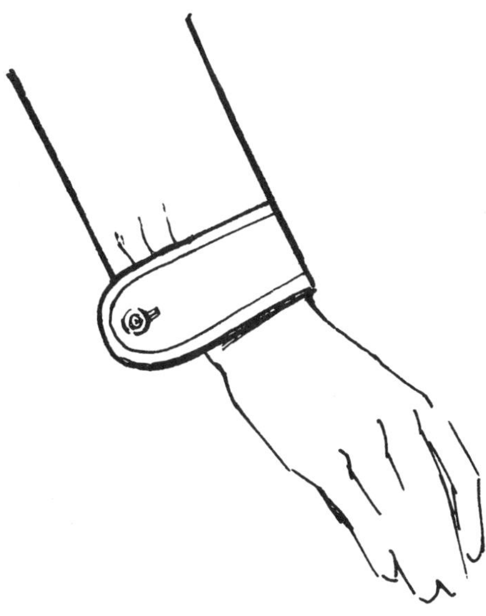

Tab Cuff

BUTTONHOLE DESIGN FOR SINGLE-BREASTED COAT

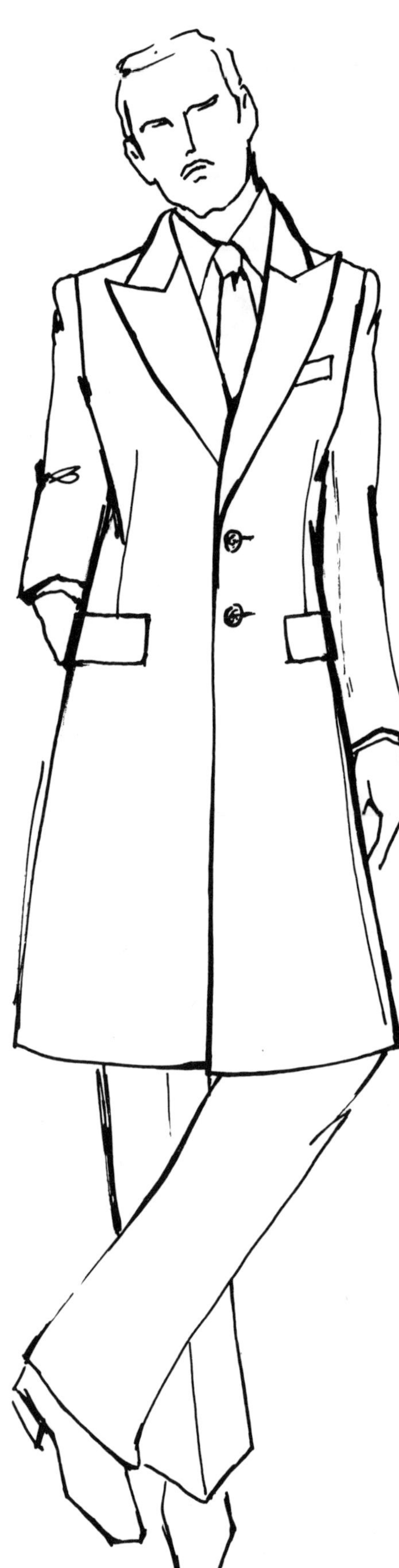

A = center front at waist.
A to B = 2".
B to C = 1/2 of button diameter plus 1/2" for extension.

Buttonhole Opening
B to D = 1/8".
D to E = button diameter plus 1/8".
A to F = A to B.
Extension and buttonhole opening are the same as above.

Note: Placement of first buttonhole can be 3/8" to 1/2" below breakpoint level depending on thickness of fabric and the button size.

Note: Buttonhole can be larger than 1/8" of button diameter depending upon the size and design of the button.

DIAGRAM—Buttonhole Design for Single-Breasted Coat

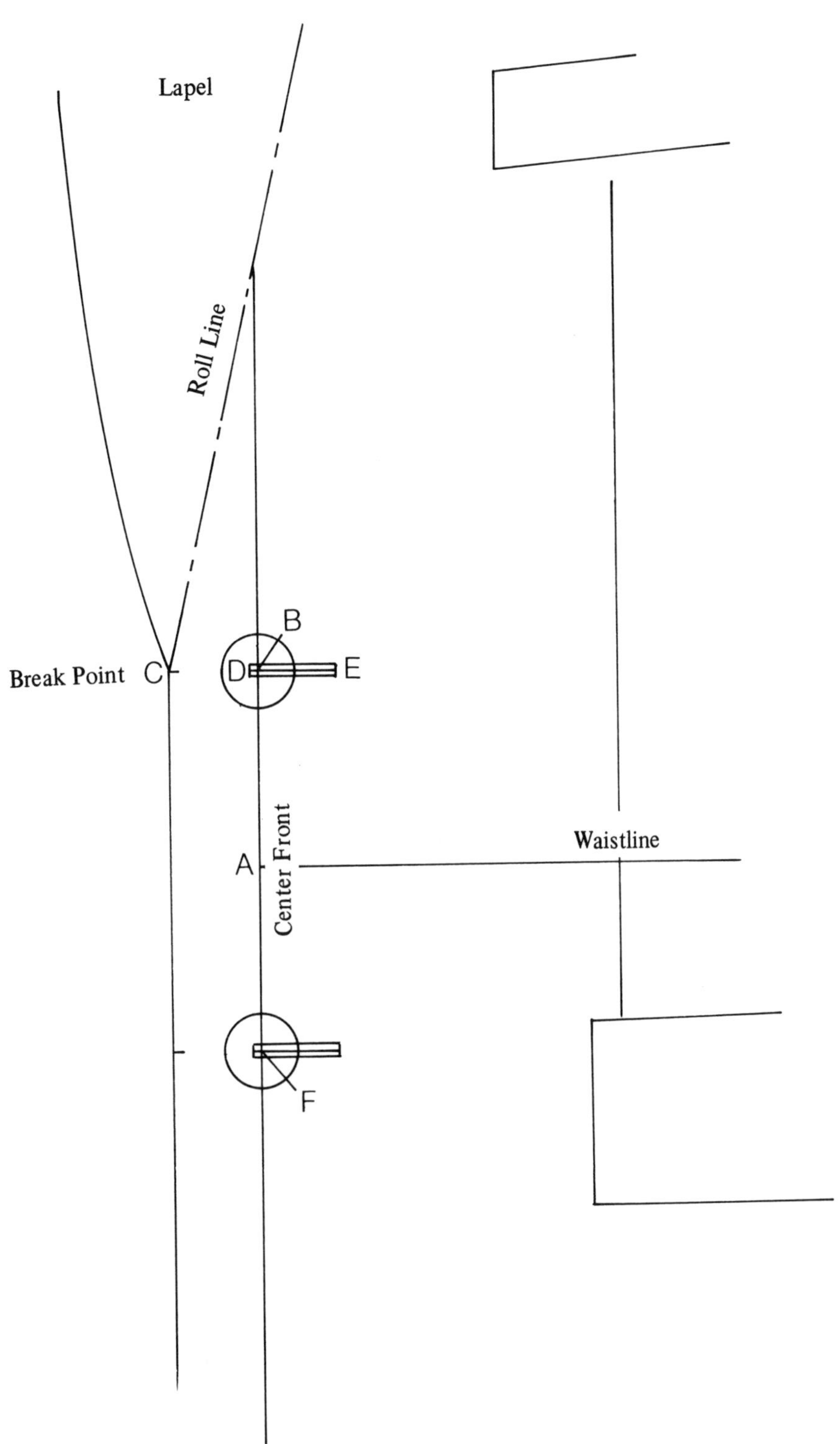

BUTTONHOLE DESIGN FOR DOUBLE-BREASTED COAT

A = center front at waist.
A to B = 2" above waist.
B to C = extension.
C to D = 1/2 of button diameter plus 1/2".

Buttonhole Opening
D to E = 1/8".
E to F = button diameter plus 1/8".
B to G = B to D.
D to H = 4".

The position of the buttonhole opening is the same as for Single-Breasted Coat.
G to D = H to I.

Note: Placement of first buttonhole can be 3/8" to 1/2" below breakpoint level depending on thickness of fabric and the button size.

Note: Buttonhole can be larger than 1/8" of button diameter depending upon the size and design of the button.

DIAGRAM–Buttonhole Design for Double-Breasted Coat

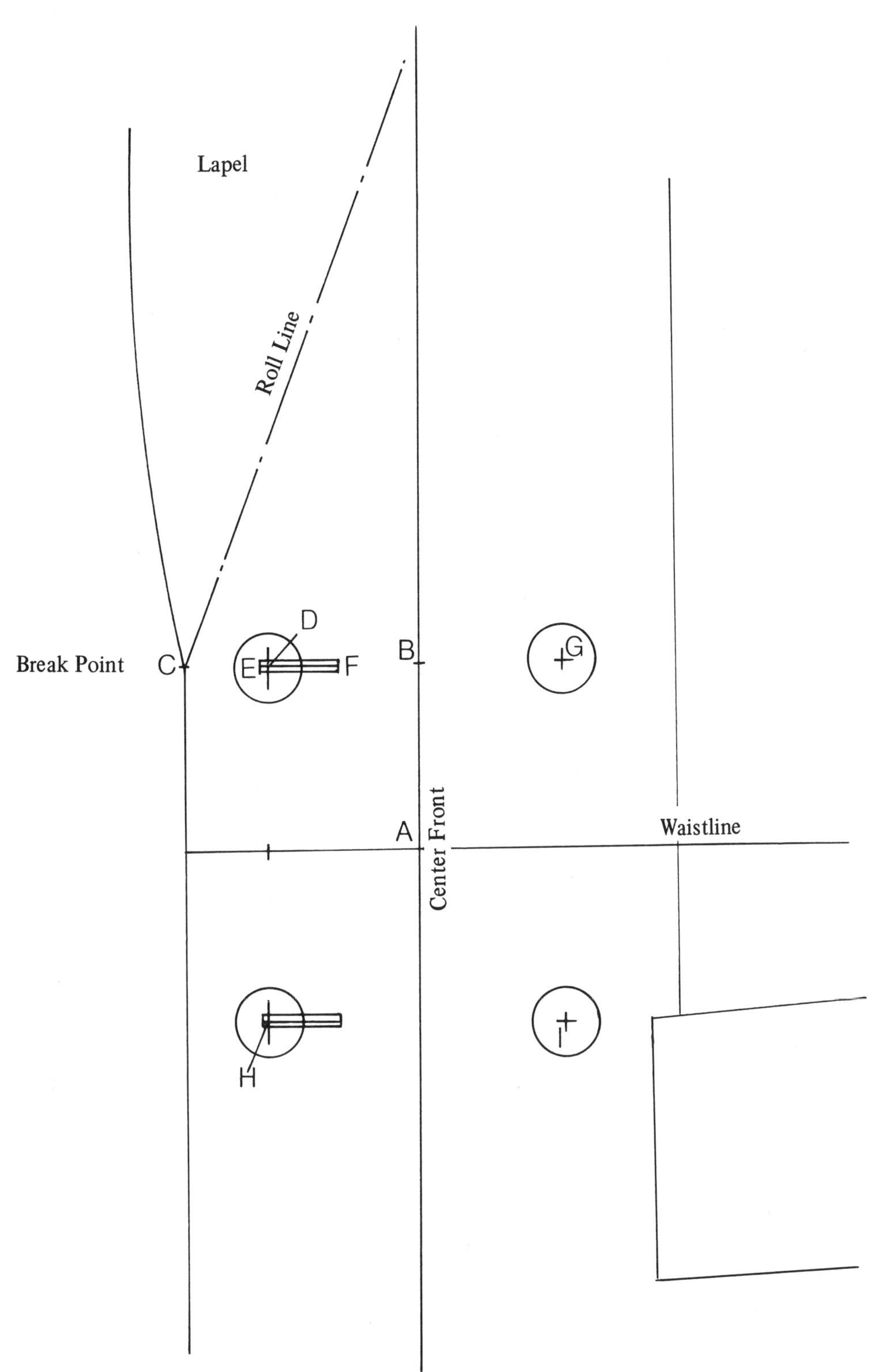

BASIC BANDED COLLAR VARIATION

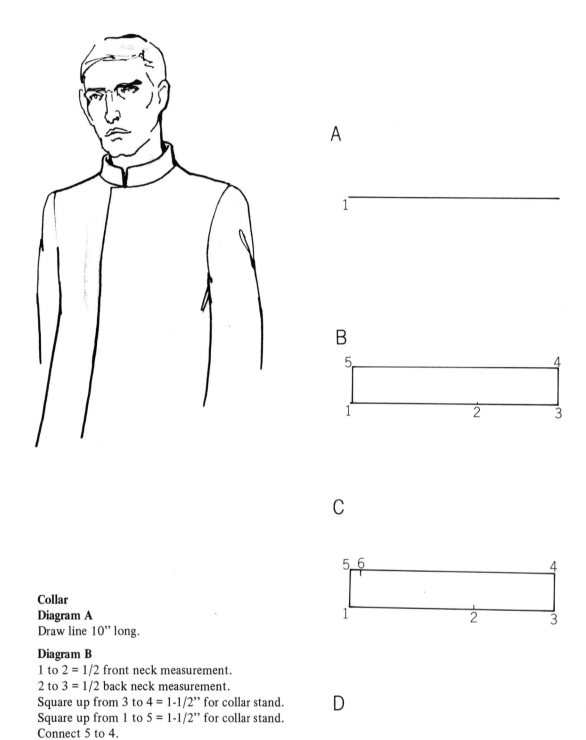

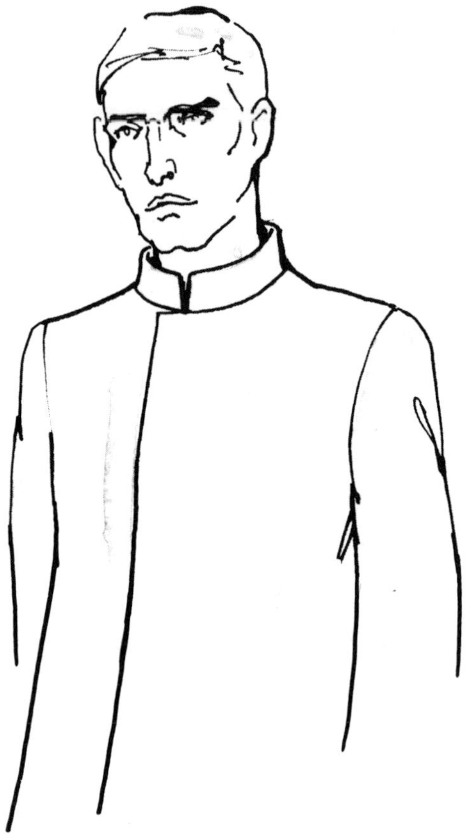

A

1

B

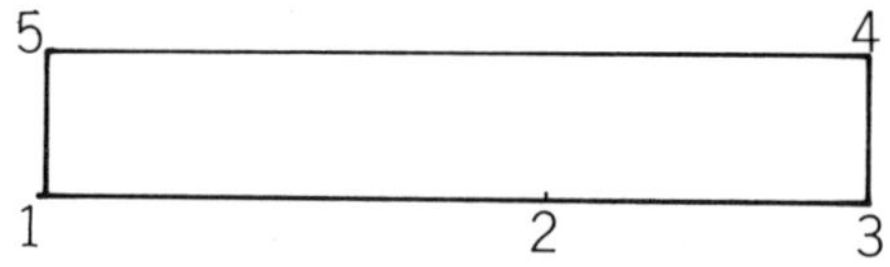

5 4

1 2 3

C

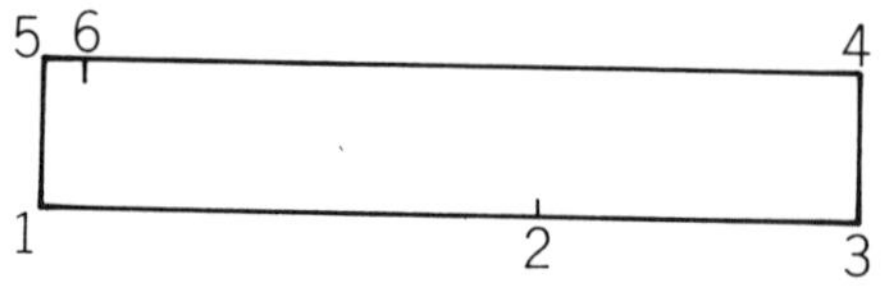

5 6 4

1 2 3

D

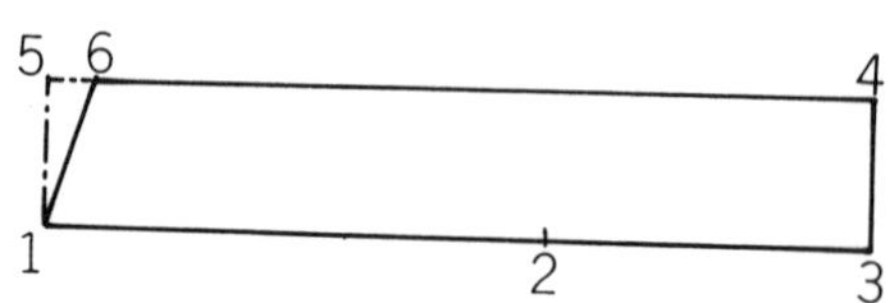

Collar

Diagram A

Draw line 10" long.

Diagram B

1 to 2 = 1/2 front neck measurement.
2 to 3 = 1/2 back neck measurement.
Square up from 3 to 4 = 1-1/2" for collar stand.
Square up from 1 to 5 = 1-1/2" for collar stand.
Connect 5 to 4.

Diagram C

5 to 6 = 1/2".

Diagram D

Connect 6 to 1 to finish banded collar.

Note: Shape and size of collar should be adjusted according to design.

MANDARIN COLLAR VARIATION

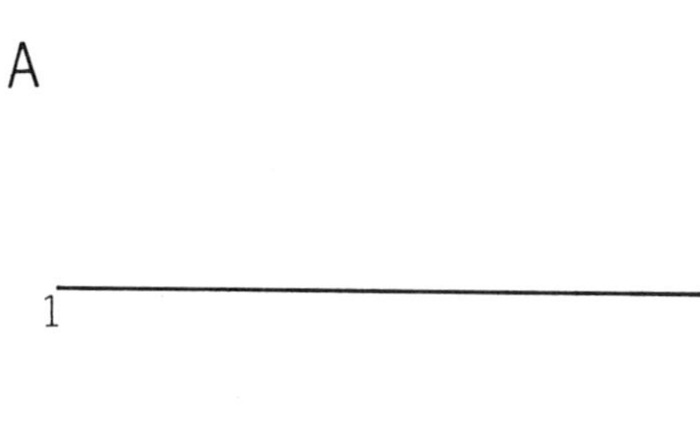

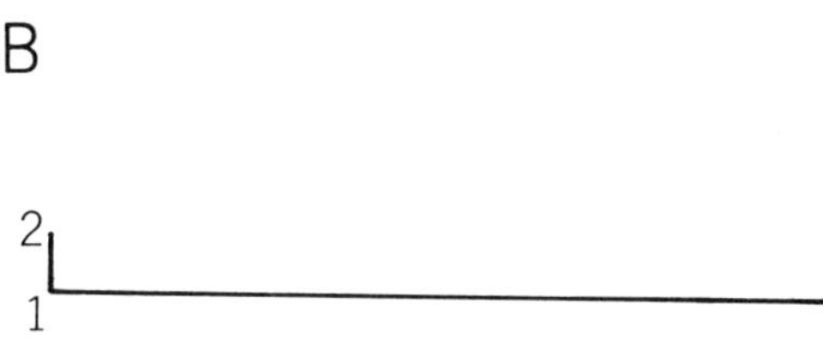

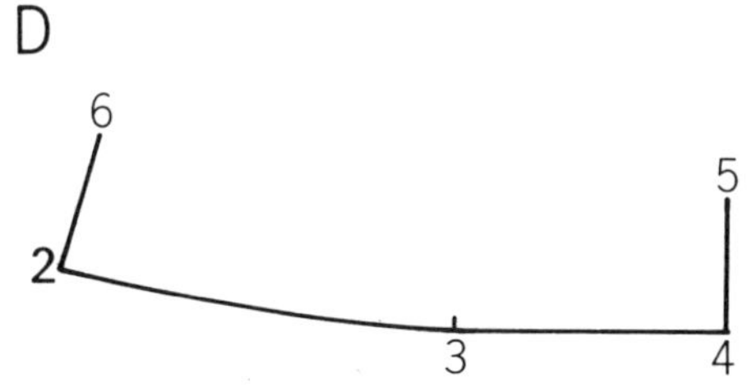

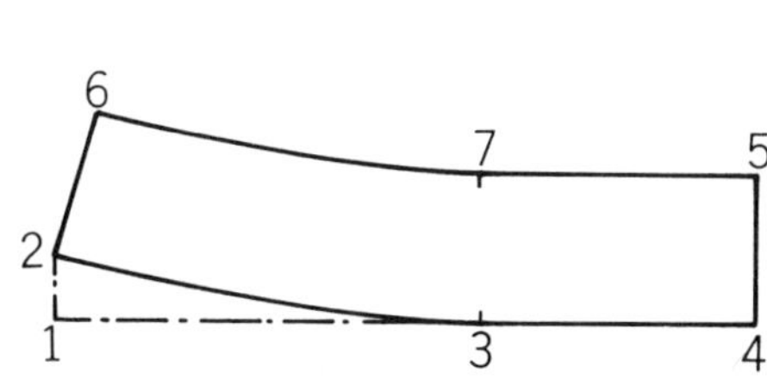

Collar

Diagram A

Draw 10" line.

Diagram B

Square up 1 to 2 = 3/4".

Diagram C

2 to 3 = 1/2 front neck measurement.
Connect 2 to 3 with hip curve ruler.
3 to 4 = 1/2 back neck measurement.

Diagram D

Square up 4 to 5 = 1-3/4".
Square up 2 to 6 = 1-3/4".

Diagram E

3 to 7 = 1 3/4".
Connect 5 to 7 with straight line.
Connect 7 to 6 with same curve as 2 to 3 to finish mandarin collar.

Note: Shape and size of collar should be adjusted according to design.

FUNNEL COLLAR VARIATION

A

1

B

2

1

C

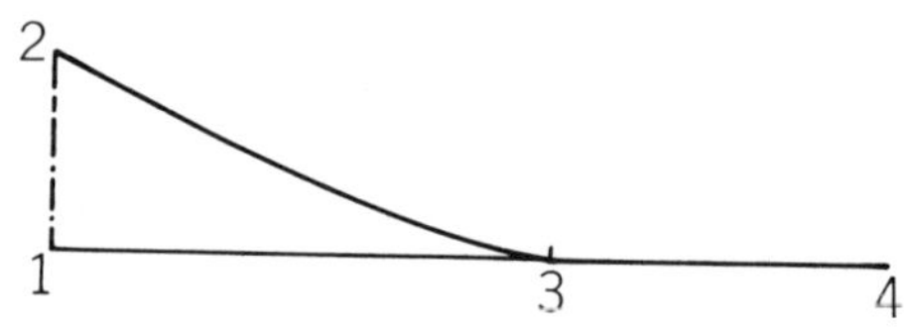

D

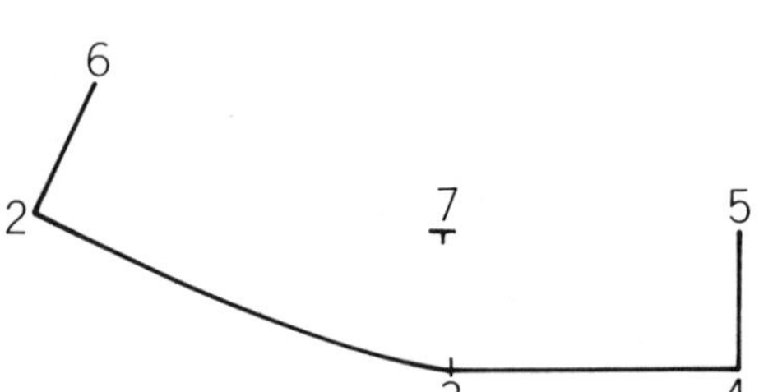

E

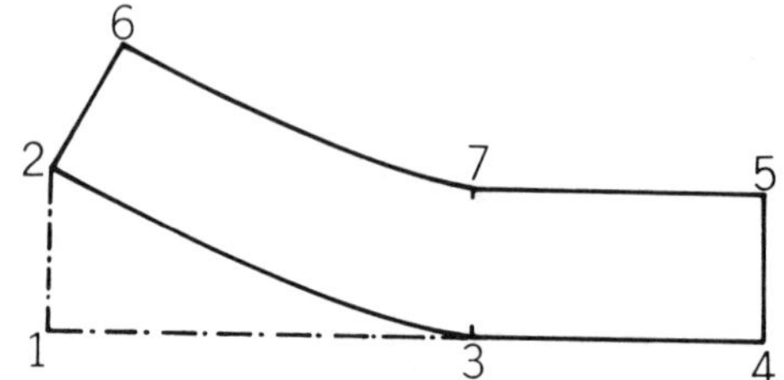

Collar

Diagram A
Draw line 10" long.

Diagram B
Square up 1 to 2 = 2".

Diagram C
2 to 3 = 1/2 front neck measurement.
Connect 2 to 3 with sleigh curve.
3 to 4 = 1/2 back neck measurement.

Diagram D
Square up 4 to 5 = 1-3/4".
Square up 2 to 6 = 1-3/4".

Diagram E
3 to 7 = 1 3/4".
Connect 5 to 7 with straight line.
Connect 7 to 6 with same curve as 3 to 2 to finish funnel collar.

Note: Shape and size of collar should be adjusted according to design.

CONVERTIBLE COLLAR VARIATION

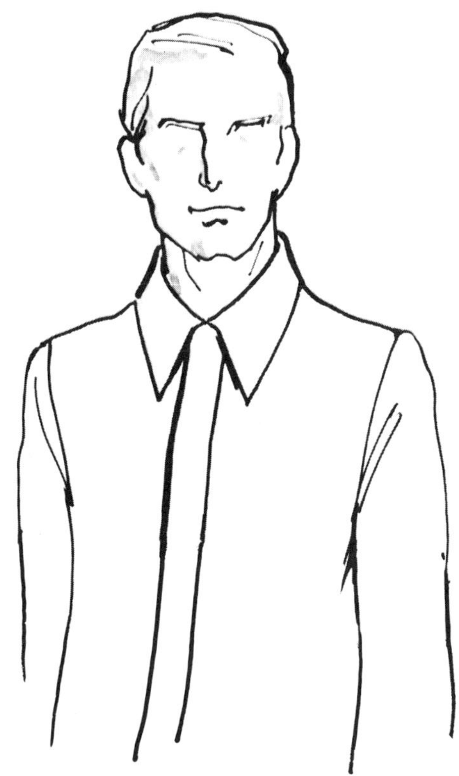

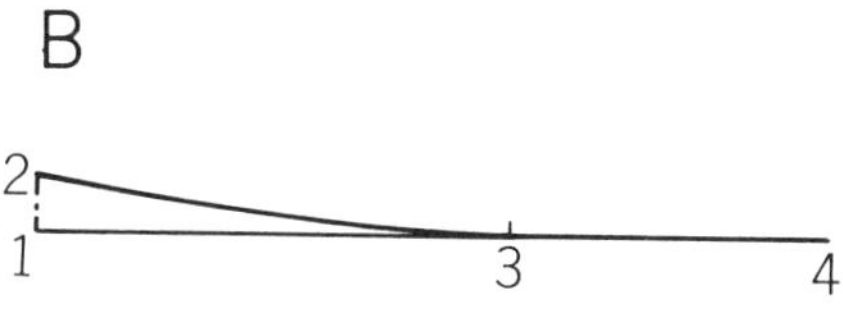

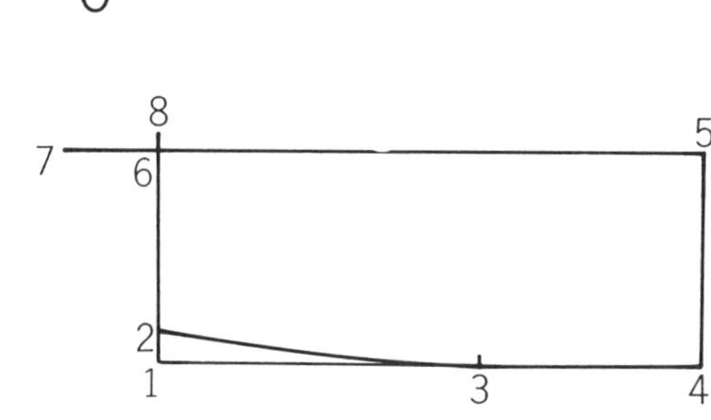

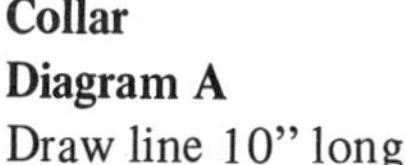

Collar
Diagram A
Draw line 10" long.

Diagram B
Square up 1 to 2 = 1/2".
2 to 3 = 1/2 front neck measurement.
Connect 2 to 3 with hip curve ruler.
3 to 4 = 1/2 back neck measurement.

Diagram C
Square up 4 to 5 = 3-1/8".
1 to 6 = 4 to 5.
Extend 6 to 7 = 1-1/2".
6 to 8 = 1/4".

Diagram D
9 = 1/2 5 to 6.
Connect 2 to 7 to 10 = 3-1/2".
Connect 9 to 8 to 10 with hip curve ruler to finish convertible collar.

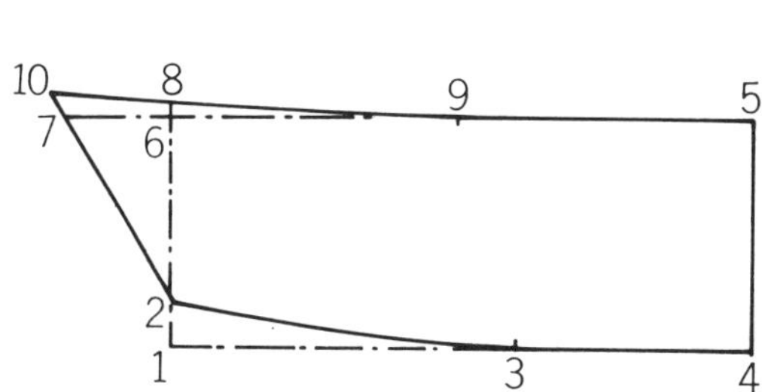

Note: Shape and size of collar should be adjusted according to design.

CONTINENTAL COLLAR VARIATION

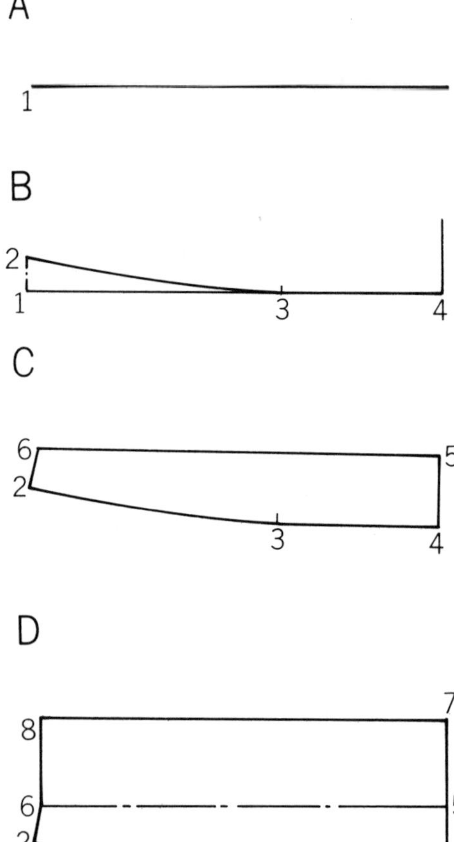

Collar

Diagram A
Draw 10" line.

Diagram B
Square up 1 to 2 = 3/4".
2 to 3 = 1/2 front neck measurement.
3 to 4 = 1/2 back neck measurement.
Square up 4 to 5.

Diagram C
Square up 2 to 6 = 3/4".
Connect 5 to 6 with straight line.

Diagram D
5 to 7 = 1-3/4".
6 to 8 = 1-3/4".
Connect 8 to 7.

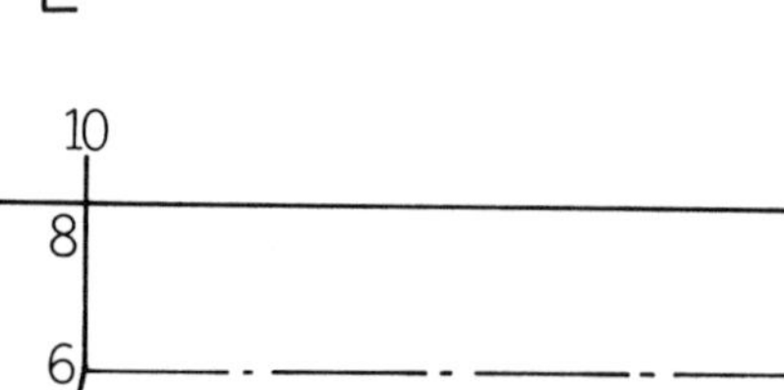

Diagram E
Extend 8 to 9 = 1-1/2".
Extend 8 to 10 = 1/2".

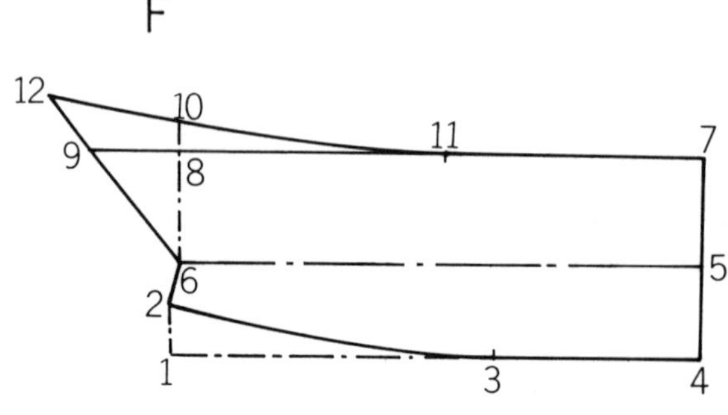

Diagram F
11 = 1/2 8 to 7.
6 to 9 to 12 = 3-1/2".
Connect 11 to 10 to 12 with hip curve ruler to finish continental collar.

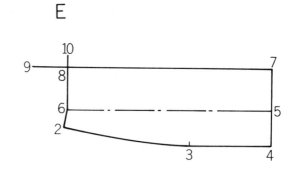

Note: Shape and size of collar should be adjusted according to design.

BANDED CONVERTIBLE COLLAR VARIATION #1

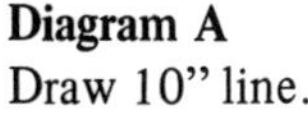

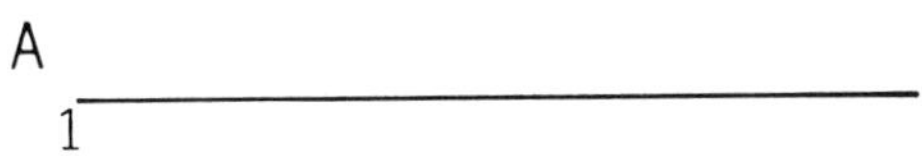

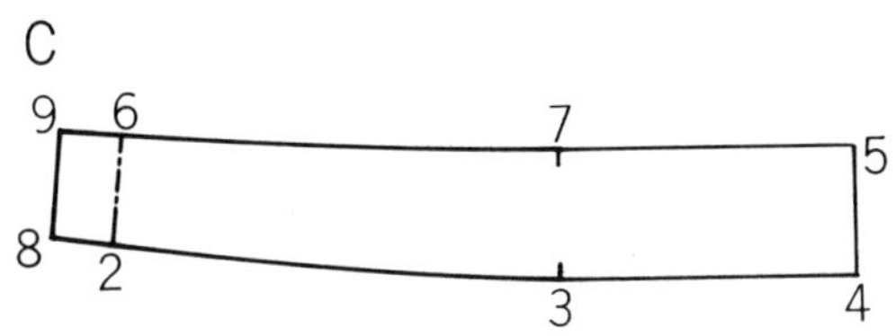

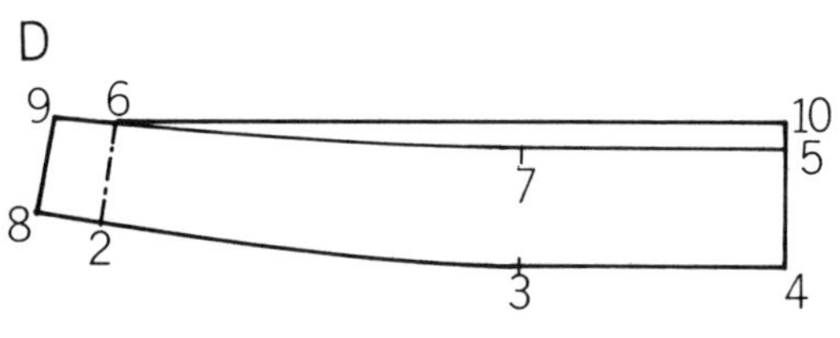

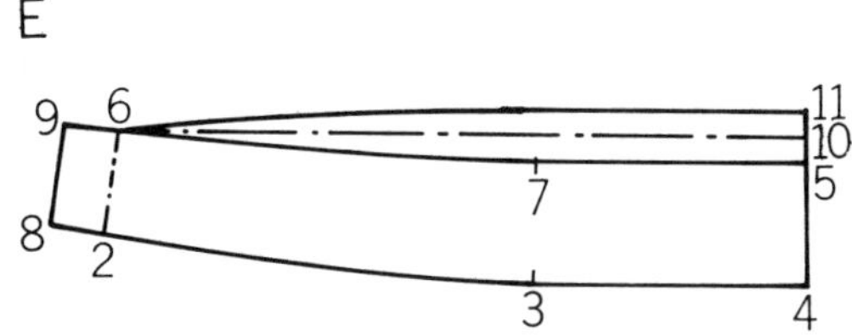

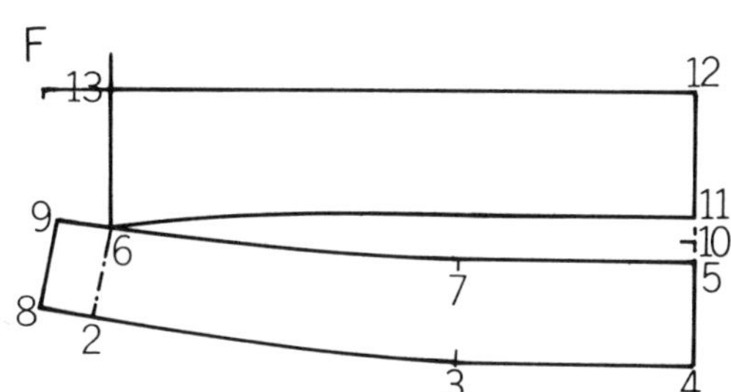

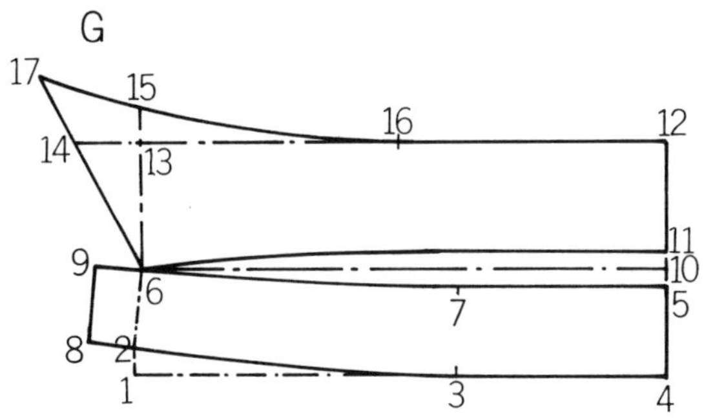

Collar

Diagram A
Draw 10" line.

Diagram B
Square up 1 to 2 = 1/2".
2 to 3 = 1/2 front neck measurement.
Connect 2 to 3 with hip curve ruler.
3 to 4 = 1/2 back neck measurement.

Diagram C
Square up 4 to 5 = 1-1/2".
3 to 7 = 1-1/2".
Square up 2 to 6.
6 to 9 = 3/4" for extension.
2 to 8 = 3/4" for extension.
Connect all points as shown in diagram.

Diagram D
5 to 10 = 1/4".
Connect 6 to 10 with straight line.

Diagram E
10 to 11 = 1/4".
Connect 6 to 11 with same curve as 5 to 7 to 6.

Diagram F
11 to 12 = 1-7/8".
6 to 13 = 10 to 12.
13 to 14 = 1".
13 to 15 = 1/2".

Diagram G
16 = 1/2 12 to 13.
Connect 6 to 14 to 17 = 4".
Connect 16 to 15 to 17 with hip curve ruler to finish collar variation.

BANDED CONVERTIBLE COLLAR VARIATION #2

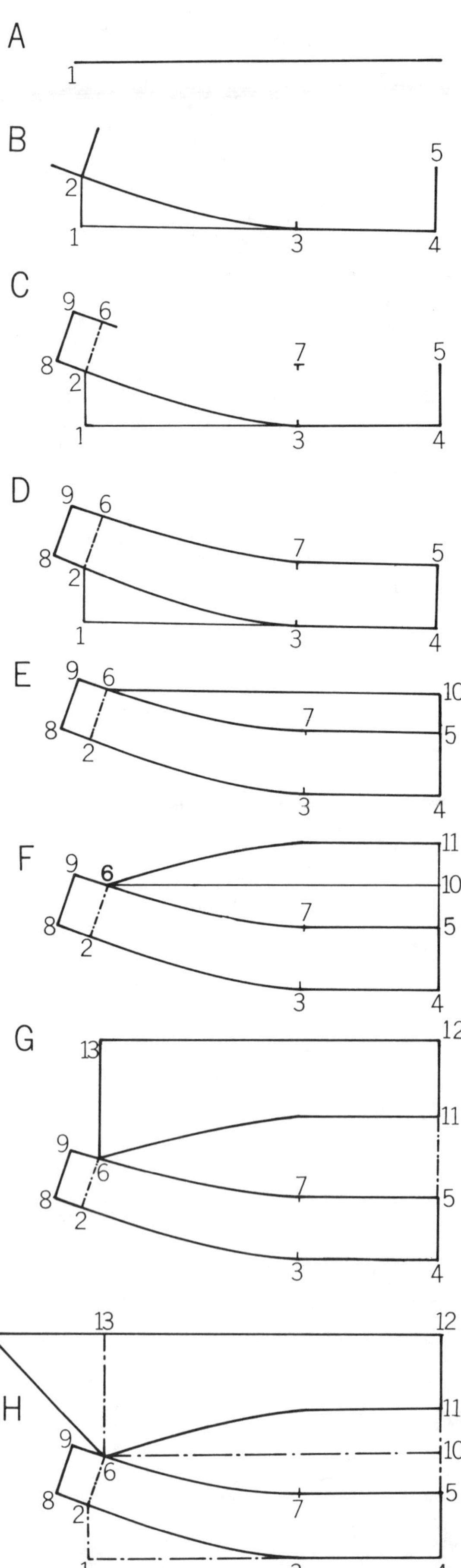

Collar

Diagram A

Draw line 10" long.

Diagram B

Square up 1 to 2 = 1-1/4".
2 to 3 = 1/2 front neck measurement.
Connect 2 to 3 with sleigh curve.
3 to 4 = 1/2 back neck measurement.
Square up 4 to 5 = 1-1/2".
Square up 2 to 6 = 1-1/4".

Diagram C

3 to 7 = 1-1/2".
2 to 8 = 3/4" for extension.
6 to 9 = 3/4" for extension.
Connect as shown in diagram.

Diagram D

Connect 5 to 7 with straight line.
Connect 7 to 6 with sleigh curve.

Diagram E

Extend line upward from 5 to 10.
Square off from 10 to 6.

Diagram F

10 to 11 = 5 to 10
Connect 11 to 6 with same curve as 5 to 7 to 6.

Diagram G

11 to 12 = 1-3/4".
6 to 13 = 10 to 12.

Diagram H

Extend 13 to 14.
6 to 14 = 4" to finish dress shirt collar.

NOTES

COLLAR PARTS AND NOTCH COLLAR SIZE VARIATIONS CHART

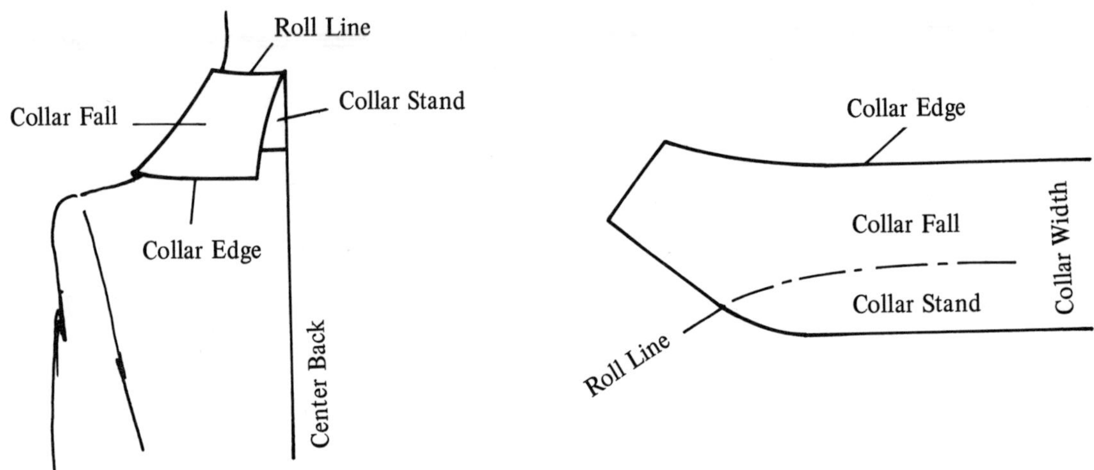

COMMERCIALLY USED NOTCHED COLLAR SIZE VARIATIONS

Shifting is a procedure which will give the correct collar-edge measurement. This will give a proper fit to the notched collar.

NOTE: In Size Charts A, B1, and B2 breakpoint = 2" above waist.

A. Both stand and collar fall change 1/8". Amount of shift is 1/2" in all sizes.

Collar Stand	1-1/8	1-1/4	1-3/8	1-1/2
Collar Fall	1-5/8	1-3/4	1-7/8	2
Collar Width	2-3/4	3	3-1/4	3-1/2
Shift	1/2	1/2	1/2	1/2

B1. Stand remains the same throughout all sizes. Collar fall gain is 1/8" in each size. Shift will then gain 1/8" also in all sizes.

Collar Stand	1-1/8	1-1/8	1-1/8	1-1/8
Collar Fall	1-5/8	1-3/4	1-7/8	2
Collar Width	2-3/4	2-7/8	3	3-1/8
Shift	1/2	5/8	3/4	7/8

NOTCH COLLAR SIZE VARIATIONS CHART

B2. Same as B1, except stand measurement is higher. Shift also changes 1/8" in all sizes.

Collar Stand	1-1/4	1-1/4	1-1/4	1-1/4
Collar Fall	1-3/4	1-7/8	2	2-1/2
Collar Width	3	3-1/8	3-1/4	3-3/4
Shift	1/2	5/8	3/4	7/8

C. Use the following chart when breakpoint on Single-Breasted Jacket changes due to styling; e.g., breakpoint 2" above waistline requires 5/16" shift in collar, etc.

Collar Stand	1-1/8	1-1/8	1-1/8	1-1/8	1-1/8	1-1/8
Collar Fall	1-5/8	1-5/8	1-5/8	1-5/8	1-5/8	1-5/8
Collar Width	2-3/4	2-3/4	2-3/4	2-3/4	2-3/4	2-3/4
Shift	5/16	6/16	7/16	1/2	9/16	5/8
Above W.L.	2	3	4	5	6	7

D. Use the following chart when breakpoint on Double-Breasted Jacket changes due to styling; e.g., breakpoint 2" above waistline requires 5/16" shift in collar, etc.

Collar Stand	1-1/8	1-1/8	1-1/8	1-1/8	1-1/8	1-1/8
Collar Fall	1-5/8	1-5/8	1-5/8	1-5/8	1-5/8	1-5/8
Collar Width	2-3/4	2-3/4	2-3/4	2-3/4	2-3/4	2-3/4
Shift	3/8	7/16	1/2	9/16	5/8	11/16
Above W.L.	2	3	4	5	6	7

NOTCH COLLAR DRAFTING PROCEDURE

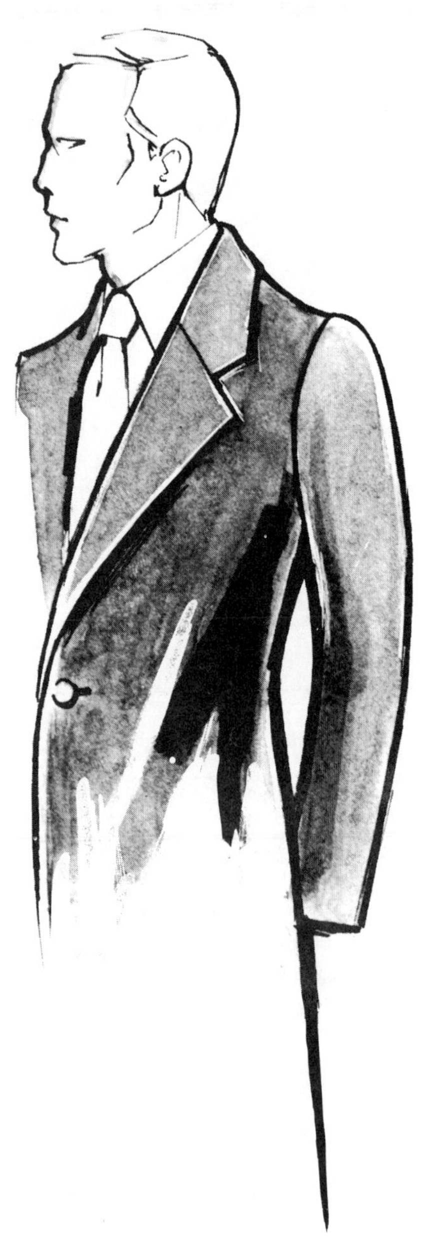

Measurements:

Collar stands 1-1/4".
Fall = 1-3/4".
Shift = 1/2".
See notch collar size variation chart on page 176.

Note: Shape and size of collar should be adjusted according to design.

DIAGRAM–Notch Collar Drafting Procedure

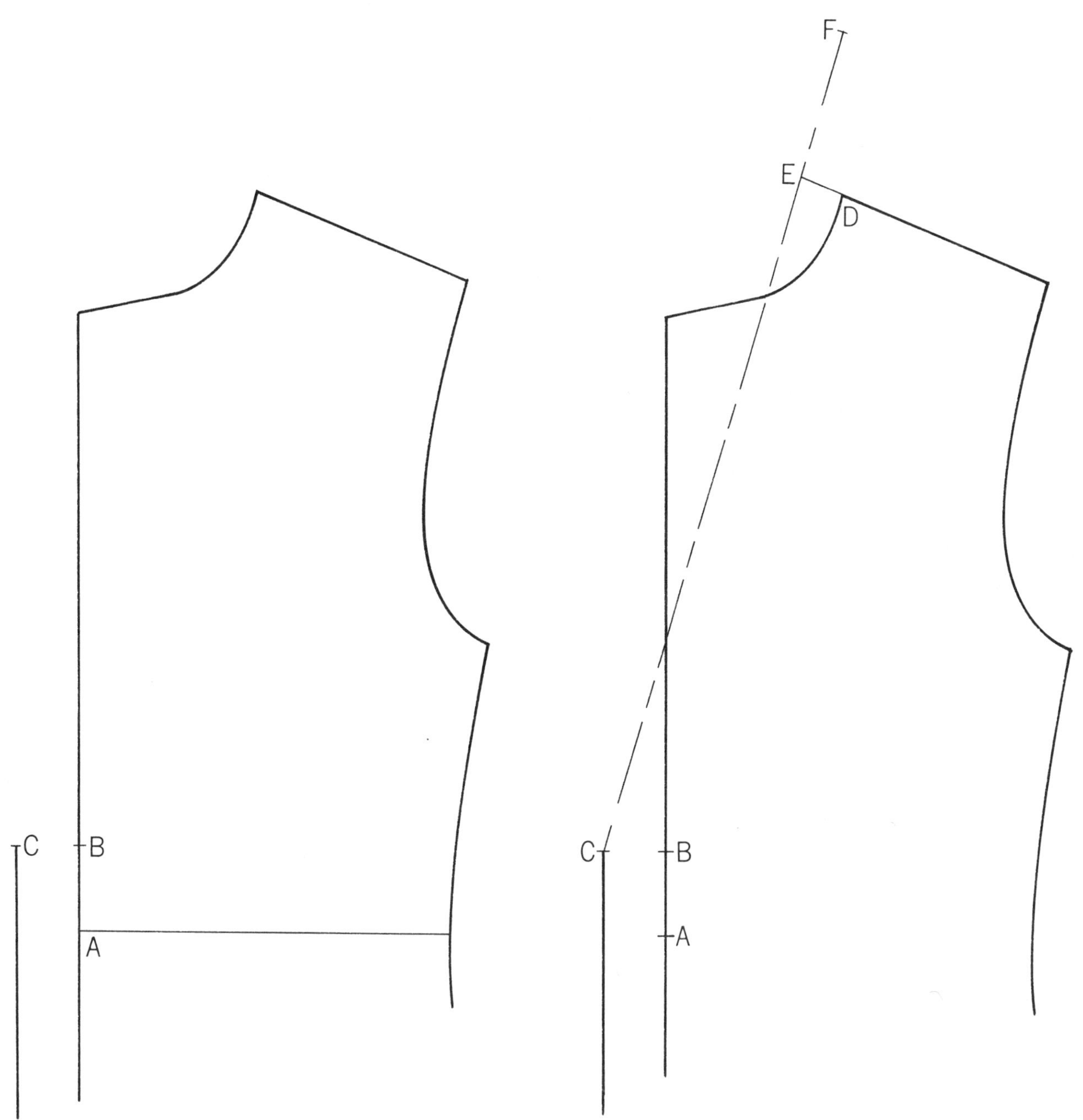

Diagram A

A = waist at center front.
B = position of first button.
B to C = 1-1/2" for extension.
C = breakpoint.

Diagram B

D = shoulder and neck point.
Extend shoulder line to E.
D to E = collar stand - 1/4".
Connect and extend C to E to establish roll line.
E to F = back neck measurement.

DIAGRAM—Notch Collar Drafting Procedure

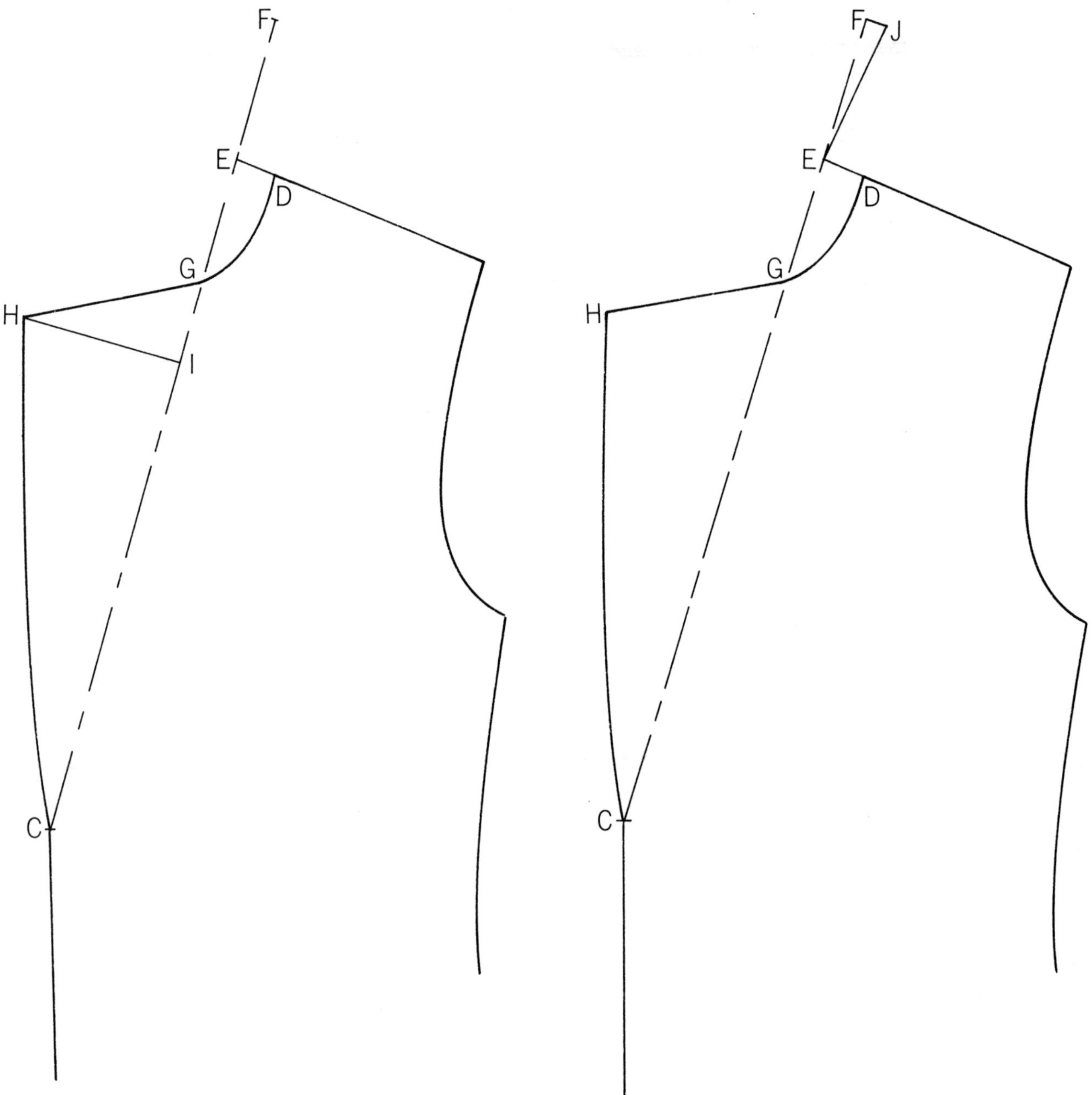

Diagram C

G = roll line at neck.
Extend neck line from G to H with straight line as a guide.
Square off from I to H for lapel width.
Connect H to C with hip curve ruler, using deeper curve toward C to finish lapel.

Diagram D

Square off from F to J = shifting amount, e.g., 1/2".
(See **Size Chart** for different measurements.)
Connect J to E to establish new roll line.

DIAGRAM–Notch Collar Drafting Procedure

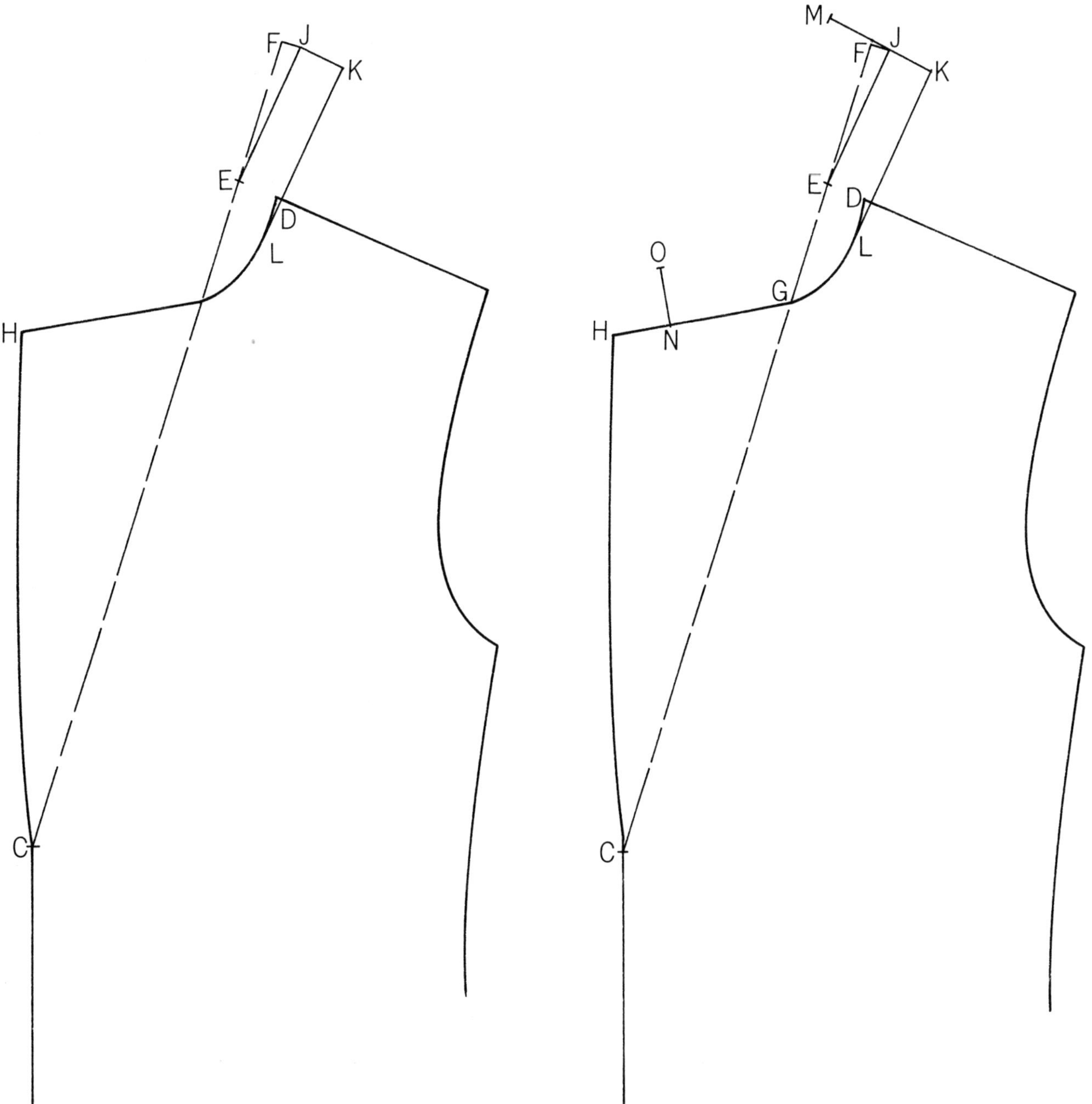

Diagram E

Square off from J to K = collar stand, e.g., 1-1/8".
Square K towards shoulder line, blend into L.

Diagram F

Extend line J to M = collar fall, e.g., 1-3/4".
M to K = collar width.
H to N = according to your design, e.g., 1-1/2".
N to O = N to H.

DIAGRAM—Notch Collar Drafting Procedure

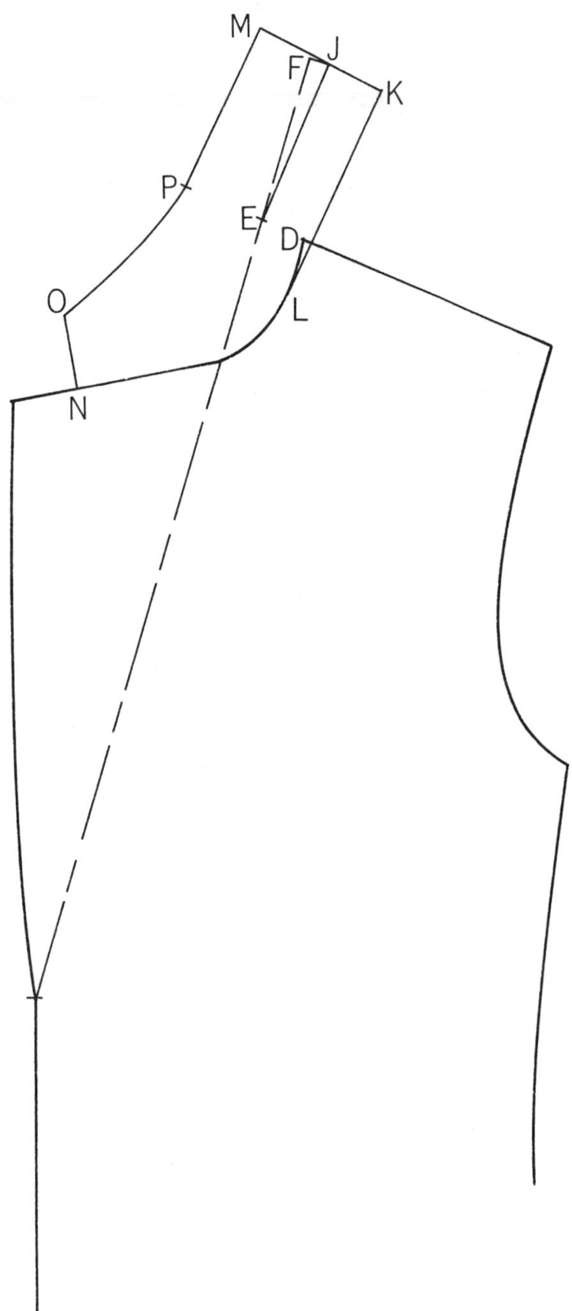

Diagram G

P = extended shoulder line.
Square off from M to P.
Connect O to P with straight line, blend in at P to finish notch collar.

NOTES

TWO-PIECE NOTCH COLLAR

Measurements:
Collar stand = 1-1/8".
Collar fall = 1-3/4".

Note: Shape and size of collar should be adjusted according to design.

DIAGRAM–Two-Piece Notch Collar

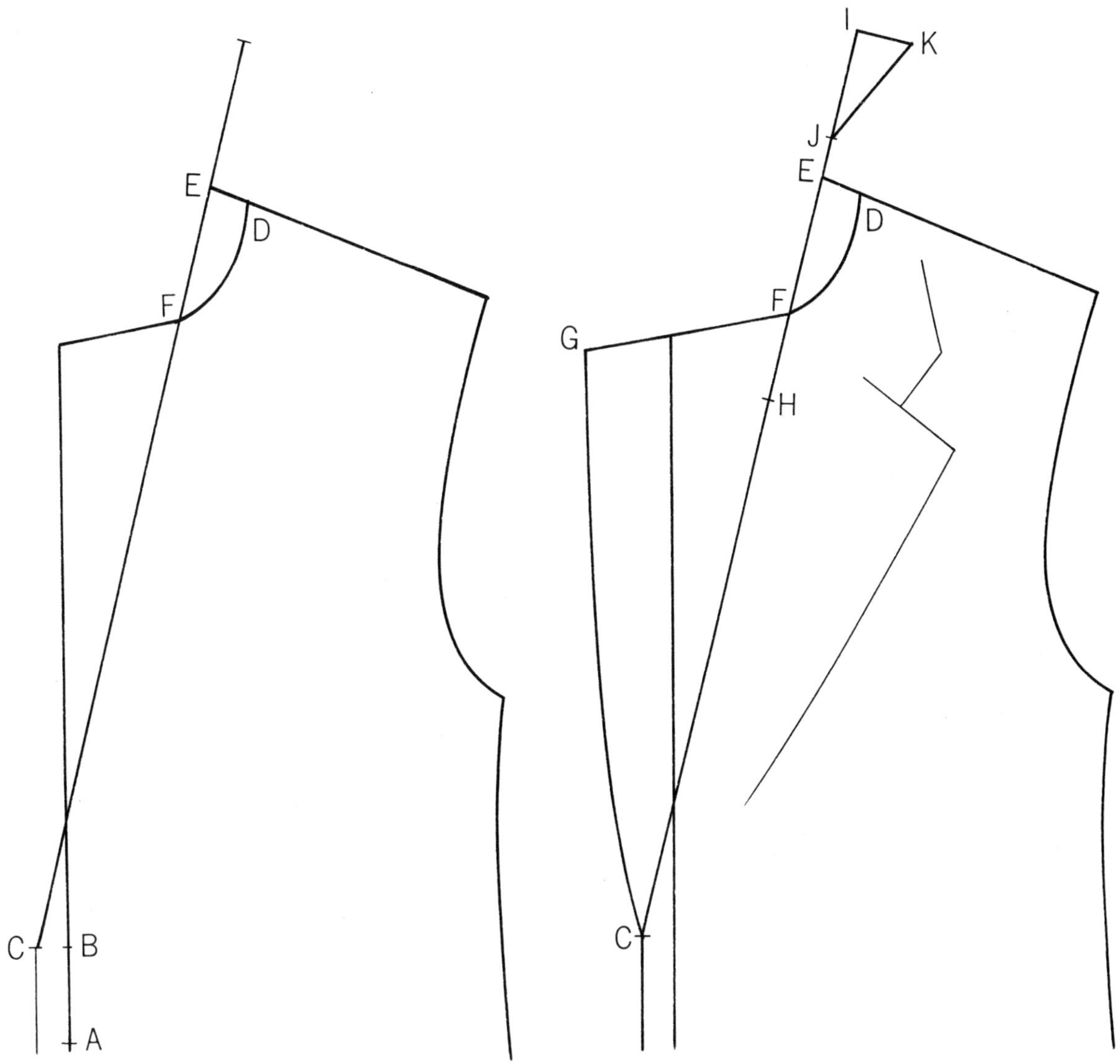

DIAGRAM A

A = waist at center front.
A to B = 2".
B to C = 3/4".
D = intersection of neck and shoulder.
D to E = collar stand - 1/4" (e.g., 1-1/8" collar stand).
Connect C to E to establish roll line.

DIAGRAM B

F = intersection of neck and roll line.
Extend neckline toward G.
Square off H to G = lapel width (e.g., 4-1/2").
Connect G to C with hip curve ruler using deeper curve toward C to finish lapel.
E to I = back neck measurement - 3/8".
Square off I to K = 1-1/4".
I to J = 2-1/4".
Connect K to J.

DIAGRAM–Two-Piece Notch Collar

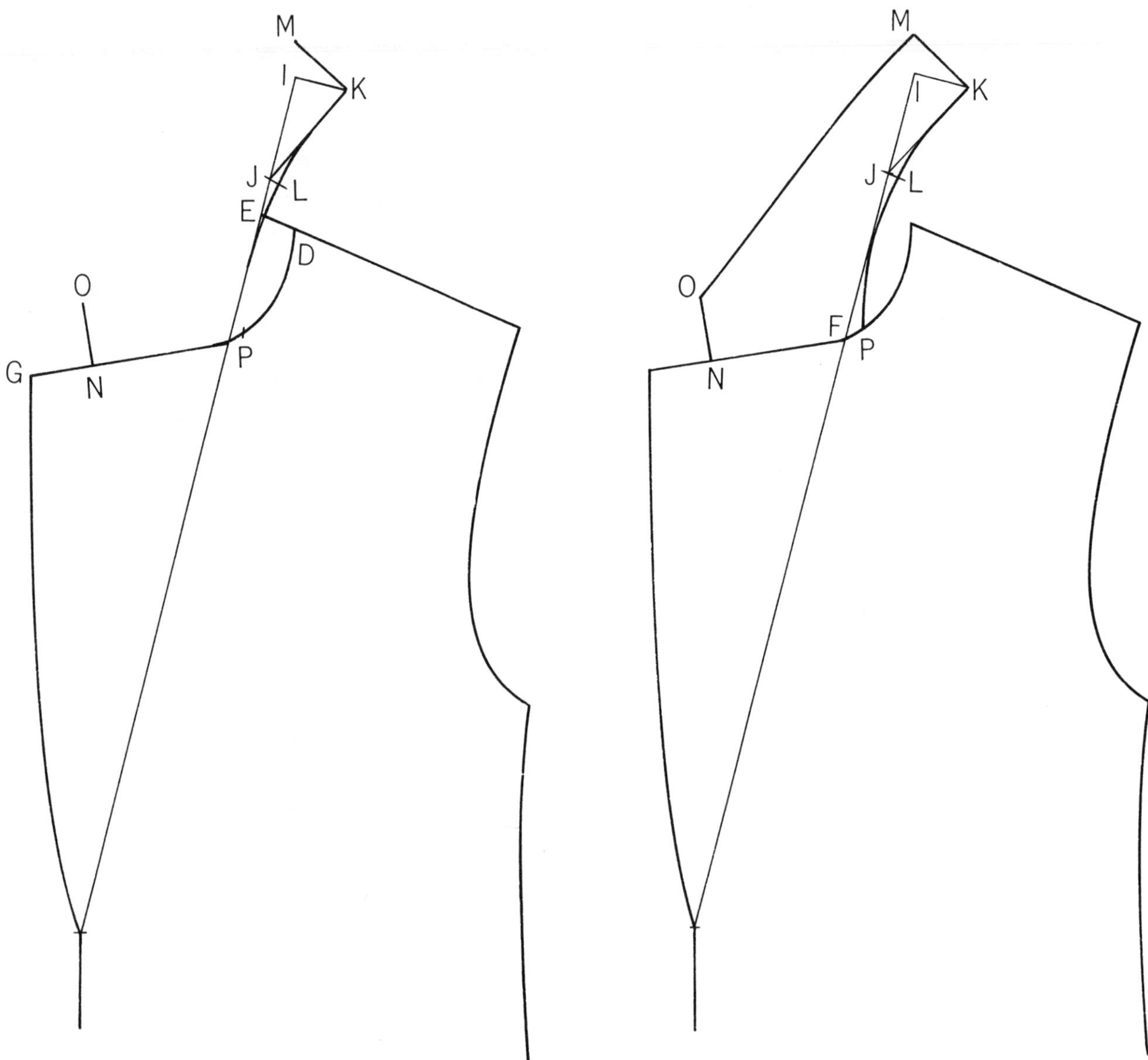

DIAGRAM C

Collar
J to L = 1/4".
Blend in at L (see diagram).
K to M = collar width (e.g., 1-5/8").
G to N = according to design (e.g., 1-1/2").
N to O = N to G.

DIAGRAM D

Connect M to O.
Square off at M for 2" (see diagram).
F to P = 3/8".
Blend in P to L to finish collar.

DIAGRAM—Two-Piece Notch Collar

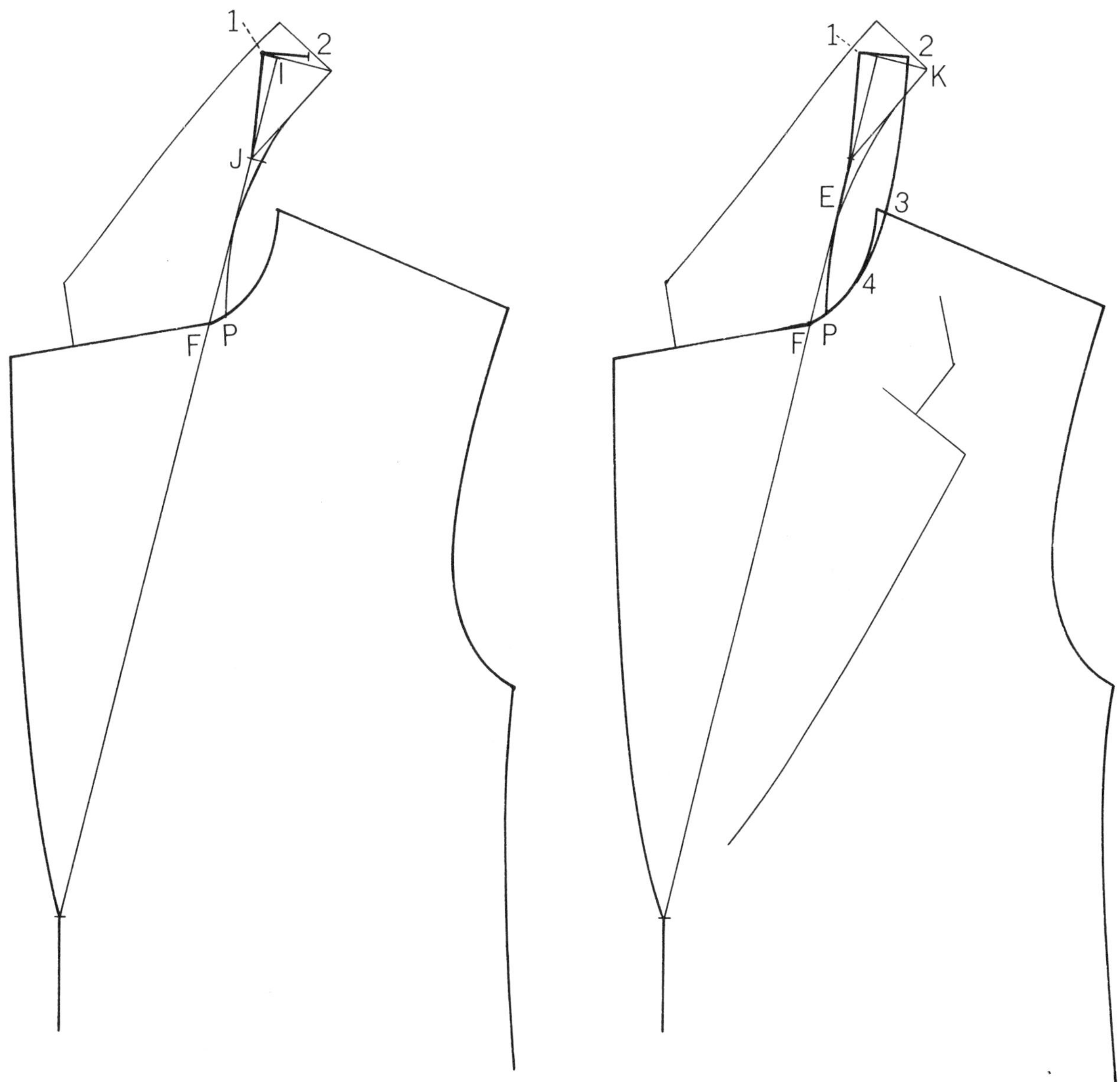

DIAGRAM E

Collar Band
I to 1 = 3/8".
Connect 1 to J.
Square off from point 1 to 2 = collar stand (e.g., 1-1/8").

DIAGRAM F

E to 3 = 1 to 2.
Connect 2 to 3 with sleigh curve ruler.
Blend in to 4.
Square off at point 2 to finish band.

P to K = P to 1 + 1/4".
1/4" ease.
Ease should be adjusted to 1/4".

TWO-PIECE BROAD COLLAR

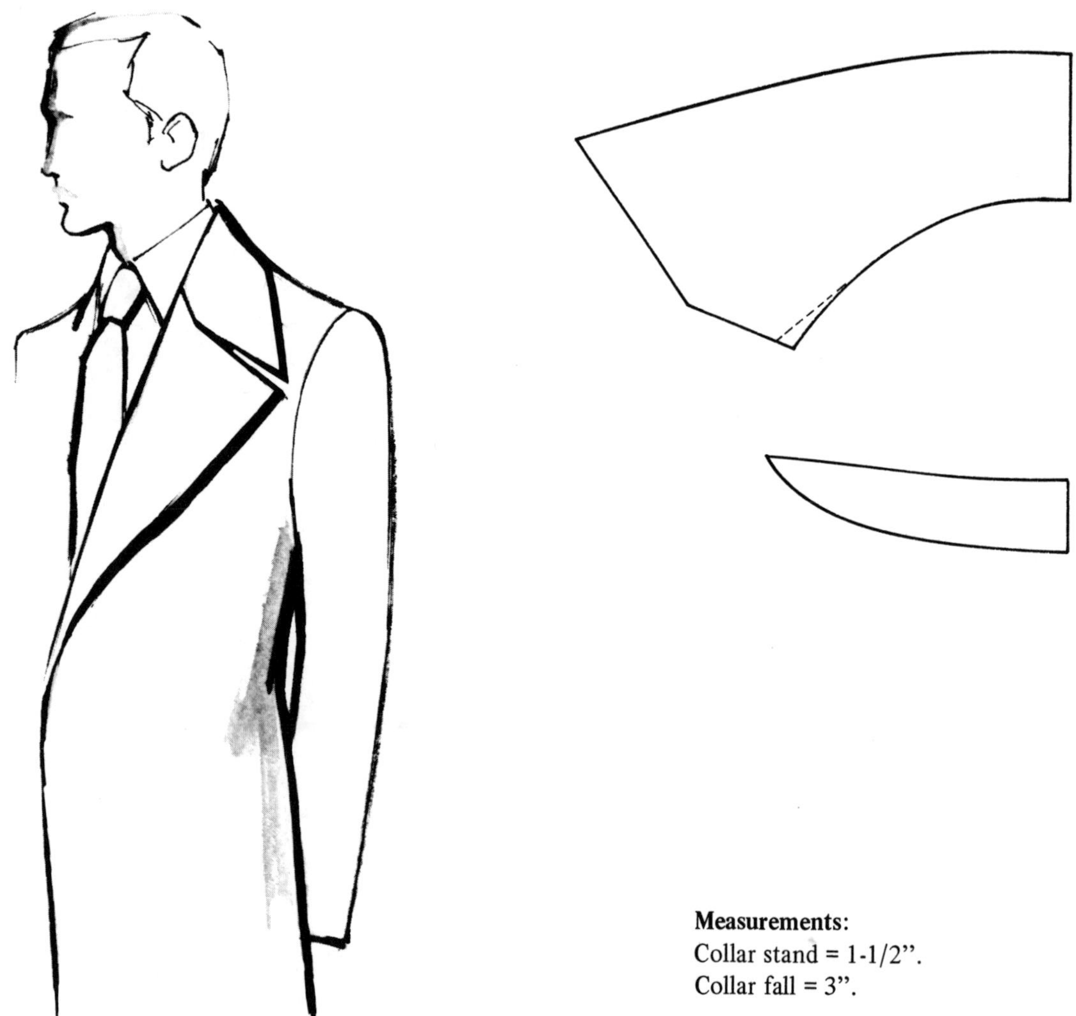

Measurements:
Collar stand = 1-1/2".
Collar fall = 3".

Note: Shape and size of collar should be adjusted according to design.

DIAGRAM—Two-Piece Broad Collar

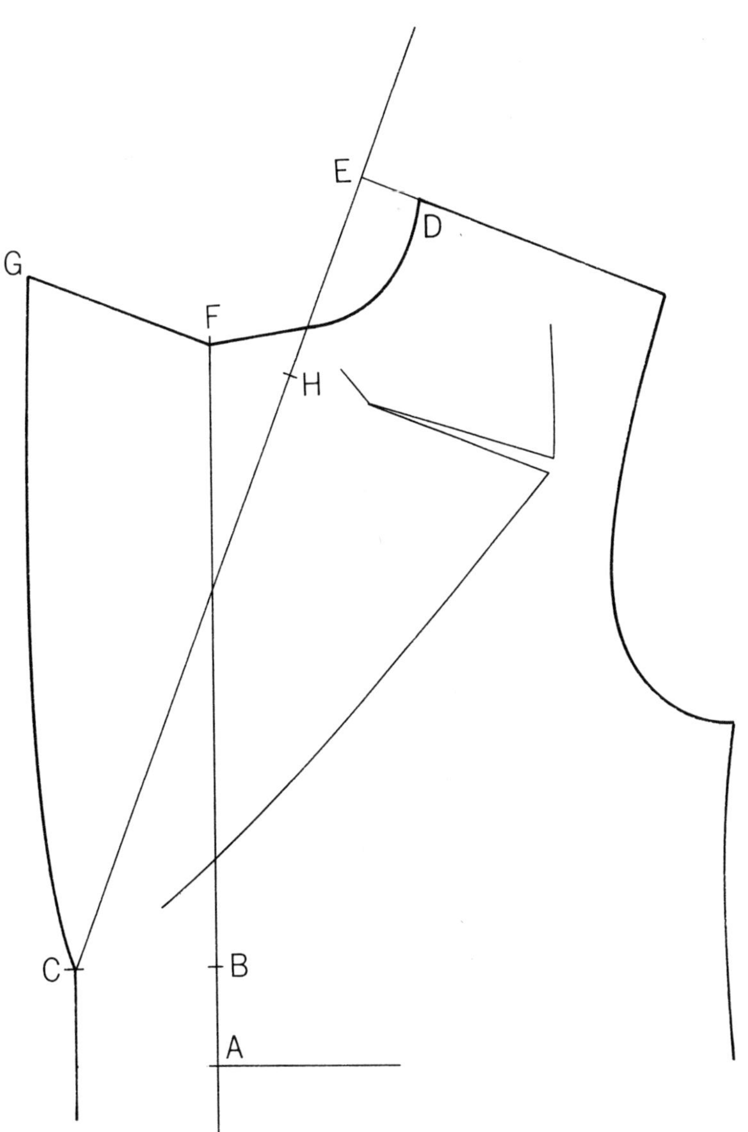

DIAGRAM A

Lapel

A = waist at center front.
A to B = 2".
B to C = 3" for extension (double breasted).
D = intersection of neck and shoulder.
D to E = collar stand - 1/4" (e.g., 1-1/2 collar stand).
Square off H to F to G according to your design (e.g., 6").
Connect G to C with hip curve ruler, using deeper curve toward C to finish lapel.

DIAGRAM–Two-Piece Broad Collar

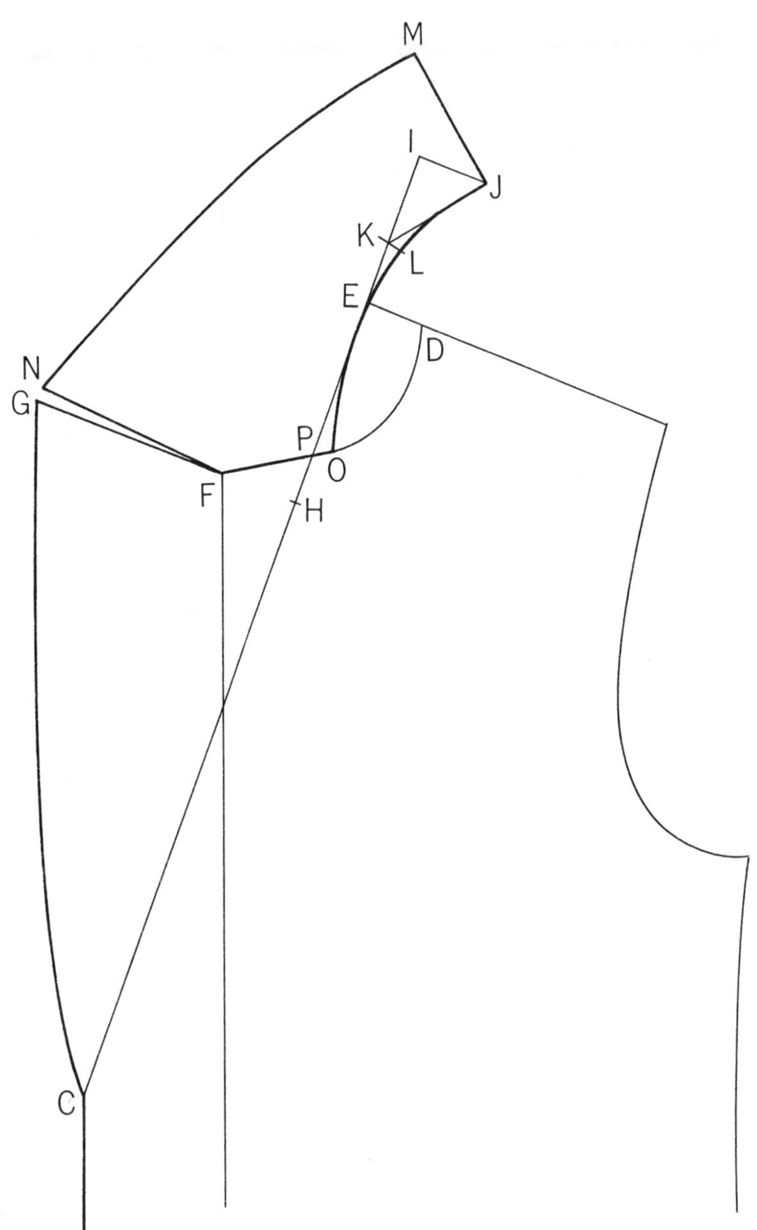

DIAGRAM B

Collar

E to I = back neck measurement - 3/8".
Square off I to J = 1-1/2".
I to K = 2".
Connect J to K.
K to L = 1/4".
Blend in at L (see diagram).
J to M = 3-1/8".
G to N = 1/4"
Connect M to N with sleigh curve ruler.
Square off from point M for 2".
P to O = 1/2".
Blend in O to L to finish collar.

DIAGRAM–Two-Piece Broad Collar

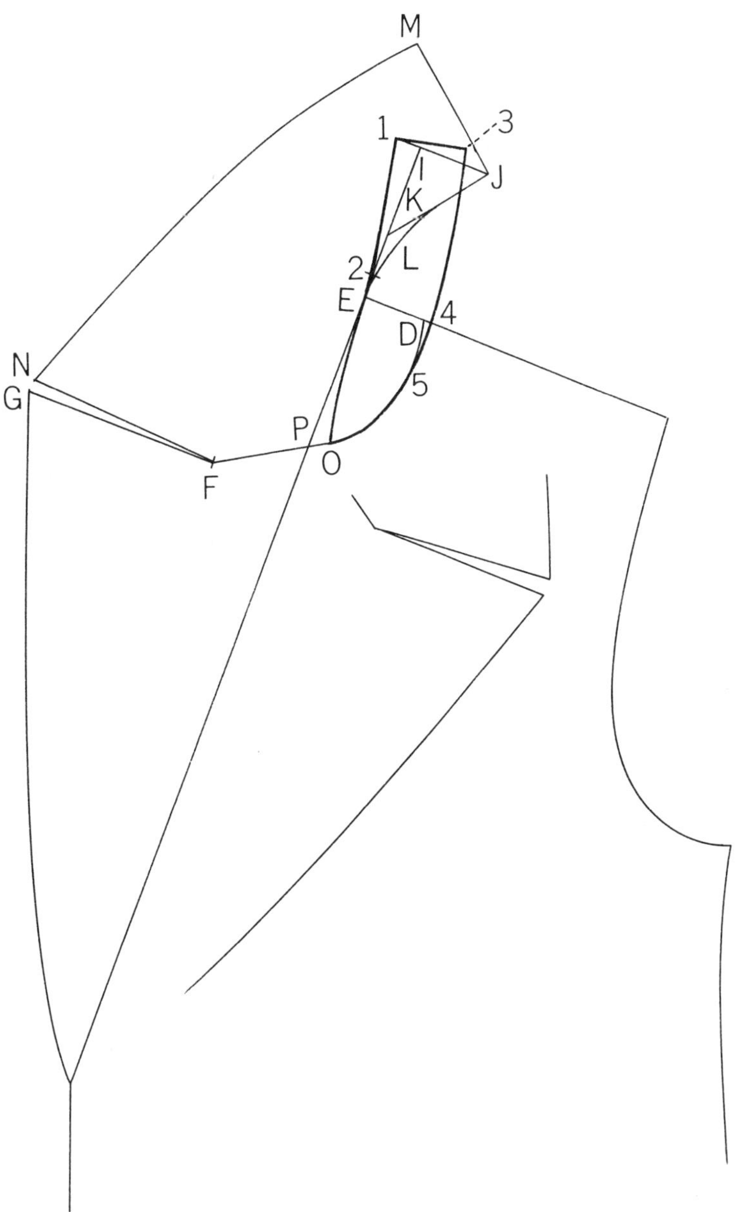

DIAGRAM C

Collar Band
I to 1 = 5/8".
1 to 2 = 2-1/4".
Connect 1 to 2 with straight line.
Then blend in at point 2.
Square off 1 to 3 = collar stand (e.g., 1-1/2").
E to 4 = collar stand - 1/8" (e.g., 1-3/8").
Connect 3 to 4 with sleigh curve ruler.
Blend in 4 to neck line to finish collar band (see diagram).

O to J = O to 1 + 1/4".
1/4" ease.
Ease should be adjusted to 1/4".

ONE-PIECE REGENCY COLLAR

Measurements:
Collar stand = 1-1/2".
Collar fall = 3-1/4".

Collar

Draw a line 12" long.
1 to 2 = back neck measurement.
2 to 3 = A to B - 3/8" (front neck).
3 to 4 = 4".
Square up 1 to 7 = 6-1/4".
Square up 2 to 8 = 3".
Square up 3 to 9 = 1"
1 to 5 = 1-1/2".
5 to 6 = 1-1/2".
Square off 5 to 10.
Square off 6 to 8.
10 to 11 = 1/4".
Connect 3 to 11 with sleigh curve ruler, then blend in toward 5.
8 to 12 = 1/2".
Connect 9 to 12 with sleigh curve ruler, then blend in toward 6 to finish collar stand.
Square up 4 to 13 = 3-1/2".
Connect 9 to 13.
Square off 7 to 14 = 2-1/2".
Connect toward 14 with sleigh curve ruler, to finish Regency Collar.

Note: Shape and size of collar should be adjusted according to design.

DIAGRAM—One-Piece Regency Collar

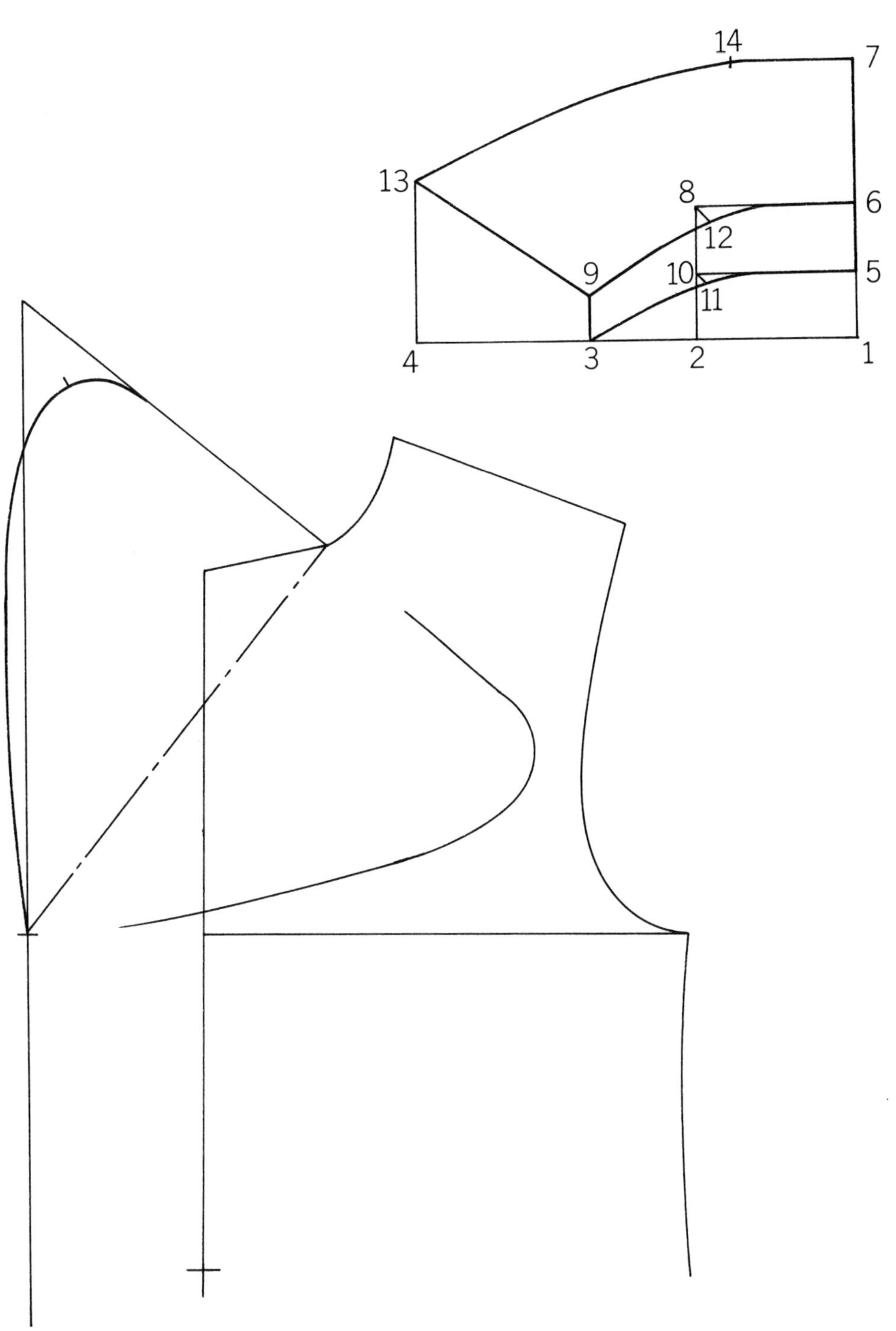

TWO-PIECE REGENCY COLLAR

Measurements:
Collar stand = 1-1/2".
Collar fall = 3".

Note: Shape and size of collar should be adjusted according to design.

DIAGRAM—Two-Piece Regency Collar

DIAGRAM A

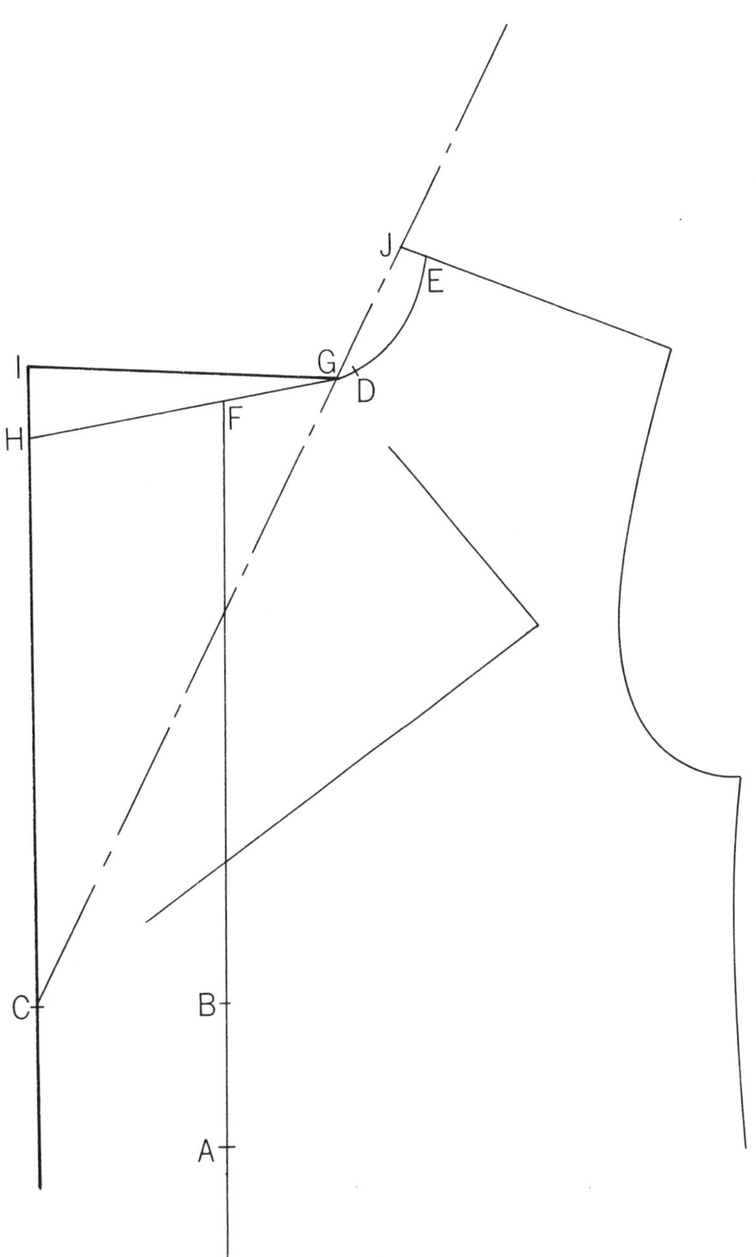

Lapel

A to B = 3".
B to C = 4".
Square up toward I.
E = intersection of shoulder and neck.
F = neck point.
D = 1/2 E to F.
G = 1/2" from D.
Connect C to G and upward for roll line.
Extend neckline H.
H to I = 1-1/2".
Connect G to I to finish lapel.

DIAGRAM—Two-Piece Regency Collar

DIAGRAM B

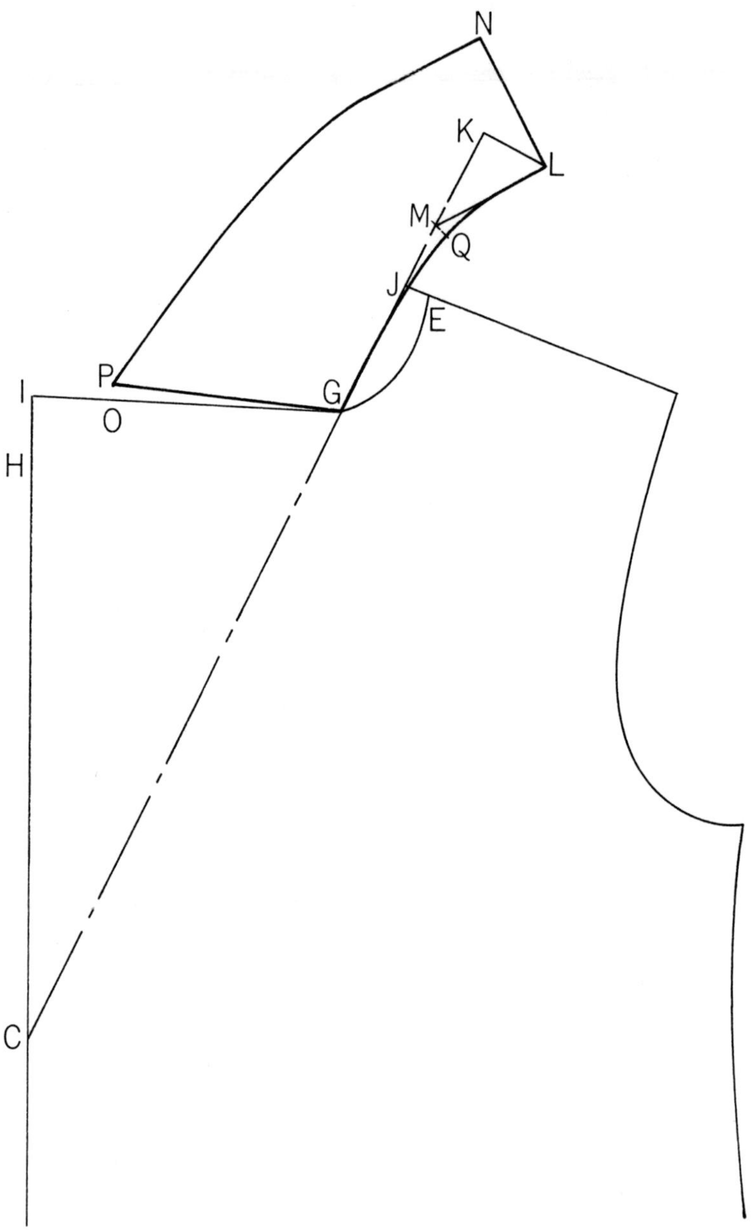

Collar

J to K = Back neck measurement - 3/8".
Square off K to L = 1-1/2".
K to M = 2-1/4".
Connect L to M.
L to N = 3".
I to O = 1-1/2".
O to P = 1/4".
Connect N to P with sleigh curve ruler.
Square off 2-1/4" from N (see diagram).
M to Q = 1/4".
Blend in neck line using Q (see diagram), to finish neckline.

DIAGRAM–Two-Piece Regency Collar

DIAGRAM C

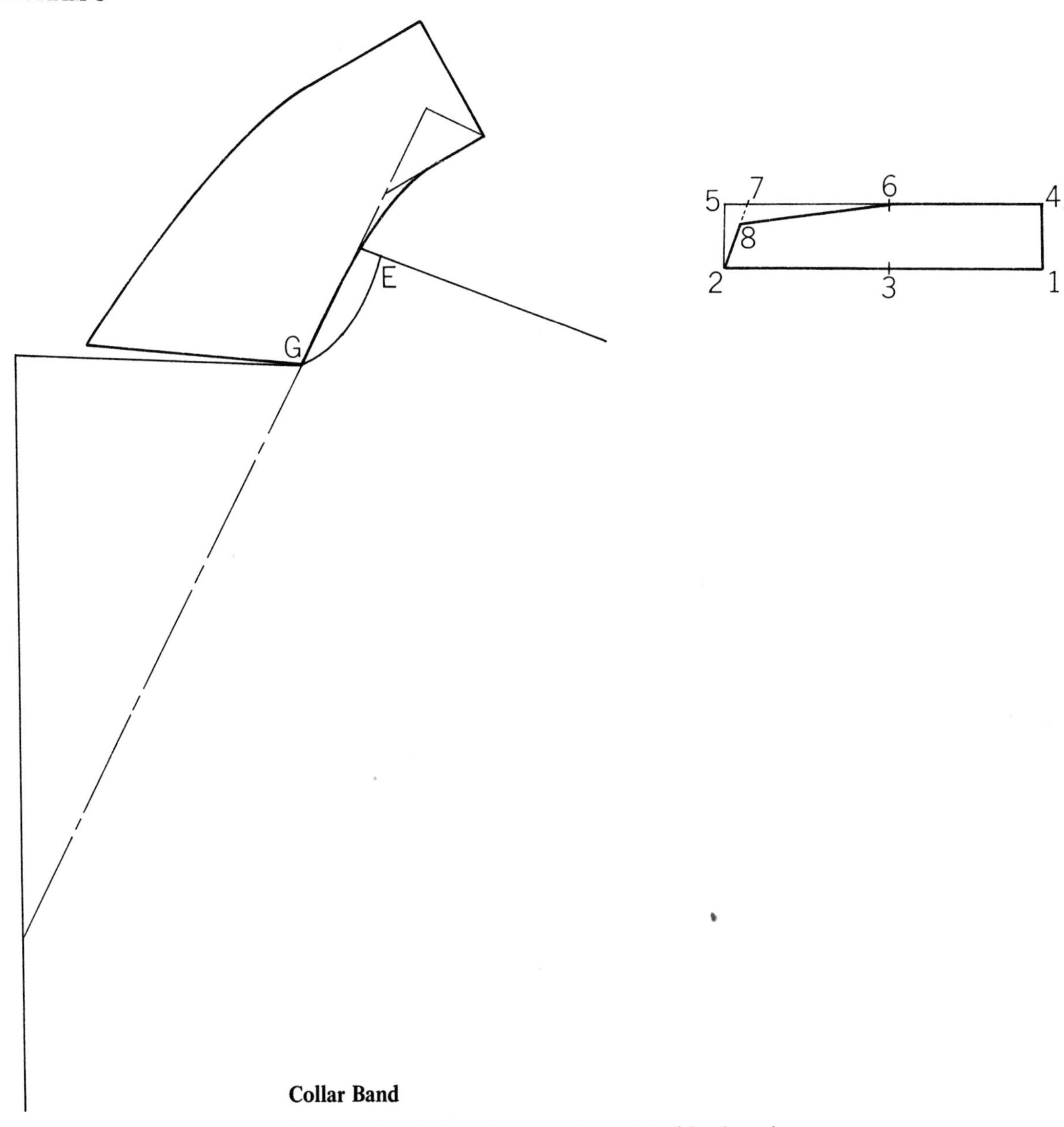

Collar Band

1 to 2 = G to E from front neck + original back neck measurement.
1 to 3 = original back neck measurement.
Square up 1 to 4 = 1-1/2".
Square up 2 to 5 = 1-1/2".
Connect 4 to 5.
Square up 3 to 6.
5 to 7 = 1/2".
7 to 8 = 1/2"
Connect 6 to 8.
Connect 2 to 8.
Blend in at point 6 to finish band.

CONVERSION TABLE (Inches to Centimeters)

Inches		Inches 1/8	1/4	3/8	1/2	5/8	3/4	7/8
		0.32	0.64	0.95	1.27	1.59	1.91	2.22
1	2.54	2.86	3.18	3.49	3.81	4.13	4.45	4.76
2	5.08	5.40	5.72	6.03	6.35	6.67	6.99	7.30
3	7.62	7.94	8.26	8.57	8.89	9.21	9.53	9.84
4	10.16	10.48	10.80	11.11	11.43	11.75	12.07	12.38
5	12.70	13.02	13.34	13.65	13.97	14.29	14.61	14.92
6	15.24	15.56	15.88	15.88	16.19	16.51	16.83	17.46
7	17.78	18.10	18.42	18.73	19.05	19.37	19.69	20.00
8	20.32	20.64	20.96	21.27	21.59	21.91	22.23	22.54
9	22.86	23.18	23.50	23.81	24.13	24.45	24.77	25.08
10	25.40	25.72	26.04	26.35	26.67	26.99	27.31	27.62
11	27.94	28.26	28.58	28.89	29.21	29.53	29.85	30.16
12	30.48	30.80	31.12	31.43	31.75	32.07	32.39	32.70
13	33.02	33.34	33.66	33.97	34.29	34.61	34.93	35.24
14	35.56	35.88	36.20	36.51	36.83	37.15	37.47	37.78
15	38.10	38.42	38.74	39.05	39.37	39.69	40.01	40.32
16	40.64	40.96	41.28	41.59	41.91	42.23	42.55	42.86
17	43.18	43.50	43.82	44.13	44.45	44.77	45.09	45.40
18	45.72	46.04	46.36	46.67	46.99	47.31	47.63	47.94
19	48.26	48.58	48.90	49.21	49.53	49.85	50.17	50.48
20	50.80	51.12	51.44	51.75	52.07	52.39	52.71	53.02
21	53.34	53.66	53.98	54.29	54.61	54.93	55.25	55.56
22	55.88	56.20	56.52	56.83	57.15	57.47	57.79	58.10
23	58.42	58.74	59.06	59.37	59.69	60.01	60.33	60.64
24	60.96	61.28	61.60	61.91	62.23	62.55	62.87	63.18
25	63.50	63.82	64.14	64.45	64.77	65.09	65.41	65.72
26	66.04	66.36	66.68	66.99	67.31	67.63	67.95	68.26
27	68.58	68.90	69.22	69.53	69.85	70.17	70.49	70.80
28	71.12	71.44	71.76	72.07	72.39	72.71	73.03	73.34
29	73.66	73.98	74.30	74.61	74.93	75.25	75.57	75.88
30	76.20	76.52	76.84	77.15	77.47	77.79	78.11	78.42
31	78.74	79.06	79.38	79.69	80.01	80.33	80.65	80.96
32	81.28	81.60	81.92	82.23	82.55	82.87	83.19	83.50
33	83.82	84.14	84.46	84.77	85.09	85.41	85.73	86.04
34	86.36	86.68	87.00	87.31	87.63	87.95	88.27	88.58
35	88.90	89.22	89.54	89.85	90.17	90.49	90.81	91.12
36	91.44	91.76	92.08	92.39	92.71	93.03	93.35	93.66
37	93.98	94.30	94.62	94.93	95.25	95.57	95.89	96.20
38	96.52	96.84	97.16	97.47	97.79	98.11	98.43	98.74
39	99.06	99.38	99.70	100.01	100.33	100.65	100.97	101.28
40	101.60	101.92	102.24	102.55	102.87	103.19	103.51	103.82
41	104.14	104.46	104.78	105.09	105.41	105.73	106.05	106.36
42	106.68	107.00	107.32	107.63	107.95	108.27	108.59	108.90
43	109.22	109.54	109.86	110.17	110.49	110.81	111.13	111.44
44	111.76	112.08	112.40	112.71	113.03	113.35	113.67	113.98
45	114.30	114.62	114.94	115.25	115.57	115.89	116.21	116.52
46	116.84	117.16	117.48	117.79	118.11	118.43	118.75	119.06
47	119.38	119.70	120.02	120.33	120.65	120.97	121.29	121.60
48	121.92	122.24	122.56	122.87	123.19	123.51	123.83	124.14
49	124.46	124.78	125.10	125.41	125.73	126.05	126.37	126.68
50	127.00	127.32	127.64	127.95	128.27	128.59	128.91	129.22
51	129.54	129.86	130.18	130.49	130.81	131.13	131.45	131.76
52	132.08	132.40	132.72	133.03	133.35	133.67	133.99	134.30
53	134.62	134.94	135.26	135.57	135.57	135.89	136.21	136.84
54	137.16	137.48	137.80	138.11	138.43	138.75	139.07	139.38
55	139.70	140.02	140.34	140.65	140.97	141.29	141.61	141.92
56	142.24	142.56	142.88	143.19	143.51	143.83	144.15	144.46
57	144.78	145.10	145.42	145.73	146.05	146.37	146.69	147.00
58	147.32	147.64	147.96	148.27	148.59	148.91	149.23	149.54
59	149.86	150.18	150.50	150.81	151.13	151.45	151.77	152.08
60	152.40	152.72	153.04	153.35	153.67	153.99	154.31	154.62

ABOUT THE AUTHOR

Born in Japan, Masaaki Kawashima, fashion designer, teacher, author has lived and worked in two countries, the United States and Japan, for the past twenty years. He has created original designs for men and women and made clothes for each. In addition to the present book, he is the author of two widely used basic texts, one in Japanese, *A Standard Text of Pattern Grading* (Bunka School of Fashion Press, 3rd Printing, Tokyo, 1972), and *Fundamentals of Men's Fashion Design: A Guide to Tailored Clothes* (Fairchild, 1974). Presently, he is Associate Professor of Fashion Design at the Fashion Institute of Technology in New York City and Consulting Professor of Fashion Design at the Bunka School of Fashion in Tokyo and the Chiyo Tanaka School of Fashion in Tokyo and Ashiya. In this latter capacity, he has conducted annual seminars for professional designers and manufacturers in the fashion field; these seminars have been the source of many contemporary fashion trends in Japan. Mr. Kawashima serves as Chief Designer and Fashion Consultant for one of the leading Japanese department stores.

Uniquely, he combines the training, talent, experience, and understanding of western ways in fashion with design techniques of Japan.